THE ORWELLIAN EMPIRE

D0813652

Gilbert Mercier

For my father, Dr. Gilles Mercier

Contents

Introduction

IT WAS IN EARLY 1981. I was still living in Paris, and the opening of the very first McDonald's restaurant, right at the bottom of the Champs Elysée, made me realize that the full-blown Americanization of France had started. The invasion began back then, even though France was still independent politically from the United States. France, at the time, was not yet a vassal of the US-led empire; it had its own military, which was not part of the North Atlantic Treaty Organization (NATO). The disease of mass consumption moved in when the junk food restaurant opened its doors in Paris. French people, at large, did not understand that the subculture of global corporate capitalism had sneaked in and would eventually, first erode, then try to annihilate France's culture. It was precisely at that moment that I started to contemplate a move to the US in an effort to study at its source what was undermining my culture. I eventually moved to the center of the lowest common denominator empire in 1983, during the first term of the Reagan administration.

I came from a country where people in office were well-educated serious people, to arrive in a surreal land where the man pretending to be in charge was a second-rate actor who read someone else's scripts. French President François Mitterrand was in charge of France, whereas Ronald Reagan was a cardboard cutout figurehead run by handlers. Vice President George Bush Sr. set himself up as the chairman of the board of America Empire Inc. Bush Sr. and his political and business friends started to manage the affairs of the US as if the country was a corporation. It was in the early 1980s that the politico-corporate bosses of the US started the systematic downgrading of all publicly funded social programs, and it was in the mid 1980s that the US homeless population exploded due to the drastic cuts in public spending on mental health.

The Orwellian Empire does not have a birthday, but it unquestionably was born from a few cancerous cells in 1980. Politics had become spectacle, and spectacle had become a grotesque farce. Within a decade, corresponding with the collapse of the Soviet Union, we were living in the imaginary territories between Orwell and Kafka. Deception and opacity had gained an unstoppable momentum. Regardless, what truly mattered in the heart of the empire back then is still what matters now: maximum profit at any social cost. The corporate rulers wanted to dismantle Franklin Delano Roosevelt's (FDR) New Deal, and this is precisely what they did. The corporate political appointees had learned their lessons from the 1960s and 1970s. Another Vietnam or Watergate scandal would not be allowed to happen. Independently inclined journalists were progressively fazed out of all major US TV networks, which were bought by diversified corporations. Many Vietnams and Watergates would, of course, happen again, but the American public was kept in the dark. Besides neutering the press, those in power also made sure that no regular Americans would be drafted in the military. The US Army became a docile mercenary-force instrument of the wars for profit. Armed and often secret conflicts, run by outfits like the Central Intelligence Agency (CIA), became the rule, and some of them, through either drug or weapon trafficking, became self financed. The writing was on the wall, considering that the man sitting as the chairman of the board between 1980 and 1992 had run the CIA.

An insidious coup took place in that decade, and it has been consolidating its control ever since. The political appointees of the corporate rulers would never willingly relinquish their power. The Internet revolution of the 1990s could have been a major threat to the officers of the Orwellian construct. After all, the Internet made the entire knowledge of mankind available for free to nearly everyone at anytime. The information superhighway could have been the path for dissenters to storm and take over the castles. Such a dangerous tool as the Internet had to be diverted from its original mission. The Orwellian Empire's helpers turned the information superhighway into countless mazes of disinformation. The Internet could have brought to the discourse a sense of clarity; instead, in its offshoots of social media, it has created confusion and induced, in many cases, a collective attention deficit disorder. It has also created the illusion that virtual action is real action. What matters is to generate as much confusion in people's minds as possible, to keep everyone brainwashed and off balance, in order to control the key narrative. Critical thinkers, not the so-called terrorists, are the real enemies of the empire, and it is very hard to practice critical thinking in an image or 140 characters. What the Orwellian Empire has on its disinformation menu is either to brainwash the public with spectacles and consumerist frenzy, or with blatant propaganda that is targeted specifically to different focus groups. In Orwellian times, lying to the people and getting them confused has become an art form. Since the Orwellian Empire feeds on paradox, the bigger or more absurd the lie, the better. Clean coal, which is an oxymoron, has become an advertising campaign. You can be all you can be in the US military, but they don't tell you that coming back without a leg or in a body bag is a probable course. In Orwellian times, nothing is what it seems. This book is a three-decade journey into a world where the narratives have become so deceitful that the application of logic and reason to get to the truth is considered to be revolutionary.

I. Fair Is Foul

1

The Illusion of Democracy

IT IS IRONIC, CONSIDERING democracy's pitiful state worldwide that, in accordance to its etymology, it literally means common people's rule or, more simply, people's power. The English term democracy and the 14th-century French word democratie come from the Greek demokratia via the Latin democratia. The Greek radical demos means common people, and kratos means rule, or power. How did we manage to pervert such a laudable notion of power to the people and diametrically turn it into a global system of rule under the principles of oligarchy and plutocracy? Everywhere, from east to west, and north to south, plutocrats and oligarchs are firmly in charge: the puppet masters of the political class. They have transformed democracy into a parody of itself and a toxic form of government. The social contract implied in a democratic form of governance is broken.

At the start of Jean-Jacques Rousseau's *The Social Contract*, written in 1762 and one of the inspirations for the French revolution 27 years later, the Enlightenment philosopher wrote: "Men was born free, and he is everywhere in chains."[1] The key argument of *The Social Contract* is that the only governments with a legitimate right to exist are those that function with the expressed consent of the governed. Further, Rousseau introduced the fundamental and revolutionary notion of sovereignty of the people, as opposed to sovereignty of the state or rulers. For Rousseau, the only legitimate form of political authority is the one agreed upon by all the people in a social contract, with full respect for everyone's natural birthrights to equality, freedom and individual liberty.

The electoral process is an essential part of the consent of the governed defined by Rousseau. In almost all of the so-called democratic countries, however, the important act of voting to elect the people's representatives has become an exercise in futility. Today, politicians, who still have the audacity to call themselves public servants, are nothing more than the obedient executors of the transnational global corporate elite. These politicians are actors who are cast to perform in opaque screenplays written by top corporate power brokers and marketed to the public like products. In this sad state of affairs that passes for democracy, citizens have become blind consumers of political figureheads who work for global corporate interests. For any organism to remain healthy, it must be able to excrete. The same applies to our collective social body, but instead of regularly eliminating our political residue and flushing it away, we recycle it.

Mark Twain wrote: "If voting made any difference, they wouldn't let us do it."[2] This quote from the gilded age is just as accurate today. A vote implies real choice, and we have none. From France to Brazil, the United Kingdom, Germany, India and, of course, the US — all of which pass for great democracies — political choices have become largely reduced to two electable political parties with different names to accommodate the local cultural flavors. This comforting idea of an option between left and right that spices up democracies' voting menus is a farce. For example, in France, the so-called socialist François Hollande and his right-wing predecessor Nicolas Sarkozy are both docile servants of neoliberal and imperial policies dictated from elsewhere. Both, Sarkozy and Hollande, are proponents of austerity measures imposed by financial institutions such as the International Monetary Fund (IMF) and World Bank, and also imperialist actions, such as rejoining NATO and intervening militarily in Libya (Sarkozy), and Mali and Central African Republic (Hollande).

The UK offers the example of the phony difference between Labor, the party of warmonger in Iraq and Afghanistan, Tony Blair, and Tory, the party of warmonger in Libya, Afghanistan and Syria, David Cameron. This observation extends, of course, to the fake choice between Democrats and Republicans in the US: the names change periodically, but the neoliberal imperialist policies remain the same. In reality, the pseudo two-party system accommodates a one-party power structure that is financed and ruled by the same people everywhere and serves identical interests. This fake two-party system maintains the appearance of democracy by giving people the illusion that voting matters.

Few people are willing to admit that democracy is broken or take direct action to create a new system, although there is a rampant global dissatisfaction with politicians. According to an October 2014 poll, only six percent of US voters thought that their Congress was doing a good job, and 65 percent rated its performance as being poor or very poor. Even more telling of the popular sense of an assumed general political corruption, 63 percent of US voters thought that most members of Congress would be willing to sell their votes for either cash or campaign contributions. In France, Hollande's approval rating had crashed to 13 percent: the lowest for any president since the early 1960s. Despite France's revolutionary history, the constitution gives its president the power to remain in office until the full term of his five-year mandate and, if necessary, to rule by decree.

In our current supra-national world order, it is a largely counterproductive undertaking to focus popular dissatisfaction on interchangeable figureheads such as François Hollande, Barack Obama, David Cameron, Narendra Modi, Dilma Rousseff, and Angela Merkel. All are expendable. Instead, the global public opinion should contest the legitimacy of unelected global-governance institutions such as the IMF, World Bank, United Nations, World Trade Organization (WTO), and other powerful non-governmental organizations (NGO), think tanks, and consortia like the World Economic Forum and the Clinton Global Initiative. These institutions largely constitute the global elite; they dictate global policies and draft secret treaties such as the Trans-Pacific Partnership (TPP) agreement concerning billions of people. For the governance of such global institutions to be viewed as being remotely democratic, they would have to be elected by the world citizenry.

"Protest beyond the law is not a departure from democracy; it is absolutely essential to it," wrote Howard Zinn.[3] People worldwide are fed up with their politicians, and they are protesting. Yet, as if most are suffering from a collective Stockholm syndrome, they are not sufficiently pro-active to rid themselves of their abusers by any means necessary. Voting was meant to be a sacrosanct civic duty, but it has become the unconscious action of sleepwalkers.

In 1789, toppling the monarchy was a tall order in France. The intellectual inspiration for this revolution came from the works of Rousseau, Voltaire, Diderot and Montesquieu, who can be viewed as the founding fathers of modern democracy. If the veneer of the Enlightenment philosophers' discourse has survived time, the spirit of it has been gutted. The elite of corporate global governance has trampled the social contract. People who had gained their freedom during the past 200 years are everywhere back in chains. An increasing number of people realize that a drastic systemic change is imperative, but few are willing to admit that nothing short of a global revolution can challenge the entrenched plutocratic world order.

In the aftermath of such a revolution, or ideally before it, we must redefine the parameters of what should guarantee representative governance today in real democracy with common people's rule. Real democracy works best on a small scale. In ancient Greece, for example, democracy worked because its practice was limited to small communities in which citizens personally knew their politicians. Today, pushes for autonomy by regions such as Catalonia and Scotland represent the aspirations of people for smaller governance and their reactions against the threat to their cultural identities. On the other hand, problems such as overpopulation, pollution, climate change, the current mass extinction, and the waste of limited resources must be dealt with globally to have any impact. Therefore a type of direct democracy is also needed to deal with global issues; this could consist, for example, of global referendums. The current systems of supposed democratic governance are corrupt and decayed; after we demolish them and reconstruct democracy, it might finally become true for our times.

United States: From Democracy to Oligarchy and Plutocracy

One hundred and thirty foreign companies sponsored Political Action Committees (PACs) and used their US-based subsidiaries to finance countless political campaigns in the 2010 US election cycle, reported the watchdog organization opensecrets.org.[4] Together, these companies donated more than $12.6 million to political campaigns through various PACs. Electoral contributions seemed to be recession proof, since this number was higher than for any previous federal midterm election cycle, and second only to the 2008 presidential election, when foreign-connected companies spent a record $16.9 million on US elections.

Up until the 2006 election, the foreign connected PACs greatly favored the Republican Party. Since then, they have hedged their bets and become bipartisan. The top companies involved in this scheme, which should be completely illegal but is not, include the UK's pharmaceutical giant GlaxoSmithKline, the UK-based defense company BAE Systems, Belgium's mega beverage producer Anheuser-Busch, and the Netherlands-based tax advisory firm KPMG. The PACs of these companies' US-based subsidiaries spent more than $500,000 on the 2010 elections.

Unfortunately for the survival of our democratic system, the Federal Electoral Commission rules state that as long as the US subsidiary of the foreign-based company has enough money in its own account to provide such donations, there is no issue in giving unlimited amounts of money to PACs. Foreign-connected PACs, by law, must raise money from US citizens or green-card holders and may not use foreign funds to finance their political efforts. Needless to say, the enforcement of laws against megacorporations with such extensive reach is a lost battle.

Beside these foreign-based corporations, US-based ones are also heavily invested in the US electoral process. From 1989 to 2010, the top-10 list of the largest US donors were: AT&T with $45.6 million, Goldman Sachs with $36.7 million, Citigroup with $27.5 million, UPS with $24.9 million, Altria (AKA Philip Morris) with $24.3 million, Microsoft with $21 million, JP Morgan with $20.3 million, Time Warner with $20 million, Morgan Stanley with $19.8 million and, last but not least, Lockheed Martin with $19.3 million.

Journalist Bill Moyers, while paying tribute to one of his mentors, John Gardner, the founder of Common Cause, on the occasion of the organization's 40th anniversary, fondly recalled the era of Lyndon Johnson, when the sense of social justice and progress still had a strong meaning in the US social system.[5] Moyers argued that 1980 was the beginning of the end for the advances made first by FDR, then later by Johnson. "The conservative movement, once embodied in Goldwater, found its new hero in Ronald Reagan, and launched a campaign to bring back radical laissez-faire, when there was no social contract and all but the privileged and powerful were left to forage on their own," said Moyers. Further in his address, Moyers said that the right "propelled by cascades of cash from corporate chieftains like Coors, the Koch brothers, and Jack Welch marched on Washington and succeeded brilliantly." Moyers also quoted a very candid but extremely revealing statement made by billionaire Warren Buffet concerning this issue: "There's class warfare, all right, but it's my class, the rich class, that's making war, and we're winning."[6] In his remarks, Moyers deconstructed the myth of limited government, which is so much at the center of the Tea Party activists' philosophy. "Freedom in America would come to mean the freedom of the rich to buy the government they wanted and to write the rules to their advantage, even if it meant leaving millions of Americans behind. Advocates of limited government were never opposed to government, only to one that would not tolerate their social Darwinism," said Moyers.[5]

On January 21, 2010, in a 5-4 vote on a decision commonly called Citizens United, the Supreme Court overturned a 63-year old law designed to limit the influence of big corporations on elections. By opening this Pandora's box, the Supreme Court rubberstamped the rise of corporate fascism. From then on, Americans would elect the best political candidates money could buy. The ruling said that corporations could spend as much as they wanted to support or oppose candidates for President and Congress. Strong dissenters in the court were Justices Stevens, Ginsburg, Breyer and Sotomayor. "The Court ruling threatens to undermine the integrity of elected institutions around the nation," said Justice Stevens in his dissent statement.[7] The decision was indeed a legal maneuver orchestrated by an ultra-activist court working to further the lock of big corporations on the already shaky US electoral process, as opposed to working in the interest of the American people and for the benefit of democracy.

According to Common Cause, a nonpartisan and nonprofit advocacy organization founded as a vehicle for citizens to make their voices heard, the Supreme Court ruling was "the Superbowl of bad decisions for Democracy."[8] Common Cause said that the decision created a political crisis, and the Supreme Court had handed down a ruling that would enhance the ability of the deepest-pocketed special interests to influence elections and the US Congress. "The Roberts Court today made a bad decision worse. This ruling allows Wall Street to tap its vast corporate profits to drown out the voice of the public in our democracy. The path from here is clear: Congress must free itself from Wall Street's grip so Main Street can finally get a fair share," said Common Cause president Bob Edgar.[8] What was left of US democracy had come under attack from an institution that was supposed to protect it. The Supreme Court, de facto, had rewritten the US constitution by scrapping the "We, the people" to replace it with "We, the corporations."[8]

Within one year, the decision to treat corporations as people had already altered the dire landscape of money's influence on politics. Thankfully, there was still some opposition to the constitutional coup. On the one-year anniversary of the decision, opponents of Citizens United were on Capitol Hill to seek a constitutional amendment to put a cap on electoral corporate spending. Common Cause accused Justices Scalia and Thomas of having ties to conservative activist groups that benefited from the court ruling during the November 2010 elections. Bob Edgar said the Justice Department should investigate whether the previous year's ruling of Scalia and Thomas on the case constituted a conflict of interest. "If the Justice Department finds a conflict on the part of either Justice, Common Cause asks that the solicitor general petition the court to vacate the Citizens United decision," said Edgar. [9]

Justices Scalia and Thomas both acknowledged that they had attended functions organized and sponsored by Koch Industries, one of the biggest financial entities behind the success of the so-called grassroots Tea Party movement. Further, Common Cause expressed concerns about the earnings of Justice Thomas' wife from the conservative think tank Heritage Foundation, and a PAC called Liberty Central that she co-founded in 2009. "The public is entitled to more detail about the nature and extent of the Justices' involvement with Koch Industries' closed-door strategy sessions. And there has been no response to the equally serious concern raised about Justice Thomas' financial conflict of interest due to his wife's role as CEO of Liberty Central, and its political activities in 2010," said Edgar.[10]

President Obama was initially highly critical of the Supreme Court decision, but he did not push the issue with a legal challenge. "Last week the

Supreme Court reversed a century old law that I believe will open the flood gates for special interests," said Obama in his January 2010 State of the Union address.[11] After this, however, he changed his tune to project a more business friendly image for his re-election bid in 2012.

2

Pepsi or Coke?

SINCE THE US became a full-blown empire in 1945, a constant factor at play has been a single political agenda with regard to foreign policy. Ever since Harry Truman, the underlying goals of all US policy decisions overseas, by Democrats and Republicans alike, have been to assert and expand US global dominance. The Cold War, curiously, presented some clarity, as the enemy, the Soviet Union (or USSR), was clearly and conveniently defined as the evil empire that needed to be contained and ultimately defeated. The Korean War was in this context; so was the Vietnam War.

The opposition to the Vietnam War in the late 1960s and early 1970s was the last time the US left had any impact on foreign-policy decisions. The collapse of the Soviet Union in the late 1980s to early 1990s allowed the only empire still standing to run amok, without any real opposition from within because the logic of empire, defined in short as America number one, had blitzkrieged the public discourse. This sense of American exceptionalism still prevails today.

For people who did not live in the US, it was hard to comprehend, with regard to the 2012 elections, that the left had so little room in the parody of democracy that had become the US political system. The left had been reduced to only two voices, lost in a political desert: Senator Bernie Sanders and Congressman Dennis Kucinich. Both men had been pre-eminent in making their points for a true left agenda but utterly ineffective at making a dent in the public discourse. To be fair, neither Sanders nor Kucinich got the attention they deserved from the corporate-controlled US media. The challenge they brought to the debate did not fit the status quo. This was a crime of lèse majesté in Washington where, despite the theatrical pseudo-fights about ideology, the order of the ruling class, profit and empire, had to remain the same.

In March 2009, I was dining with some French journalists who were reporting on President Obama's wave of so-called hope and change, and what it could mean for US policy. I had to be the cold shower on their parade. When I told them that Obama would wind up implementing policies more right wing than Sarkozy, they looked at me in disbelief. In their minds, US Democrats were the left, and Obama was a liberal democrat.

Later on, I think my French colleagues would have fought less against my arguments. Obama is a Reagan Democrat in the mold of his political boss, corporate Democrat Bill Clinton. In the US, there is no representation from the left; there is the right calling themselves Democrats, and the far right calling themselves Republicans. In this political landscape, bad actors like Ronald Reagan become mythological politicians and politicians like Barack Obama are good actors. Regardless of the Democrat or Republican nametag, elections are always about preserving the same interests, and Americans are the ultimate victims of this giant con game.

The so-called progressives who got sucked into supporting candidate Barack Obama over Hillary Clinton were tricked into a carbon-copy scheme. They were not the only ones. The members of the jury for the Nobel Foundation were also easy marks when they awarded war-President Obama a Nobel Peace Prize; so were my French colleagues who had bought into the bogus concept of hope and change when they should have known better.

When Obama unleashed his reelection campaign for 2012, the challenger lineup from the far-right Republican Party (GOP) was weak, and there was little chance of a surprise candidate coming from the left to seize the moment. Dennis Kucinich had given it an unsuccessful try in 2008, and Senator Sanders seemed not to believe in himself enough to give it a shot.

United States politicians have little time to focus on the real business of government, because they are almost always campaigning for election or re-election. Every two years American voters go to the polls to elect a House of Representatives and part of the Senate; or part of the Senate, the House of Representatives, and a President. In any case, because of the lack of options, the political pendulum swings in highly predicable ways.

In 2010, according to Obama, the Democrats were shellacked by the GOP and their allies from the Tea Party.[12] The Democrats were blamed by part of the US electorate for the aftermath of the 2008 economic crash. The 2012 US elections would tell a different story. If, in 2010, some Americans bought the rhetoric that painted Obama as a socialist, in 2011 this ludicrous notion had completely lost traction, as people realized that Obama had a lot more in common with Reagan than FDR in domestic policy. As far as foreign policy, Obama was even more a war president than his predecessor, George W. Bush. Bush's wars in Iraq and Afghanistan were ongoing, and Obama had added Pakistan and Libya to the endless wars of the empire.

The small minority within the Democratic Party who opposed the war-mongering policies of the Obama administration would not be heard, just as in 2008. If any challenge at all came from the left leaning progressive portion of the US electorate, the Obama campaign-money machine would bury it. Obama's goal was to raise a record $1 billion for his reelection bid, and he would meet his target. After all, he was in bed with Wall Street and the military-industrial complex, not to mention a sizable part of the so-called Hollywood left.

Aside from the comic-relief pseudo candidates, such as Donald Trump, the options for Republican voters were unconvincing. Newt Gingrich had managed to eliminate himself from the race, and Mitt Romney was the most likely contender to finish ahead of the Republican pack. Romney had two major hurdles that he was unlikely to overcome in a run against Obama. First, the far right of the Tea Party viewed Romney as being too liberal, and therefore he would not get their enthusiastic support; second, he was a Mormon, which would prevent a large number of Christian fundamentalists from voting for him.

Even though Obama was elected president in 2008 on the false hope-and-change premise, when it came to the implacable logic of maintaining the empire, change was out of the question for a vast majority of Americans. The assassination of Osama bin-Laden gave Obama a six-percent boost in the polls, and the effect would linger well into the 10th anniversary of 9/11, on September 11, 2010, when the sitting president would remind Americans that he was the one who got enemy number one.[13] The assassination of bin-Laden transformed the image of the Commander in Chief from the reluctant warrior who won a Nobel Peace Prize to the ruthless killer who returned home from the battlefield with his archenemy's head. The hope-and-change slogan was, of course, a convenient gimmick to get elected. By and large, Americans did not want change as far as foreign policy was concerned; instead they wanted to maintain the status quo of the empire, and Obama was the right man for the interests of US imperialism.

Obama or Romney Mattered as Little as Pepsi or Coke
Most US citizens believe that they live in a democracy, which implies an availability of choices, and they think the US has a two-party system with real differences between Democrats and Republicans. In reality, the very same unelected officials have pulled the strings and made policy decisions for decades, for the sake of the same interests. Alan Greenspan is a typical example of this; so are Henry Kissinger and Zbigniew Brzezinski on issues of foreign policy. Larry Summers, a Clinton man who had a big responsibility in creating the real-estate bubble and subsequent 2008 crash, quickly became one of Obama's key economic advisers. Ben Bernanke was Obama's Chairman of the Federal Reserve and was also Bush's. The same troubling continuity of powerful policy players took place between the Reagan and Bush Sr. administrations, and the Clinton administration.

It is hard to pinpoint when US democracy took a wrong turn towards a plutocracy where oligarchs stay in power from one generation to the next, where a political aristocracy has the impudence to maintain an incestuous relationship with bankers and corporations at the expense of the people that they are supposed to represent, and where a small group of unelected supposed wise men pull the strings in the dark, of one puppet administration after the other. Americans are not, in general, very well informed. This being said, US citizens intuitively understand the corruption and failures of their political class. Five months before the presidential and congressional elections, in June 2012, the public's approval rating of the US Congress was 17 percent, compared to 75 percent disapproval: one of the lowest levels of confidence in US history.[14]

A few politicians could have mustered the courage to challenge the plutocracy's status quo or at least open a necessary discussion. Some were putting their hopes in Congressman Ron Paul on the right, and Senator Bernie Sanders on the left, to disrupt the smoke-and-mirrors maze of the appalling political discourse. Each could have challenged the monstrosity that had become the monolithic Republicrat one-party system. But it would not happen that time around, and it might never happen at all unless money is taken out of US politics.

In the US, just like in branding and marketing, only money talks. There is no room for small brands, and there are only minute differences between the big brands. Unless you have developed a branding fixation or addiction for either Pepsi or Coke, they are hard to tell apart. Both soda concoctions have a lot of sugar and caffeine, and one could argue that they represent, unless consumed in moderation, a hazard to health. In a society where consumption is king, politics and politicians have become products and brands. When consumers go to supermarkets, they might buy Pepsi or Coke if they like soda. The same consumers have a choice between Democrats or Republicans if they want their votes to count. In this staged election process, politicians have slightly different flavors, but they are basically the same. Most are millionaires who defend the interests of the establishment, as opposed to the interests of the people. Politicians, either Republicans or Democrats, valiantly fight for the banks, Wall Street, giant corporations and the pursuit of war for the profit of the military-industrial complex. Just like their soda counterparts, Republicans and Democrats make you fat and sick so that their good friends from the health-pharmaceutical industry can reap the financial rewards. In November 2012, voters, the consumers of talking points of their favorites cable news stations, faced a similar dilemma. Did it really matter? Domestically, the big corporations would still call the shots, and Congress would display its usual inertia. Internationally, the imperialist policies would be maintained or expanded. The winner of the elections mattered as little as buying a Pepsi instead of a Coke.

On November 6, 2012, the new leader of the so-called free world was crowned, but the corporate puppet masters would maintain their grip on the levers of power. Gore Vidal wrote: "There is only one party in the United States, the Property Party, and it has two right wings: Republican and Democrat."[15] This one-party Republicrat system has gone on for decades. The election cycle was a circus, but a highly profitable one: Obamney, i.e. the Obama and Romney wing, raised $2 billion, which were lavishly spent mainly on TV advertisements. This astronomical sum was endlessly recycled, or laundered, from corporate entities (after all, according to the US Supreme Court, corporations are people) back into the pockets of the mega-corporations that control the US media and so on. The US is not the best democracy money can buy, it is a sad circus act with a few elephants, some donkeys and some predictable clowns who have run out of ideas on how to make people laugh.

In the run-up to the elections, the argument of voting for the lesser of two evils was often heard, both on the left and from libertarians. This argument immediately fell apart when those who expressed it were pushed for a justification. One was: "I hate the US foreign policy, but on gay rights...." Another one said, and this was on Twitter's open feed: "Republicans are hard on pu**ies!" Not much articulation there. Meanwhile, the resident of the White House was running a kill list and acting like a worldwide assassin; Guantanamo Bay Detention Camp was still open for business; fascist legislation such as the National Defense Authorizations Act (NDAA) and the Patriot Act were part of the US legal system; the police state was growing, with police forces becoming militarized, and wars for profit were spreading across the globe like a cancer, making all the real players of America Empire Inc. very rich and happy.

"But he saw too that in America the struggle was befogged by the fact that the worst Fascists were they who disowned the word 'Fascism' and preached enslavement to Capitalism under the style of Constitutional and

Traditional Native American Liberty," wrote the novelist Sinclair Lewis.[16] Corporate fascism is in the US, and it has been here for a while. It is plastered by the brands that sponsor it: Coke, Pepsi, Walmart, GE, Chevron, Wells Fargo, etc. Americans are the quintessential consumers. Politics are no exception. Anybody with experience in advertising knows that brand fidelity is the key to a successful product. In 2012, Obamney came in two different flavors and packages, although it was manufactured by the same corporation: America Empire Inc. Consumers had the freedom to choose between Pepsi or Coke, and McDonalds or Burger King, just as they had the freedom to choose who would read the teleprompters in the White House. It was not a matter of governance or policies but of consumer taste.

From Nobel Peace Prize Winner to Assassin in Chief

There should be a return policy on the Nobel Peace Prize. President Obama did a remarkable bait-and-switch job by conveying that he would be a head of state always seeking peaceful diplomatic solutions. Obama not only convinced many US voters but also an overwhelming proportion of the international community that he would respect the rule of international law. He criticized his predecessor, George W. Bush, for the detentions of suspects without trial at the Guantanamo prison camp and in the secret overseas CIA facilities of the rendition program. If Bush Jr.'s forte were torture and the arbitrary detention of suspects, Obama had become the chief of America's illegal drone assassination program: the empire's judge and executioner.

A report, published on May 29, 2012 in *The New York Times,* revealed that Obama had personally approved the targets on a secret kill list of the US' extensive drone assassination program.[17] If in many corporations in the US, office workers have a casual Friday, at the White House the big day is assassins' Tuesday. It is when, according to *The New York Times,* about two dozen counter-terrorism security officials meet with the president in the situation room. The decisions can deal with terror suspects anywhere in the world, as the Obama administration seems to view countries' sovereignty as an insignificant detail. In the past few years, the main targets have been in Yemen and Pakistan, but the sky is literally the limit for the secret program. "Mr. Obama has placed himself at the helm of a top secret nomination process to designate terrorists for kill or capture, of which the capture part has become largely theoretical," wrote *The New York Times'* Jo Becker and Scott Shane.[17] The evolution of Obama has stunned some of his current and former advisers who told *The New York Times* that it is without precedent in US history to have a president personally heading this type of shadow war.

Obama's management of the drone kill list and the maintenance of Guantanamo were shrewd, callous and fundamentally hypocritical. On the second day of his presidency, he signed several executive orders to honor some of his campaign promises. He declared that brutal interrogation techniques would be banned, and that the infamous Guantanamo prison camp would be shut down. "What the new president did not say was that the executive orders contained a few subtle loopholes. They reflected a still unfamiliar Barack Obama, a realist who, unlike some of his fervent supporters, was never carried away by his own rhetoric," wrote Jo Becker and Scott Shane.[17] Basically, in a covert manner, Obama, using his legal skills, had preserved three major Bush policies that he had attacked so vehemently during his campaign: rendition, military commissions and indefinite detention.

In 2008, then-candidate Obama said that Guantanamo and what it represented was the best recruiting tool for al-Qaeda and terrorist enemies of America. Near the end of his second term in 2015, the shameful prison was still open, and adding to this, the assassination program had expanded to become state policy. Despite the lies of the Obama administration, drone strikes are never clinical, and most of the time they kill countless civilians in what is casually called collateral damage. Drone attacks fuel anti-American sentiments all over the world, most notably in Pakistan, Yemen and Somalia. These attacks are in breach of the most basic international laws, and they also represent an extremely dangerous precedent. Besides being a war fought in a cowardly manner, where the pilot operates the drone thousands of miles from his victims, the drone program could also be arbitrarily extended to domestic use, or it might become a weapon of predilection worldwide. Israel has drones and does not hesitate to implement assassination programs not only in Gaza but also as far as Syria and Iran. Furthermore, the label of terrorist is so elastic that it could be applied to any perceived enemy of the state and become dangerously broad. Might this include in the near future someone like Julian Assange and other prominent dissidents? Most Americans probably like having their president's hand on the trigger: a scary prospect for freedom and democracy.

A few weeks before the November 2012 reelection of Barack Obama to the presidency, *News Junkie Post* tried to secure interviews with prominent African-American media figures for a project titled: "Obama's first term: what would MLK have said?" The people approached for this project were regarded to be on the very left of the US political spectrum and had been, a few months before the election, highly critical of Obama's first term in office. As election day approached, however, they avoided the interview. Like many African-Americans, members of other minority groups, and other groups of so-called progressive voters, at the last minute they decided to mute their attacks on Obama to make sure he would be reelected, following the dubious logic: Obama is not as bad as the other guy. Considering Martin Luther King Jr.'s own words, if he had been alive as we approached his birthday in 2013, he would probably have been a leading voice against Obama's domestic and foreign policies.

"Letter from Birmingham jail" was one of MLK's most eloquent statements against social injustice, and "A time to break the silence" was his major statement against war.[18] [19] The latter was delivered in 1967 in the context of expressing his staunch opposition to the Vietnam War and the escalation policy of Lyndon B. Johnson; but MLK's words could easily address the Obama administration's warmongering policies in Afghanistan, Pakistan, Libya, Yemen and Syria. As a matter of fact, it is likely that MLK would have broken his silence as soon as Obama, a war president, had received a Nobel Peace Prize in 2009.

Just like today in the US, MLK's moral protest against the war was a minority position. Even his supporters in the black community were concerned that his anti-war position would withdraw energy from the Civil Rights movement. Dr. King also pointed out — and this remained the same in 2013 — that the poor and minorities in the US were the primary components of the military. "Over the past two years, as I have moved to break the betrayal of my own silence and to speak from the burning of my own heart, as I have called for radical departure from the destruction of Vietnam, many persons have questioned me about the wisdom of my path: 'Why are you speaking about the war, Dr. King'; 'Why are you joining the voice of dissent?'; 'Peace and civil rights don't mix', they say.... The Nobel Peace Prize was also a commission, a commission to work harder than I had ever worked before for the brotherhood of man. This is a calling that takes me beyond national allegiances," said Dr. King.[19]

In his book *Humanitarian Imperialism,* published in 2006, Jean Bricmont argued that since the end of the Cold War, human rights have been used as a justification for war or foreign interventions, sometimes under the auspices of the UN like in Haiti, by the world's leading economic and military powers, and above all the US.[20] The criteria for such interventions are usually arbitrary and self-serving. They can involve the muscle of global imperialism in the form of NATO, or a softer version like the US Agency for International Development (USAID). Obama, during his first term, became expert in this type of double language and hidden agenda. It was used in Libya to justify the intervention against Gaddafi, and the same discourse about protecting human rights was recycled in early 2013 against Bashar al-Assad in Syria. The same rationale of humanitarian imperialism was used by Obama's NATO ally, France's President François Hollande, to wage a war in Mali. Jean Bricmont wrote in February 2012:

> US interference in the internal affairs of other states is multi-faceted, but constant and repeatedly violates the spirit and often the letter of the UN Charter. Despite claims to act on behalf of principles such as freedom and democracy, US interventions have disastrous consequences. Every aggressive action led by the US creates a reaction. Development of an anti-missile shield produces more missiles, not less. Bombing civilians — whether

deliberately or by so-called 'collateral damage' produces more armed resistance, not less. Trying to overthrow or subvert governments produces
more internal repression, not less.[21]

In appearance, MLK and Obama have a lot in common. Both are
intelligent individuals and excellent orators. But this analogy, cultivated by
Obama, only holds water near the surface. Obama actually has more in
common with Ronald Reagan than with the Civil Rights leader. Obama is a
consummate actor. It is by design that his public inaugural ceremony, which
should have been scheduled for January 20, 2013 when he took his oath,
coincided instead with the celebration of MLK Day on Monday, January 21.
By paying a made-for-TV tribute to the Civil Rights leader, Obama revived
the false analogy between himself and MLK.

Despite superficialities, Obama's reelection did not embody what MLK
longed for in his famous statement, "A man should not be judged by the
color of his skin but by the content of his character."[22] Judging by his first
term in office, it was impossible to know the content of Mr. Obama's
character. George W. Bush had very few qualities, but at least he had the
merit of being unapologetic and transparent about who he was: the quintessence of the ugly American, aggressive and uncultured. Obama, on the
other hand, gave the illusion of being a polished humanist despite being as
imperialist as his predecessor. Obama was both a Nobel Peace Prize recipient and the US' hitman in chief. He was both a president who used executive power to try to force a gun control law on US citizens, despite the second amendment, and the most successful salesman for the military-
industrial complex in US history.

Human Rights in the Morning, Raids in the Afternoon

During the Vietnam War, the saying that best illustrated the schizophrenic
aspect of the US involvement there was "candy in the morning, napalm in
the afternoon." Decades later, the US administration still displays the same
signs of this disturbing behavior, where one hand takes away what the other
hand has given. The twisted logic of this insanity was playing out in Pakistan in summer 2010. On one hand, the US was making helicopters available for desperately needed food supply drops for flood victims, on the other
hand drone attacks were conducted in the same areas on almost a daily
basis. Obama's war in Pakistan could be portrayed as "food drops in the
morning, drone attacks in the afternoon."

On September 23, 2010, Obama delivered the second speech of his
presidency at the UN General Assembly. He did not receive as many cheers
as the first time around, because the international delegates were starting to
understand the deep dichotomy between the words of the President and his
actions. At the UN, Obama painted the US as a benevolent superpower
concerned with human rights. He said:

America has also embraced unique responsibilities that come with our power. Since the rains came and the floodwaters rose in Pakistan, we have pledged our assistance, and we should all support the Pakistani people as they recover and rebuild. And when the earth shook and Haiti was devastated by loss, we joined a coalition of nations in response. Today, we honor those from the UN family who lost their lives in the earthquake, and commit ourselves to stand with the people of Haiti until they can stand on their own feet. Amidst this upheaval, we have been persistent in our pursuit of peace.[23]

The achievements of the Obama administration explained above were mere fiction. The help given to Pakistani flood victims by the US and the international community had been not only slow coming but also completely anemic. This was in contrast to the robust not-so-secret war that the Obama administration was fighting in Pakistan. As far as the situation in Haiti, more than eight months after the earthquake, over one million people were living under mildewed tents, and no significant progress had been made in reconstruction.

Later in his speech, the US President asked: "What is the world that awaits us when today's battles are brought to an end?"[23] Of course, this was a purely rhetorical question, because the policies of the Obama administration, just like those of its predecessors for decades, had bred and fostered a state of permanent war. Obama further said in his UN address:

> One of the first actions of this General Assembly was to adopt a Universal Declaration of Human Rights in 1948. That declaration begins by stating that, "recognition of the inherent dignity and of the equal and inalienable rights of all members of the human family is the foundation of freedom, justice and peace in the world…."
>
> Human rights have never gone unchallenged — not in any of our nations, and not in our world. Tyranny is still with us — whether it manifests itself in the Taliban killing girls who try to go to school, a North Korea regime that enslaves its own people, or armed groups in Congo that use rape as a weapon of war.
>
> In times of economic unease, there can also be an anxiety about human rights. Today, as in past times of economic downturn, some put human rights aside for the promise of short-term stability or the false notion that economic growth can come at the expense of freedom. We see leaders abolishing term limits. We see crackdowns on civil society. We see corruption smothering entrepreneurship and good governance. We see democratic reforms deferred indefinitely.[23]

Simultaneously with this speech, Anwar Awlaki's father filed a lawsuit that asked a US federal court to enjoin the president from assassinating his son, a US citizen, without any due process. In an article published on September 25, 2010, Glenn Greenwald wrote: "At this point, I didn't believe it was possible, but the Obama administration has just reached an all-new low in its abysmal civil liberties record."[24] Greenwald was referring to a brief in which the Obama administration asked the court to dismiss the lawsuit without the possibility of hearing the merit of the claims by invoking state secrets privilege. "That is not surprising: both the Bush and the Obama administrations have repeatedly insisted that their secret conduct is legal, but nonetheless urge courts not to even rule on its legality. But what is most notable here is that one of the arguments the Obama DOJ raises to demand dismissal of this lawsuit is 'State Secrets': In other word, not only does the President have the right to sentence Americans to death with no due process or charges of any kind, but his decision as to who will be killed and why he wants them dead are state secrets, and thus no court may adjudicate their legality," wrote Greenwald in his article.[24] The first paragraph of the Obama administration's legal brief argued the dismissal of the case as follows:

> Defendants Barack H. Obama, President of the United States, Leon E. Panetta, Director of the CIA, and Robert M. Gates, Secretary of Defense, hereby move to dismiss Plaintiff's complaint, pursuant to Federal rule of Civil Procedure, an the grounds that Plaintiff lacks standing and that his claims require the Court to decide non-justiciable political questions. Alternatively, the court should exercise its equitable discretion not to grant the relief sought. In addition, Plaintiff has no cause of action under the Alien Tort Statute. To the extent that the foregoing are not sufficient grounds to dismiss this lawsuit, Plaintiff's action should be dismissed on the ground that information properly protected by the military and state secrets privilege would be necessary to litigate this action.[25]

On September 24, 2010, the Federal Bureau of Investigation (FBI) confirmed that they had begun a number of raids against the homes of antiwar activists in several states, on the grounds that they were "seeking evidence in support of an… investigation into activities concerning the material support of terrorism."[26] Raids were conducted in Minneapolis, Chicago, the state of Michigan and the state of North Carolina. In Minneapolis, many of the homes targeted were related to the Marxist group Freedom Road Socialist Organization. One of the loudest voices speaking out and denouncing this crackdown on dissent by the Obama administration belonged to Paul Craig Roberts. The next day, Roberts wrote an opinion piece titled, "It is official: the US is a police state."[27] Referring to the FBI raids and to what he viewed as being the practices of a police state, Roberts wrote: "Now we know what Homeland Security (sic) Secretary Napolitano meant when she said on September 10, 2010: 'The old view that, if you fight the terrorists abroad, we won't have to fight them here is just that; the old view.' The new view, Napolitano said, is 'to counter violent extremism right here at home.' Violent extremism is one of those undefined police state terms that will mean whatever the government wants it to mean."[27]

Guantanamo: Betrayal of Campaign Promises and Rule of Law
President Obama issued an executive order setting up indefinite detention
at Guantanamo Bay Detention Camp, on March 7, 2011.[28] Detainees' cases
would undergo a periodic administrative review. The Obama administration
also announced that it would use military commissions to review new
terrorism cases. Some of the prisoners rotting at Guantanamo had been
detained by the US, without trial or even any kind of charge, for nine years.

The American Civil Liberties Union (ACLU) had already voiced its outrage over the Obama administration's decision about Guantanamo. The
organization called the detention facility illegal, and wanted Guantanamo to
be shut down. The ACLU also opposed what it called "the illegitimate military commissions" and asked for the cases to be prosecuted in the federal
criminal court system. "The best way to get America out of the Guantanamo morass is to use the most effective and reliable tool we have: our
criminal justice system. Instead the Obama administration has done just the
opposite, and chosen to institutionalize unlawful indefinite detention —
creating a troubling 'new normal' — and to revive the illegitimate Guantanamo military commission," said Anthony Romero from the ACLU.[29 30]

What a difference a few years made in the flip-flop politics of broken
promises. On the campaign trail in 2008, candidate Obama's most emphatic
promise was to close the Guantanamo detention facility, which he viewed as
a stain on US international reputation. Candidate Obama said that
Guantanamo should be shut down and that habeas corpus should be restored for the detainees. "The US should have developed a real military system of justice that would sort out the suspected terrorists from the acci-
dentally accused," Senator Obama said in 2006.[31]

In June 2008, candidate Obama praised a Supreme Court decision that
allowed Guantanamo's prisoners to challenge their detention in civilian
courts. Obama said: "This is an important step toward reestablishing our
credibility as a nation committed to the rule of law and rejecting a false
choice between fighting terrorism and respecting habeas corpus."[32] Back in
2008, candidate Obama also said that the trials were "too important to be
held in a flawed military commission system that has failed to convict
anyone of a terrorist act since the 9/11 attack, and that has been embroiled
in legal challenge."[33] Yet another blatant contradiction between then and
now: back in 2006, Senator Obama had voted against the Military
Commission Act.

Obama's "announcement takes us back a step when we should be
moving forward toward closing Guantanamo and ending its shameful policies," concluded Romero in his statement.[29 30] This decision by the administration would enlarge the stain on the US' international reputation and
also make Obama lose the little credibility he had left overseas.

Bush-Clinton Mafia Dynasties

If a space or a time traveler would set his time ship's dial to 2015, with the US as its destination, one could think that a mandatory preparation for the journey to understand the US' political system would be an attentive study of the constitution. After all, the document, drafted in 1787 by the so-called founding fathers and finally ratified three years later in 1790 in its original form, is supposed to be the foundation of the US political edifice. Two hundred and twenty-five years later, the document had been so thoroughly gutted of its substantial original merits, at least in its spirit if not its letter, that the foundation of the building had become a superfluous architectural ornament. While the US Constitution was far from being revolutionary and granted equal rights only to white male landowners, it marked, in conjunction with the French Revolution of 1789, a resolute break from the European kingdoms. No king or queen could ever claim this land again, under any circumstance. A republic, ruled by a meritocracy of well-educated Anglo-Saxon patrician men, was born. Since 190 years after the US Constitution's ratification, however, which is exactly since 1980, the country has been ruled by two dynasties or their surrogates: the Bushes and the Clintons.

To understand the undemocratic and extremely seedy side of US modern-day politics, it would be imperative for our time traveler, de Tocqueville in training, to watch two classics of American cinema: The Godfather, and The Godfather Part II. Director Francis Ford Coppola, in his fictional, yet extremely well researched and documented films, invited us inside the US' underbelly. During the 19th century and up to the early 20th century, massive numbers of poor immigrants, mainly Italians, Irish and Jews from Eastern Europe, were lured to the Americas largely to escape economic hardship. Those who landed in the US quickly understood that they were excluded from, or at best marginalized in, this promised land run by white Anglo-Saxon protestants. The more ambitious ones, unencumbered by moral boundaries, developed their own form of government and social code of conduct in the form of a tightly knit family-like structure that usually strictly followed ethnic lines. The birth of organized crime in the US, either Italian, Jewish or Irish, was a direct consequence of the fight for survival of communities that were deliberately excluded from power or even political discourse.

Mafia families had a strictly enforced code of conduct and precise hierarchy, with a don (boss) at the top; a consigliere (adviser to the head of the family) directly picked by the don; an underboss who was usually groomed to be the don's successor; capos (the lieutenants), and soldiers. In the 1930s, under the supervision of Lucky Luciano, the don of all dons, not only the five Italian mafia families worked together, but they also collaborated on many occasions with the Jewish and Irish mafia. In this parallel brand of power and economy, mafia families extracted contributions, i.e. a primitive form of taxation of usually 10 percent of income, from businesses, ironically to protect them from random criminal activities. By the mid-1930s, mafia families controlled large sections of the US economy. The prohibition of alcoholic beverages, which spanned from 1920 to 1933, marked the apogee of the mafia families, either Italian, Jewish or Irish. The mob controlled the flow of liquor, and Americans were thirsty.

During the prohibition era, Joe Kennedy, father of John F. Kennedy and Robert F. Kennedy, the patriarch of a family that passed for being true US aristocracy, although he had been the grandson of a dirt-poor potato-famine Irish immigrant, substantially increased his vast fortune by importing, from the UK and Canada, and selling illicit liquor in association with Italian-American don Frank Costello and Jewish gangster Meyer Lansky. Joe Kennedy had an edge on the competition: he went into the prohibition era in 1920 with large stocks of booze from his father's stores. In what cannot be a coincidence, on the day prohibition ended 13 years later, Joe Kennedy had three exclusive deals to import British whiskey and gin, as well as an extensive network of retailers already in place. Kennedy understood that his political ambitions for his sons would require vast amounts of money. Like any mafia bosses, don Joe Kennedy wanted to start a dynasty at any cost and regardless of moral or even legal considerations. In the US, money meant power, and this notion was the motto for both supposed blue-blood patriarch Kennedy and don Lucky Luciano.

Arguably, the first term of George H. Bush, founder of the Bush dynasty, started in 1980 when he officially became Vice President or, to use the mafia term, super underboss to Ronald Reagan, an aging actor, perhaps already senile, hired to perform the role of global don: leader of the free world and most powerful man on earth, according to US mainstream media propaganda. Bush Sr. had previously run the CIA. During the two terms of the Reagan administration, from 1980 to 1988, it was common knowledge that Bush Sr. was the boss who led US policy. He officially became the don in 1988 and ran his own operation with pretty much the same crew until 1992. James Baker was the key consigliere to don Bush Sr., but he also listened closely to the Talleyrand of US politics, consigliere extraordinaire Henry Kissinger. Bush Sr.'s underboss was Donald Rumsfeld, who picked his capo in the person of Dick Cheney. George W. Bush or Bush Jr., when his turn came, kept most of the old don's crew with some minor changes and additions. Cheney became the underboss, while Rumsfeld took the vital Pentagon portfolio.

Before George W. Bush's turn, the Clinton dynasty came along in 1992, courtesy of Walmart, and with the firm intention, as an obligation to their sponsors, to facilitate a global corporate imperialist agenda. With the North

American Free Trade Agreement (NAFTA), don Bill Clinton went the extra mile for the benefit of his friends in transnational corporations. Bill Clinton became a favorite of Wall Street investment banks, such as Goldman Sachs, by being instrumental in the repeal of the Glass-Steagall Act, which was voted in 1933 during the Great Depression in the aftermath of the 1929 Wall Street crash. The Glass-Steagall Act limited commercial banks' securities activities, and it clearly separated commercial banking from investment banking, to curtail speculation. The repeal of this act allowed Wall Street investment banks to gamble money that was held in commercial banks, and this was arguably one of the lead systemic factors in the 2008 global financial-market crash.

Don Clinton's consigliere was mainly First Lady Hillary, but he also took the advice of the other super-consigliere besides Kissinger: Polish-born Zbigniew Brzezinski. Consigliere Brzezinski started his career in 1966 when he advised Lyndon B. Johnson. He returned in the late 1970s to advise Jimmy Carter. When he was Carter's consigliere, Brzezinski came up with the idea to finance and arm the mujahideen in Afghanistan to fight the Soviet Union. Don Clinton's underboss was Leon Panetta, and the lead capo was Rahm Emanuel. When dona Hillary Clinton lost what she viewed as being her turn in the driver's seat, both the Clinton and Bush mafias made sure that young capo Barack Obama, who had not patiently waited for his turn in the limelight, was surrounded by trusted hands. One can imagine the deal imposed on Obama by Bill and Dick. The Bush mafia would keep the Pentagon for the time being; Hillary would run US foreign policy from the State Department; don Bill's underboss Leon Panetta would become Obama's CIA director from 2009 to 2011, and boss of the Pentagon from 2011 to 2013. Clinton's trusted lead capo Rahm Emanuel became Obama's underboss. Don Bill did not stay idle after the 2008 election; he became Obama's lead consigliere, with the occasional help on geopolitical dossiers such as Ukraine from... Brzezinski, of course. The 88-year-old anti-Russian Democrat uber-consigliere's latest contribution had been to bring back the Cold War into international affairs. Bill Clinton's main task was to replenish the family coffers through the Clinton Global Initiative, a fundraising operation disguised as humanitarian. After the 2010 earthquake, Haiti became don Bill's pet project and personal fiefdom.

By now, our time traveler realizes that the premise of the 2016 US presidential election fight was already set. It would be a rematch of an old time classic: Bush against Clinton, dona Hillary versus don Jeb Bush. For good measure, and to give American consumers of elections a sense that their democracy is not an illusion, there would be unelectable challengers in the fake primaries. This would be strictly for entertainment purposes and to indulge the so-called American left. On a short list of likely seat warmers for Hillary were Elizabeth Warren, Bernie Sanders, perhaps even Joe Biden. On

the Bush side of the ring, the supposed primary challengers would be harder
to find: perhaps Donald Trump again, or phony Libertarian Rand Paul. But
let us listen to what consigliere extraordinaire Henry Kissinger said on the
issue; after all, he has advised more US presidents than anyone else alive. In
a September 6, 2014 interview with National Public Radio's *(NPR)* Scott
Simon, when asked if Hillary Clinton would make a good president,
Kissinger said: "I know Hillary as a person, and as a personal friend. I
would say, yes she would be a good president. But that would put me under
a great conflict of interest if she were a candidate, because I intend to support the Republicans.... Yes I would be comfortable with her as a president." Our time traveler is dazed, confused and disgusted by what the US
has grown into: the sort of charade that notions like democracy, the
common good and morality have become in this display of vile and raw
power for power's sake.

RADIO SPUTNIK, SEPTEMBER 12, 2015
Andrew Korybko of *Red Line*: If Joe Biden decides to throw his hat into the
ring, how could this affect the dynamic of the elections?

Gilbert Mercier: Ultimately, Joe Biden, if he runs, will serve an
entertainment purpose: sort of what is going on with Donald Trump in the
GOP primary. Biden might try to cater to the vote that seems to be gelling
for Bernie Sanders. He might be targeting that vote by talking about wealth
inequality and social justice and all of that. But Joe Biden is nothing new.
He cannot run on another ticket of "hope and change." Biden has been the
Vice President and part of the handlers of Obama for almost eight years. I
don't see the point. He makes a lot of gaffes and can be pretty sharp, but
what can he give to the show?

Overall, the 2016 US election will be like it was four years or eight years
ago: a political charade. If I was the editor of *The Onion,* a satirical
newspaper in the United States, I could write something today or tomorrow
like: "Breaking News: Hillary Clinton is Elected President of the US," and I
would likely be right. Because, in a way, it is all a make believe that there is a
real democracy in this country. In fact, there has not been a real democracy
in the US, with someone really in charge in the White House, since the
departure of Jimmy Carter in 1980.

It doesn't matter if Biden runs. Bernie Sanders will keep the former
Occupy folks, and they can vent some steam. Then maybe he will become
Secretary of Labor for Hillary Clinton. Regardless, what it is going to be is
the return of an old-time classic: Clinton versus Bush, and Hillary Clinton
will win. There could be only one real contender in the Democratic primary,
and it is John Kerry, but I don't think that he is going to run.

Andrew Korybko: I want to ask you about Sanders: What can Biden do
to steal his thunder?

Gilbert Mercier: I do have respect for Sanders, but I think that if he had wanted to be a real contender he would have run in 2008 or 2012. At the time, I was suggesting to the people of Occupy that he should run. Now he is going to run on the Occupy themes. I am not saying he is not sincere; he is sincere. But the question is: if he really wanted to win, he should have run as an independent, he should have done a Ralph Nader, if you wish. He would have run with a solid Libertarian like Ron Paul — not the son, Rand Paul — because both of them stand for less US intervention worldwide. This being said, Sanders is not doing it, which makes me think that he will, one way or another, operate as a seat warmer.

The US election is like a Hollywood script or, actually, more like a TV reality show. There is a cast, it is scripted, and it is about TV ratings. Donald Trump is perfect for it. This is what it is all about: to give people the illusion that they live in the greatest democracy in the world. Women will vote for Hillary; gays will vote for Hillary; Hillary has the support of Goldman Sachs; Hillary has the endorsement by Henry Kissinger; Hillary has the support of the military-industrial complex; they have been doing very good business.

II. Lowest Common Denominator Empire

3

In God We Trust, but Money We Worship

IN A MATTER OF A FEW hundred years the US has managed to rewrite its history into a mythological fantasy. The concepts of liberty, freedom and free enterprise in the land of the free, home of the brave are a mere spin. The US was founded and became prosperous based on two original sins: firstly, on the mass murder of Native Americans and theft of their land by European colonists; secondly, on slavery. This grim reality is far removed from the fairytale version of a nation that views itself in its collective consciousness as a virtuous universal agent for good and progress. Ronald Reagan expressed the most recent version of this mythology when he said: "America is a shining city upon a hill whose beacon light guides freedom-loving people everywhere."[1]

In rewriting its history about Thanksgiving, white America tells a Disney-like fairytale about the English pilgrims and their struggle to survive in a new and harsh environment. The pilgrims found help from the friendly and extremely generous Native-American tribe, the Wampanoag Indians, in 1621. Unfortunately for Native Americans, the European settlers' gratitude was short-lived. By 1637, Massachusetts Governor John Winthrop ordered the massacre of thousands of Pequot Indian men, women and children. This event marked the start of a Native-American genocide that would take slightly more than 200 years to complete, and of course to achieve its ultimate goal, which was to take the land from Native Americans and systematically plunder their resources. The genocide that began in 1637 marked the beginning of the conquest of the entire continent until most Native Americans were exterminated, a few were assimilated into white society, and the rest were put in reservations to dwindle and die.

When Christopher Columbus supposedly discovered the Americas in 1492 during his quest for gold and silver, an estimated 15 million Native Americans lived north of current-day Mexico, whom he erroneously called Indians. This was, by all considerations, a thriving civilization. Three hundred and fifty years later, the Native-American population north of Mexico would be reduced to fewer than a million. This genocide was brought upon the natives by systematic mass murder and also by disease, notably smallpox, spread by the European colonists.

Columbus and his successors' proto-capitalist propensity for greed was foreign to Native Americans. They viewed the land as tribal collective ownership, not as property that could be owned by individuals. "Columbus and his successors were not coming to an empty wilderness, but into a world which, in some places, was as densely populated as Europe, and where the culture was complex, where human relations were more egalitarian than in Europe, and where the relations between men, women, children and nature were more beautifully worked out than perhaps in any other places in the world," wrote Howard Zinn in his masterful *A People's History of the United States*.[2]

In many ways, the US celebration of Thanksgiving would be analogous to setting aside a day in Germany to celebrate the holocaust. Thanksgiving is the American holocaust. The original crimes of genocide and slavery are not limited to US early history but have found an extension in the policies of modern-day US. The systematic assault on other nations and cultures still goes on under various pretenses or outright lies. United States wars of empire are going on today more than ever before. These wars have left millions of people dead across the world in the course of American history, and they are still fought for the same reasons behind the Native-American genocide and slavery: namely, to expand the wealth of the US elite.

Defenders of Thanksgiving will say that whatever the original murky meaning of the holiday, it has become a rare chance to spend time with family and show appreciation for what one has. For most Americans today, however, it is hard to be thankful. As matter of fact, unless you belong to the two percent who represent the US ruling class, you should not be thankful at all. How can you be appreciative for what you have if you have lost your house to foreclosure, don't have a job and can't feed your family? How can you be appreciative if you are a homeless veteran? How can you be appreciative when you are poor or sick in a society without social justice?

On Thanksgiving Day, rich celebrities and politicians make a parody of what should be real charity by feeding countless poor and homeless. This eases their conscience, at least for a while. Charity, however, should not be a substitute for social justice. Just to ruin some people's appetite before they attack that golden turkey: keep in mind that Thanksgiving celebrates genocide.

Empires Come and Go

Like a bottle of milk, all empires have their expiration date. Long ago, national entities and cultures enthusiastically aspired to build empires, and the impulse for this was the erroneous assumption of being a superior civilization. It was about exporting an extensive set of aspirations, a culture, and a value system. Romans thought that their aqueducts and paved roads for the supposed savages of the north were the selfless gifts of a more advanced civilization. In what could be an indication that history is on an accelerated course, the life span of empires has become shorter. The Egyptian empire lasted more than 3,000 years, the Mayan empire survived 2,900, and the Chinese empire more than 1,600. Rome lasted a millennium: as a united empire, the Roman empire remained for 500 years, and the Eastern Roman empire or Byzantine empire lasted an extra 1,000 after the split from the Western Roman empire. The French and British empires had a global reach for centuries. Others were not as successful and disappeared in a few years. This was, of course, the case for the psychotic empire that Adolf Hitler tried to create. He thought that his empire, the Reich, would last a thousand years, and he was delusional, needless to say. To do well against the stress of time, empires must deliver a beneficial management to the local populations under their control. By contrast to the superior Roman technology that brought water to the occupied countries via aqueducts, Hitler built concentration camps to exterminate dissidents, Jews, Gypsies and gays.

The British and French empires competed for centuries to control the resources in Africa, the Americas and Asia. Africa was neatly divided: England controlled large swaths of the East, while France controlled the West and some countries in North Africa. In Asia, the British ruled India and what is now Pakistan, and the French called Indochina home. Both empires lasted about 100 years, mostly respecting each other's zones of governance. Despite the atrocities committed on the local populations, both the British and French did positive things to buy peace with the locals. Even though France was in Vietnam for the rubber, Saigon was built like a French city. Both empires built a better infrastructure from scratch: roads, education, some basic healthcare and a more efficient agriculture. The goal of the improvement wasn't humanitarian at all; it was about the efficiency of the exploitation of resources and labor.

World War II marked the beginning of the end for both France's and Britain's empires. The deal was sealed in Yalta in 1945 between Stalin and Roosevelt, with Churchill being present but already taking a back seat. In a matter of five years, and about 60 million deaths, from the ruins of Britain, France, and Japan emerged two new empires: the US and the Soviet Union. The spoils of war for the Soviet Union and the US were a split global hegemony. The former allies of necessity quickly became enemies in proxy wars, but both completely agreed on one thing: the time to rule globally was over for Britain and France. The old imperial powers were slow to understand the nature of the new game. It took the loss of India in 1948, the UK's biggest piece of imperialist real estate, and the loss of Indochina in 1951 after France's defeat by a communist movement in a colonial war of independence in Vietnam, to make the UK and France begin to see that they might have from then on an ever-shrinking role on the world stage. Nevertheless, it took them nine years to digest fully the consequences of Yalta. In 1956, France and Britain enjoyed their very last joint imperialist venture by attacking Egypt over the ownership of the Suez Canal. The fiasco of the Suez Canal was the final wake-up call for the decrepit empires, which were told to back off by the US and the Soviet Union.

The Cold War between the US and the Soviet Union was the conflict of the post-1945 era until the fall of the Soviets. In a way, compared to today's uncertainties, this was a stable time. It was all highly predictable, and despite flashpoints like the Cuban missile crisis, some positive achievements resulted from the competition between the two empires. The Russians were ahead in their space program, which made John F. Kennedy push for a space program spearheaded by NASA. The sense of balance achieved by the conflict of the two superpowers was smashed to smithereens when the Soviet Union collapsed in the late 1980s. The US empire got a clear shot at a one-man show and seized the opportunity.

In this new US empire, a cultural race to the bottom is underway, and it is not only helped but also partly instigated by the major US media outlets. The news divisions of TV networks have become the bullhorns and drum machines of sideshows. For example, news outlets, from *CNN* to *MSNBC* and *Fox News* became so obsessed with a story about Anthony Weiner, a Clintonite footnote politician, who had sent photographs of himself in his underwear to some of his followers on Twitter, that they called the incident Weinergate and devoted to it weeks of coverage in summer 2011. Certainly, real news organizations should not invest so much of their time to gossip, in a country that is falling apart and is involved in countless wars. On the other hand, the media's goal is not to inform the American public but to keep it entertained and therefore distracted from the mass of real problems that are piling up. The road to success in the former land of opportunity has mostly become a dead end. The public school system is in a shambles, and only money can buy a decent education. While the poor and minorities are often basically illiterate and without any chance at upward mobility, the sons and daughters of the elite go to the same prestigious Ivy League schools where their parents went. Bush's No Child Left Behind initiative was a political farce; it should have been called: no rich child left behind, to conform to the reality of the US education system.[3]

When is the US empire's expiration date? Hard to tell, but the decline has already begun. The empire is nearly bankrupt and indebted to some potential competitors like China. If China should sell all the trillions in assets that it owns in US Treasury Bonds, the US financial market would collapse. The large octopus that has become the US military eats more than $1 trillion a year from the country's coffers. No empire can sustain such follies for a very long time.

The Unending Rat Race

The back of every dollar bill features the inscription: In God We Trust. While this inscription seems to be borderline unconstitutional in the context of separation of church and state, there is an even more disturbing and contradictory aspect to it, which is the mixture of religion and money. Although a large majority of US citizens claim to believe in God, their actions are largely motivated by material gain.

For most, running the money rat race is an imperative to survive and make a meager living. For the wealthy small minority, the money race is a way to keep score and represents an insatiable urge to get more. The richest two percent of the US population live in an existential impasse of confusion between need and want. This is the psychological cornerstone of capitalism and consumerism driven by marketing and advertising: turning a desire for a product into an artificial need so that enough is never enough.

We live in a society where quantity supersedes quality in all aspects of life. Real talent and hard work have little chance of success. The time of Ernest Hemingway and Jackson Pollock is long gone. In the US, money talks, and it defines social values in a perverse system where what you have determines who you are. Money does most of the talking for celebrities with sometimes not a hint of talent but with a pretty face, a famous derrière, a busy sex life and a knack for publicity. The TV networks enhance their ratings as a slew of interchangeable and forgettable personalities supply the fodder for the insatiable American appetite for gossip about the sex lives of the rich and famous. Without any sort of moral questioning, overpaid CEOs, movie stars, popular musicians, athletes and other celebrities feel they deserve the obscene wealth they accumulate. This new aristocracy is rarely based on merit, intelligence, wisdom or entrepreneurship, but rather on the ability to tap into fleeting trends or collective erotic fantasies.

Even more concerning is the part that money plays in public life, not only as a measure of success but also as an overriding principle. Politicians are supposed to be public servants, yet without very large quantities of cash, it is impossible for them to get elected to public office. Consequently the rich, the corporations, the banks get de facto control over the political process by financing political campaigns.

The global financial meltdown of 2008 was a perfect opportunity to change course and reassess our individual and collective priorities in this difficult balancing act between quality and quantity. A few have undertaken the necessary introspection, but most still live in the mental la la land of I want more. The narcissistic and compulsive natures of this desire to accumulate more material possessions undermine any real social progress, because this urge can never be fully satisfied. The unfair social pyramid has its basis in social injustice, exploitation and oppression.

Mahatma Gandhi once said: "Earth provides enough to satisfy every man's need, but not every man's greed."[4] This wise statement made decades ago applies today more than ever. Greed and appetite for power were the underpinning psychological forces that sustained the dictator Mubarak in Egypt, motivated Gaddafi in Libya, Assad in Syria, and a few kings in Saudi Arabia, Bahrain, Jordan and Morocco. From time to time, as in the Arab world in early 2011, the pawns revolt against the kings and tell them loudly and clearly that, at the end of the game, we will all be put in the same box. Maybe the rest of the world will catch up and tell their respective ruling classes, CEOs, celebrities and other fat cats that it is time to share their wealth or face the consequences of their greed. Buddha said: "An act to make another happy inspires the other to make still another happy, and so happiness is aroused and abounds. Thousands of candles can be lighted from a single candle, and the life of the single candle will not be shortened. Happiness never decreases by being shared."[5] If only we could learn that happiness can be infinitely shared, we would not confuse it with financial success, and we might work together for the common good.

4

Idiocracy with ADD and Stockholm Syndrome

THE 2010 HOLIDAY SEASON was good for US retailers, as Americans were back on a shopping spree, often buying what they did not really need, and foremost what they could not afford unless they put themselves further into debt. Despite the recession, consumerism was still the US' favorite addiction. Strangely enough, while consumer spending was up to a level similar to the one before the global financial meltdown of 2008, the Consumer Confidence Index fell in December 2010 and scored at a very low 50 percent.[6] As an indicator, in periods of economic prosperity, the index is at around 90 percent. Was this trend yet another confirmation of the fundamental irrationality of consumerism, when people who were worried about the economy were spending more? Or was consumerism a way for Americans to cope with their deep anxiety?

MasterCard reported that sales from early November through Christmas Eve 2010 were up 5.5 percent from the previous year.[7] Sales were especially strong for luxury goods and jewelry, which obviously meant that rich people were feeling bullish about their own financial predicament, if not about the overall economy. Two very different realities were at play in the dysfunctional US economy: on one hand, for those few who benefited from the vast and fast growing transnational corporate wealth, the recession was over; on the other hand, for most Americans, they were still the victims of the Great Recession and could barely make ends meet.

The fact that consumer confidence was down was anchored in the reality experienced by the overwhelming majority of Americans. The housing market was very bad, with real estate values still eroding nationwide; the unemployment rate remained at around 10 percent; gas prices were skyrocketing and some analysts said they could pass $5 per gallon in 2011. However, and this was the only good news in the economic forecast, the stock market was doing well.

So once again, we had this big and unsustainable social dichotomy. For the well-off few with investments on Wall Street, it was the best of times, whereas for the majority of Americans, it was the worst of times. The US now has two separate economies that move on completely different tracks, in a form of economic apartheid, separate and unequal, between transnational corporate interests on one side and everyone else on the other. While it was good times again for mega-corporations and the wealthy at the top, 2011 would bring more despair and misery for most Americans.

In 2010, big corporations made giant profits as they focused on the expanding markets of China, India and other fast growing emerging economies. Meanwhile, the same corporations, while sitting on large piles of cash reserves, cut down on their US operations and did not hire US workers. For example, General Motors, a company that was bailed out by the Obama administration with US taxpayers' money, was making more cars in China than in the US. General Electric was keeping its payroll down in the US but would invest $2 billion in China and $500 million in Brazil, in a venture that would create 1,000 jobs in Brazil and none in the US.[8]

Road Kills on Rove's Crossroads

By 2010, Karl Rove had returned as a major player in American politics. The man known as Bush's Brain had successfully engineered a move of George W. Bush's administration, with some additions, to *Fox News*. Sarah Palin, Newt Gingrich, and everyone in the Republican Party (GOP) with political ambition had become a pundit on the supposedly fair-and-balanced propaganda outlet. Besides *Fox News,* the key to the coming gains by the GOP and their Tea Party bedfellows and foot soldiers was an electoral money machine which, as a super-PAC, had raised $30 million from undisclosed sources: more money than anyone else in that election cycle. This was Rove's creation: American Crossroads.

If you read the friendly, and almost inclusive sounding fuzzy propaganda concocted by Karl Rove for American Crossroads, you would understand that Rove was not only controlling the political message of the right, but also the funds of the GOP. By controlling both the money and the message, Rove had positioned himself as the ultimate kingmaker among the Republicans. For example, in the case of Tea Party newcomer Christine O'Donnell, Rove decided that she was not viable or needed (after all who needs two Sarah Palin), and he made sure that her campaign was not generously funded. Here is how Rove's American Crossroads defined its mission:

> American Crossroads is a new kind of non-profit political organization dedicated to renewing America's commitment to individual liberty, limited government, free enterprise and a strong national defense. In 2010, America faces much more than a choice among various candidates for public office. We face a crossroads. A fundamental decision about the future direction of our country that will impact America's strength and character for years to come. We face a decision between two starkly different visions of America: one where the human creativity and initiative that are unleashed by liberty and free enterprise generate the economic growth this nation needs – and one where an increasingly powerful, all controlling federal government decides how to allocate the economic spoils.[9]

The trick for Karl Rove was to create a money-raising machine for the GOP and capitalize on the anger and pseudo-libertarian philosophy of the Tea Party movement. This worked and American Crossroads quickly acquired a large number of followers on all social media.

As early as January 2010, the Democrats had to cope with the shock of Scott Brown's Republican victory for Ted Kennedy's Senate seat in Massachusetts. Ted Kennedy died a second time. The vote gave the Obama administration the major headache of trying to get bills voted in the Senate without the Democrats' previous super majority. With the Democrats' magical 60-vote majority gone, the legislative process would become gridlocked on important issues including immigration, health care reform, and climate-change policy. If nothing else, it seemed that the White House would use the sharp elbows of Chief of Staff Rahm Emanuel against the left rather than the right of the Democratic Party. After Ronald Reagan's landslide victory in 1980, Ted Kennedy made the following statement, which strangely applied to the Democrats' political predicament: "If Democrats run for cover, if we become pale carbon copies of the opposition and try to act like Republicans, we will lose, and we deserve to lose.... The last thing this country needs is two Republican parties."[10] The enthusiasm that had carried Barack Obama to the White House in 2008 had already been replaced by a raw populist anger that the GOP managed to ride. General De Gaulle made the following statement more than half a century ago: "You may be sure that the Americans will commit all the stupidity they can think of, plus some that are beyond imagination." This was exactly what a majority of voters had done in Massachusetts.

Subsequent months of the 2010 election campaign were long on negative ads, personal attacks and plain stupidity while being short on real debates on most key policy issues. Comedian Jon Stewart held a rally one week before the elections to restore sanity. It was alarming that political satirists were those who advocated restraint while the politicians rambled and ranted.

The hodgepodge that was the Tea Party was more remarkable for what it was against than what it was for. Poujadisme, a French conservative reactionary movement of the 1950s, was probably the best terminology to qualify the far-right American Tea Party. If the hope-and-change slogan had been the emotional thematic behind Barack Obama's victory in 2008, anger and fear were the emotions that fueled the Tea Party activists. The wave of unrealistic optimism that had brought Obama to power had crashed into a wall of negativity. The Tea Party activists said they were for liberty, free enterprise and the US Constitution, even if some of their leaders were completely clueless about these. They opposed what they called big government, the handouts of entitlements programs, ObamaCare, immigration reform, and the supposed Islamization of America. Although they were against the Wall Street bailout, they had opposed cracking down on banks through financial reform. The Tea Party movement claimed to be concerned about the US budget deficit and to want a crackdown on wasteful government spending, yet the biggest item of wasteful spending in the US, representing 25 percent of the overall budget, was not even debated and questioned. If the Tea Party had been a real libertarian movement and not a hodgepodge of rednecks and Christian fundamentalists operating as Karl Rove's foot soldiers and serving corporate interests, especially big oil and the military-industrial complex, they would have forcefully opposed the wars in Afghanistan and Iraq.

It was a given that the GOP and Tea Party voters would show up at the polling stations on election day in early November 2010. But what was problematic was whether the left, Green, and Latino voters would show up and if so, whether they would register a protest vote against the Obama administration. Progressives had plenty to be upset about. Despite Obama's electoral promises, Guantanamo was still in business, the Patriot Act was still in effect, the war in Iraq was not over, the war in Afghanistan had spread to Pakistan, the health care bill had not gone far enough, and the Democrats had failed to crack down on Wall Street. The Greens were not happy. The climate change bill had not been passed by Congress, the handling of the British Petroleum oil spill by the Obama administration had been badly botched, and Obama had caved in to the oil company and drill-baby-drill crowd by lifting the moratorium on offshore drilling in the Gulf of Mexico. The Latino vote was also compromised by the failure of a Democrat-controlled Congress and Obama to push through an immigration reform bill giving 12 million illegal immigrants a pass to citizenship, as candidate Obama had promised during his 2008 campaign.

In the end, for all these reasons, the Republican Party and their Tea Party allies secured a majority in the US House of Representatives and made gains in the Senate by picking up more than four seats in November 2010. A large majority of Americans cast their ballots more with their guts than with their heads and against their own interests. In the case of the Tea Party, it was all anger and primal fear. It was not the first time, and it would not be the last. After all, Bush had been reelected in 2004 after starting two wars during his first term in office.

The voters said enough, in 2006, a slogan of the Democrats, and decided that they wanted to kick out the GOP. They maintained this momentum in 2008, and the Democrats took advantage of the left's anti-Bush, anti-war energy, and they rode this wave to win the Congress and the White House. But by 2010, the real American left had been shut out of the political discourse. The US had no left with proper representation, but instead had a center-right president by the standards of any European country, a GOP right, and a Tea Party far right. The unrealistic enthusiasm that had taken Barack Obama to the White House had also not been fully rational, but at least it had the merit of being based on naive optimism rather than negativity.

In 2010, the voters had a change of heart again and elected the same people they could not stand in 2006 and 2008: brawn was in, and brain was out. Russ Feingold, arguably one of the smartest guys in the US Senate, lost his seat in Wisconsin. To compensate for this poor performance in the Midwest, Californians gave a victory to Jerry Brown for the governorship, and Barbara Boxer defeated Carly Fiorina. Also in the west, Harry Reid beat the Tea Party favorite Sharron Angle by a narrow margin. The voters blamed many of the incumbent Democrats for two years of government inaction. The attention span of many American voters is so incredibly short that it qualifies as a psychological disorder. They blamed a group of people and not a system for their lack of jobs, the global recession and the general sense of malaise in America. A majority of US voters had rewarded Rove and his latest accomplices with a political comeback, although the previous Bush administration had started two wars and crashed the global economy.

Americans had elected Obama in 2008, to clean up the mess of the Bush administration. Yet, because the US is like a teenager who suffers from attention deficit disorder (ADD), few realized that the new president would not have at his disposal a magic wand to make all their problems disappear overnight. Like teens who suffer from ADD, many Americans expected immediate gratification in whatever they did, or they would throw a tantrum. That is what the Tea Party was: the expression of a tantrum created by fear, anxiety and confusion.

Besides ADD, it turned out that in 2010 the US was very much like an abused wife who had returned to her brutal husband for another beating, in what has become known as the Stockholm Syndrome. On August 23, 1973 two automatic-machine-gun carrying criminals entered a bank in Stockholm, Sweden. They started to blast away with their guns and terrified the bank employees. One of the robbers, a prison escapee, told the employees: "The party has just begun."[11] For the next five days, the two robbers held four hostages, three women and one man, in a bank vault and strapped with dynamite. After the hostages were released, despite the fact that they had been threatened, abused, and made to fear for their lives for five days, it quickly became apparent from interviews that they had supported and established a strong emotional bond with their captors. A woman hostage later became romantically involved and engaged to one of the criminals, and another started a fund to help the bank robbers with their attorneys' fees. The oblivious US voters were just like the two Swedish women: they had been beaten, but they had fallen in love with their torturers. They perceived only two choices, both of them unacceptable, and they oscillated from one to the other with nearly every election cycle.

Panem, Circenses and Brainwashing

Little has changed in empires in 2,000 years. Panem et circenses, i.e. bread and circuses, described the methods used by Roman rulers to exert control on the populace and distract them from important matters of public affairs, by having them feast and watch gladiators fight to the death. If the Roman Empire can be compared to the US of today, its rulers and media associates are using similar tools to brainwash most people into oblivion.

In the US, the Super Bowl gets higher ratings than any other TV broadcast. It is truly the quintessence of US culture. It is violent and flashy. It showcases some sexy cheerleaders during breaks in the game and, just like the Roman games, has a lot more brawn than brain. In a nutshell, it is a representation of what most Americans would want to be but are not, or would want to have but do not. Top football players are on multi-million dollar a year contracts and are huge celebrities. Unlike gladiators, who were expendable slaves, the media and the public adoration have given top athletes almost a god status. After all, they have what most Americans want: fortune and fame, and all the trimmings to go with these. Even if a large proportion of Americans are barely scrapping by, they still want to be entertained by a bunch of extremely overpaid athletes whose achievement in life is being big, fast and able to either throw or catch a ball.

This would not be such a problem if the politics of distraction applied by US mainstream media were not across the board and around the clock. Just like the fascination with the Super Bowl hypnotizes Americans by making them comfortably numb, US elections are also part of a circus: the circus of politics as farce and distraction. I could have written an article in February 2012 and titled it: Breaking news: Mitt Romney wins the GOP nomination. Although I am not a gambling man, the odds of me losing this kind of bet would be minute. In this sort of cynical but realistic perspective, where one can predict American politics well ahead of the game, I could also have easily written something titled: Breaking news: Obama gets reelected for a second term.

In the US system, which is neither a democracy nor a republic but rather a pluto-oligarchy, politics seem to be preordained, as if going to the polls does not really matter that much. Intuitively and unfortunately, with every new election cycle, Americans become more resigned to the fact that their voices will not be heard yet another time. In 2012, some managed to stay engaged with the Occupy movement despite a complete blackout from the mainstream media about real issues, but most Americans would rather get their daily feeding of talking points. Everywhere in the world citizens are confusing talking points with news; they are confusing politics with endless charades, and they have been played in this way for decades. Like US politics, the Super Bowl is a giant circus, but the outcome is slightly less predictable and has fewer consequences. Maybe one day, Americans will want more than just to be entertained, either by athletes, celebrities or politicians, and instead they will want to get involved and do what needs to be done to take charge of their own destiny.

Sex, Lies and Politics

General David Petraeus had to resign from his position as Director of the CIA three days after the US elections, on November 9, 2012. He admitted to an affair, but some, such as the *New York Times*, said that the convenient timing of the resignation was related to an intelligence failure in a September 11, 2012 attack on the US Consulate in Benghazi, Libya.[12] We will probably never know whether Petraeus was blackmailed for money by his lover or framed for internal CIA reasons or political ones. His resignation will excuse him from being called to testify before Congress about the security breach in Benghazi. This was an embarrassment for the Obama administration. Petraeus had been credited with turning around the Iraq war at its worst stage for the US, in 2007. But the fact was that this resignation left a new slot open for an appointment by Obama during his second term.

In the Orwellian world we live in, a four-star General became a spy, and a Clinton spy, Leon Panetta, was switched to the Pentagon as Secretary of Defense. Petraeus' affair was supposedly discovered by the Federal Bureau of Investigation (FBI), which had spied on a CIA director from a compromised computer he had used. This is nothing new in the US, in the rarefied circle of power, considering that Bush Sr. had been a CIA director before becoming Reagan's Vice President. Often in the US, sex scandals have been motivated by politics. From Marilyn Monroe's affair with John F. Kennedy, to more recent sex scandals involving Bill Clinton, John Edwards and Arnold Schwarzenegger, it seems that sex is always linked to power. It is often — this could be the case with Petraeus — a way to hide a forest behind a tree.

Sex, in a less schizophrenic culture than America's, should not be this way. It brings life and death, propels and paralyzes, compels rebellion and collaboration, inspires love and hate. It is free most of the time, but it sells always. The media relentlessly serve up made-up teenagers, with no natural talent except their sex appeal, as the ideals of beauty in TV advertisements; reality shows promote premises that border on pornography, and the serious news are presented alongside the shenanigans of out-of-control pop stars. This is the more obvious form of sexual manipulation. There is also a more insidious use of sexuality for political ends.

Consider, for example, the spectacle of the 2012 US Democratic National Convention. This followed a public debate, not on US aggressions throughout the world, but on abortion and gay marriage. It was a seduction on a national scale. The incumbent President's wife looked as if on a hot date, and the next day, the newspapers discussed her well-sculpted bare arms, designer dress that gave the illusion of being short, and high-heeled red shoes. There followed former President Bill Clinton, and later President Obama himself, both of whom wowed the public with the deliveries of their speeches rather than any relevant content. The public reacted as anticipated. Some of its response in social media was quite graphic, and it was all about sex.

Between consensual adults, sex should be fun, free, creative and absolutely nobody else's business. Private life, even for public figures, should be private in sexual matters, unless it is criminal. Most of us know what constitutes a sex crime, and this is rather simple: non-consensual sex, such as rape or sex with youths below the age of consent, or sex that is associated with actions that are criminal. One example would be the fraudulent expenditure of public funds to support a mistress.

In countries that are non-puritanical like Italy, France, or Haiti, the threshold for a sex scandal is rather high. In the case of Dominique Strauss-Kahn, for example, it took an accusation of rape — some said Sarkozy set him up — to finish his career in the IMF simultaneously with his political campaign for the French presidency as a Socialist contender.[13] Silvio Berlusconi had to engage in sex orgies with underage girls, combined with graft and tax-fraud allegations to lose his position and be sentenced to prison.[14] In Haiti, where Michel Martelly has cultivated the persona of a bisexual sex fiend as musician, the only sexual scandals that have received any significant attention have been homosexual rapes by UN personnel.[15] In the US, however, the threshold for a sex crime is much lower. It is an issue of puritanical morality in complete contradiction with the reality of a hyper-sexualized culture.

While the US faced catastrophic problems such as floods followed by winter storms and homelessness, a second round of a recession that might eclipse the 2008 crash, a real estate market still shaky, a build up of tension between Turkey and the Assad regime in Syria, and millions of Americans unemployed, the US and its sad excuse for media were focused mainly on the sex scandals of politicians.

The US remains a borderline schizophrenic country living in delusions and lies. On policy issues, the US claims to support freedom and democracy while the real concerns are to secure resources, their transit routes and to maintain the empire by the use of either military or economic power. The US, especially in the Obama era, boasted endlessly about its positive role in world affairs, while it supported repressive and authoritarian regimes world-wide. This was the case under dictators Ben Ali in Tunisia and Mubarak in Egypt before the Arab Spring. It is still the case, in a flagrant double standard, in Bahrain, Yemen and Saudi Arabia.

On sexual matters, America's pathological contradictions are just as acute. In many ways, the US is still a puritanical country that was left behind by the 1960s sexual revolution. Americans do not talk much about the fact that 60 percent of married men and 40 percent of married women have af-fairs at some point in their marriages. Since the degree of infidelity is corre-lated with the number of people with whom these married adults come into contact, it stands to reason that the figures are much higher for politicians. Yet, the US has an obsession for sexual topics when it comes to its celebrities and politicians, and quite often the distinction between the two is blurred. The US has a serious dichotomy problem when it comes to sex: while it eroticizes violence, it is also a sexually repressed culture.

The Petraeus scandal in 2012 and the Weiner scandal in 2011 were among several sex scandals in recent years that had involved US politicians and caught the media's attention. Former California governor Arnold Schwarzenegger started a nightmarish journey of public humiliation and private hell after it was revealed that he had a love child with one of his staffers; US news outlets relentlessly headlined the rage of his wife.[16] Former Democratic presidential hopeful, John Edwards, was indicted by a federal grand jury on charges related to his efforts to cover up an affair and child that he had when his wife was fighting cancer; Edwards had allegedly used campaign donations to fund the cover up of the sex scandal.[17] What is truly pathetic in all this is that the US media and journalists were paying attention to side stories of this nature. Editors were putting up all this meaningless nonsense as headliners. There is one thing that the American press knows well: Americans cannot get enough of sex scandals. People on the East Coast were still dealing with the aftermath of tropical storm Sandy;

the job market was still shaky in most states; another major financial crisis was looming on the horizon due to a more than $17 trillion national debt, yet most so-called reporters and media organizations were talking and writing about a CIA director and well-respected general having an affair and being forced to resign.

American Exceptionalism Is No Shining City on a Hill

The concept of American exceptionalism is as old as the US, and it implies that the country has a qualitative difference from other nations. The notion of being special gives Americans the sense that playing a lead role in world affairs is part of their natural historic calling. However, there is nothing historically exceptional about this: the Roman empire also viewed itself as a system superior to other nations and, more recently, so did the British and the French empires.

On the topic of American exceptionalism, which he often called Americanism, Seymour Martin Lipset noted that "America's ideology can be described in five words: liberty, egalitarianism, individualism, populism and laissez-faire. The revolutionary ideology, which became American creed, is liberalism in its eighteenth and nineteenth-century meaning. It departed from conservatism Toryism, statist communitarianism, mercantilism and noblesse-oblige dominant in monarchical state-church formed cultures."[18] Naturally identifying America's system as a unique ideology, just like calling its successful colonial war against Britain a revolution, is a fallacy. For one, the US was never based on social equality, as rigid class distinctions always remained through its history.

In reality, the US has never broken from British social and economic models. American exceptionalism implies a sense of superiority, just like in the case of the British, French and the Roman empires. In such imperialist systems, class inequality was never challenged and, as matter of fact, served as cornerstone of the imperial structure. In American history, the only exception to this system based on social inequality was during the post World War II era of the economic miracle. The period from 1945 to the mid-1970s was characterized by major economic growth, an absence of big economic downturns, and a much higher level of social mobility on a massive scale. This time frame saw a tremendous expansion of higher education: from 2.5 million people to 12 million going to colleges and universities, and this education explosion, naturally, fostered this upward mobility where the American dream became possible for the middle class.

Regardless of real domestic social progress made in the US after the birth of the empire in 1945, for the proponents of American exceptionalism — this includes the entire political class — the myth of the US being defined as a shining city on a hill has always been a rationale to justify the pursuit of imperialism.[1] For example, when President Barack Obama addressed the nation to justify the US military intervention in Libya, he said that "America is different," as if the US has a special role in history as a force for good. In a speech on US foreign policy, at West Point on May 28, 2014, Obama bluntly stated:

> In fact, by most measures, America has rarely been stronger relative to the rest of the world. Those who argue otherwise — who suggest that America is in decline or has seen its global leadership slip away are misreading history. Our military has no peer.... I believe in American exceptionalism with every fiber of my being.[19]

In his book, *Democracy In America,* Frenchman Alexis de Tocqueville was lyrical in his propaganda-like adulation of American exceptionalism, defining it almost as divine providence. De Tocqueville wrote:

> When the earth was given to men by the Creator, the earth was inexhaustible. But men were weak and ignorant, and when they had learned to take advantage of the treasures which it contained, they already covered its surface and were soon obliged to earn by the sword an asylum for repose and freedom. Just then North America was discovered, as if it had been kept in reserve by the Deity and had risen from beneath the waters of the deluge.[20]

This notion, originated by the French author and amplified ever since, which defined the US as being the divine gift of a moral and virtuous land, is a cruel fairy tale. It is mainly convenient to ease up America's profound guilt. After all, the brutal birth of this nation took place under the curse of two cardinal sins: the theft of Native-American lands after committing a genocide of their population; and the hideous crime of slavery, with slaves building an immense wealth for the few, in a new feudal system, with their sweat, tears and blood.

5

A Broken Social System Exposed

FIVE YEARS AFTER HURRICANE Katrina, the Gulf Coast and New Orleans had to deal with another large-scale disaster, in this case purely man-made, in the form of the BP oil spill. It seemed that New Orleans could not get a break, but again the Crescent City was far from being the only town at the epicenter of a looming ecological and social disaster.

Most people in the mainstream media had failed to establish a link, which should have been rather obvious, between climate change, global warming, the deadly fires in Russia, and the unthinkable human tragedy that was unfolding for Pakistanis under flood waters in 2010. The highest temperatures on record had triggered the fires in Russia, and the torrential monsoon rains in Pakistan had caused the wrath of the Indus River. In both cases, we were dealing with extreme weather, which scientists view as a consequence of global warming. In other words, global warming caused climate change, which in turn produced extreme-weather phenomena such as hurricanes, floods, and droughts.

In 2005 New Orleans, hurricane Katrina exposed more than just a poorly managed city and state.[21] It revealed, not only a completely ineffi- cient and careless federal government, but also the biggest fairytale of global consciousness: the US as a model of democracy, and a system for all countries to look up to and copy. Katrina gave the US a bad reputation worldwide and offered outsiders a glimpse of the real country: the one of racial divide, despite the Civil Rights gains of the 1960s, and even more importantly the one of class divide. The world saw the America of disaster capitalism. Class is a dirty word in US politics because of its Marxist connotations. It is, however, the right one to use. In late August 2005 New Orleans, those who could afford airline tickets or had cars were able to get out of harm's way.

When journalists report on a story — providing that they embrace a pseudo-neutral *Associated Press (AP)* style — they are not supposed to get emotionally involved with their subjects. The unreachable goal is to provide readers, listeners or viewers with copies or segments that appear to be objective, impartial and loaded with facts and data. This is of course never the case, because mainstream journalists always serve a few masters. Therefore, elements of truth are tailored to serve specific agendas. Despite this, when a big story happened, like Katrina's wrecking of New Orleans in late August 2005, the pseudo-clinical *AP* neutrality was thrown out the window, and the occasion became emotional, especially for the mainstream's star journalists. Cold clinical analyses do not sell copy or get high TV rating; emotion and personal stories do.

For me, Katrina's arrival to the Crescent City was always personal. I used to own a place in New Orleans: a beautiful Victorian house Uptown. When Katrina arrived and wrecked the town, I was in Canada doing location scouting for a film. Regardless, before the hurricane hit, I managed to keep a constant eye on the coming landfall and focused my effort into moving my tenants out of town and getting a good friend to put plywood on all the windows and doors. I got my people evacuated, and once this was done, I made travel arrangements to New Orleans. Despite the lockdown of the town that had been ordered by the governor of Louisiana, I managed to get in, and I arrived on September 4, 2005.

While worldwide audiences were glued to their TV screens watching wall-to-wall coverage, at times honest and accurate and at other times tall tales made up by the likes of Brian Williams, I first made my way through Katrina's war zone to check on my house and on some friends who had decided to ride out the storm. To my surprise, the house was spared any significant damage. My new goal became to document the event as accurately as I could. For more than a week, I drove everywhere: Midtown, Uptown, the Garden District and, of course, the areas that had taken the biggest blow, such as the Lower 9th Ward and Lakeshore. The surreality of the level of destruction did not even come close to the inept and borderline criminal inaction of local, state and federal officials. New Orleans' rich left the town two or three days before the hurricane hit, whereas the poor were left behind to fend for themselves. The number-one priority for officials quickly became security: protecting their own assets and properties and those of their rich friends.

Along with the mercenaries of Blackwater — the Praetorian Guard of the Bush administration — the Louisiana National Guard was deployed. In early September 2005, most people carried guns in New Orleans to protect their properties from looting. The poor, in majority African Americans, received very little help and were mad. Most storeowners became vigilantes armed to the teeth. Looting took place, but not at all to the extreme depicted by the mainstream media to drum up fear and paranoia.

For about 10 days, New Orleans post-Katrina was a story of complete government failure at all levels. The world realized that, right under a veneer of power projected by the empire, there was a hidden third-world country with deep racial divisions and astonishing inequality. More than 1,600 people died in the aftermath of Katrina, and almost all of them were poor and black.

Up until 2008, I came back every year, not only to take care of my house, but also to compile what had become my photographic story: the progress report of New Orleans post Katrina. In three years, besides some punctual initiatives from NGOs and celebrity-driven efforts that turned out to be largely self-promotions, nothing really happened. The brutality of the storm became a slow death by decay. More than 100,000 people left New Orleans with nothing and were scattered to the winds. They became the internal refugees of disaster capitalism. Within a year, the nice parts of town were fixed, while areas like the Lower 9th Ward became no-man's land urban jungles. The vegetation took over the abandoned structures, creating a surreal landscape of rot and decay.

Katrina played a big part in the undoing of the Bush administration, yet neither Democrat nor Republican has learned the lessons from the storm. Some people from the left have categorized the BP oil spill as being Obama's Katrina, and indeed it was, but unfortunately it was not the only disaster for Obama. There was, of course, Obama's Vietnam in Afghanistan, and what could be viewed as his biggest domestic policy mistake: the bailout of Wall Street with essentially no questions asked. In regard to New Orleans, the shortcomings of the Obama administration were numerous. Ten years after the devastation of hurricane Katrina, the Lower 9th Ward, which had been hit hardest by the floods and had been home to a large majority of the city's poor and African Americans, is still desolate. With little infrastructure and very few businesses, fewer than 25 percent of residents have returned to the Lower 9th Ward. Even for those who had the knowledge and resources to rebuild, daily life is a constant struggle. A major lesson from Katrina, and from the 2008 financial collapse, is how cruelly the US treats those of its citizens who have nothing.

The lights from Reagan's shining city upon the hill have dimmed. The American dream is still alive and well for those two percent of the population who control more than half of the wealth. For 98 percent, the dream has been exposed as a farce, an elaborate Ponzi scheme cooked up by Wall Street. In the fetid waters of post-Katrina New Orleans, the US saw a disturbing reflection of itself. None of the uncomfortable questions raised by Katrina have been answered. How was it that a country that was able to send hundreds of thousands of troops halfway around the world to topple Saddam Hussein could not protect one of its cities? How could a third-world disaster happen within the borders controlled by the leader of the first world? Why did black Americans suffer the most?

A record number of Americans are homeless or have lost their houses to banks. Almost 50 million rely on food stamps to eat. Many states are on the verge of insolvency. Meanwhile, the US has no problem spending the bulk of its financial resources on repressive entities such as the police, the prison system and, of course, the military, instead of allocating more funds to education, health care, and social services. The ravages of Katrina in New Orleans and the financial crash of 2008 were the first and second blows of a devastating one-two punch, yet Americans behave as if they don't understand that the current US system is past due for a drastic makeover.

Once upon a time, the business model of the US empire was to rebuild after either a man-made or natural disaster. The Marshall Plan rebuilt Germany after World War II, and a similar program, headed by General Douglas McArthur was tailored to Japan. The empire of disaster capitalism has come up with a new business plan for the world: after destruction, nothing gets rebuilt. Haitians are still waiting for Godot and wondering who stole the money given to them by the international community. Godot has not visited Detroit, Michigan, either. Godot will certainly not pay a visit to the ruins of Iraq and Syria, courtesy of the empire of chaos. What will it take for the countless victims of the managers of disaster-for-profit to come out of their lethargy? What will it take for them to emerge from their semi-comatose state engineered by the mainstream media on the payroll of disaster capitalism? Will it be a hurricane bigger than Katrina sweeping through the Gulf of Mexico and destroying the bulk of the oilrigs? Will it take the destruction of another country following the model of Afghanistan, Iraq and Syria? Godot or a providential man will not come. People worldwide must understand that we have already entered a stage of general systemic failure, and that it is time for action, not for change of window dressing. Godot will not come; it is time for people of the Earth to grab their destiny by the scruff of the neck, time for drastic and concerted action.

COUNTERPUNCH RADIO, SEPTEMBER 1, 2015

Eric Draitser: We are marking the 10th-year anniversary of Katrina, and I am joined by Gilbert Mercier, the editor in chief of *News Junkie Post.*[22] He had some interesting experiences around Katrina and New Orleans. I came around your piece on Katrina, it is really powerful and it took me back 10 years ago. Please take us through your personal experiences.

Gilbert Mercier: For me the nightmare of Katrina was completely personal from the get go. I used to own a lovely Victorian house in an area of New Orleans that is called Uptown. When Katrina was starting to form and roam through the Gulf of Mexico, I was in Toronto, Canada working. I made my way back to New Orleans as quickly as I could, and I landed in town the 4th of September. I landed when the people of the mainstream media were already starting to phase out Katrina. I was very lucky my house didn't have any damage, and I started wondering around in a war zone. There were no traffic lights, nothing… very few civilians. Everybody in the aftermath of Katrina, for at least two weeks, was carrying a gun. You had the guns-for-hire, which our colleague Jeremy Scahill calls the Praetorian Guard of the empire, who were the mercenaries of Blackwater. They were first to come in, and I saw a few. Then, very quickly, they deployed the National Guard. Also, the storeowners were heavily armed, and pretty much everybody in New Orleans, including myself, was wearing combat fatigue. It was a very tricky situation.

ED: Yes, I think that it is definitely true. Actually you touched on two different important points: on one hand, the collapse of our urban infrastructure, especially in lower-income areas; on the other hand, something you pointed to is the militarization of this country, of the responses. Since Katrina, it has become a routine: we saw it in Boston after the bombing; we saw it in Baltimore and Ferguson.

GM: Absolutely Eric! This is the reflex of the empire. The reflex of the empire is not to help the helpless, it is to send people with guns: as many as they can. That is the issue. There was a lot of hoopla on mainstream media about the looting. There was barely any looting at all!

ED: Let's talk about that a little bit. How did you perceive the media treatment of that issue? Do you think it was constructed for political reasons or do you think that it was the natural racist reaction?

GM: They just covered it. There are, of course, the stories of Brian Williams digging up dead bodies, which were complete lies! Brian Williams, whom I saw, was staying at the Ritz Carlton in the French Quarter. The French Quarter barely got affected by the flood at all; neither was my area of Uptown or the Garden District. The wealthy areas of New Orleans are on higher ground. They covered the story the way they cover stories, which is: "it is very sad, we must do something." Everybody was panicking. Mayor Ray Nagin was panicking and trying to pretend he was doing something. It is a joke! The government at the time was inept, and so is the government now, because things have not improved. It is just absolutely phenomenal!

ED: Right! It just reminds me of the coverage of looting. There is a politic behind the way it is covered. I read accounts of armed white people being able to protect their homes, while armed black people were singled out and targeted.

GM: Absolutely! Let's give the listeners of *CounterPunch* some data. New Orleans before Katrina had about half a million inhabitants. In the Katrina aftermath, 50 percent left. Before Katrina, New Orleans was a black town with a black mayor; it became a white town with a white mayor. There is an anecdote that I must tell. I was having a drink at a bar in the French Quarter. There was a Blackwater guy talking with the bartender. They were using the N word and were saying: "The wrong people will leave, and that could be a good thing." Katrina, in a sense, is sort of like ethnic cleansing with a strong socio-economic ingredient. The poor had to leave, such as the people who did not carry flood insurance, which was by the way part of a federal program. Of course I had flood insurance because I could pay. But the poor couldn't, so they lost everything. In 10 years, New Orleans has lost 100,000 people, mainly blacks who were scattered to the winds to Texas, Georgia, etc., wherever they had family who could welcome them.

ED: Yes. It reminds me of Rahm Emmanuel saying: "Never leave a natural disaster go to waste." The exploitation of Katrina to achieve what the white bourgeois class in that city had wanted for generations.

GM: $120 billions of federal money was allocated to New Orleans; 75 percent of it was spent on emergency relief: not to rebuild the city. They had no intention to rebuild. They had no intention to rebuild the Lower 9th Ward or the Lower 7th Ward. They had no intention to rebuild the poor areas.

ED: Yes, I want to add to that. We are not talking about rebuilding structures but about institutions like public education or public low-income housing. They managed, and I am not saying this randomly, to capitalize on Katrina.

GM: You see, Eric, Katrina is a snapshot of a type of philosophy, if you can call it that; I call it disaster capitalism. That type of politics is what happened to Detroit, Michigan. It is a policy of when there is a natural disaster, you don't rebuild. You allocate some money that changes hands and disappears, like for example in Haiti. My *News Junkie Post* colleague Dady Chery writes extensively about that. As matter of fact, there is an anecdote about this. One of the big expenditures after Katrina was to give people the wonderful FEMA trailers manufactured in Florida. Unfortunately, the trailers had a big problem with toxic formaldehyde from the insulation. Of course, the infamous New Orleans FEMA trailers were recycled to Haiti in 2010.

ED: And just like New Orleans, Haiti is not being rebuilt, and it seems to be by design.

GM: Design or complete stupidity, it could be one or the other. Bottom line: they always seize the opportunity. You write a lot about Syria. It is the same thing. You destroy a place, like they did in Iraq; you never rebuild it. That is the model!

ED: I want to touch on your view of the situation in New Orleans now. Is it forever scarred?

GM: I love New Orleans. New Orleans is to me the most fabulous city of America! I am a French citizen, and of course New Orleans was French, just like Haiti. It was sold by Napoleon to Thomas Jefferson in 1804. It has culture, jazz, the people are lively, but it is not the same feeling that it used to be. Midtown got rebuilt. I met wonderful people that did it on their own. The strong did it. This country is an experiment in social Darwinism.

ED: I would totally agree with you here. The notion of progress, of post-racial America with Obama...

GM: That is nonsense! Since the election of Obama, the core values of policies, both foreign and domestic, have not changed. Look at Ferguson.

ED: Or Baltimore.

GM: This country, since Katrina, has manufactured internal refugees from disaster capitalism!

ED: New Orleans is not an isolated incident, but emblematic of a clear process.

GM: What happened with Katrina, and people became aware of it worldwide, is the realization that this superpower has a third-world country within. But they quickly forgot, because people suffer from amnesia. That is the problem. None of the primary issues has been addressed. Climate change: no. Oil is cheap. Absolutely nothing! They follow, one way or another, a simple model, and I am not saying that it is a plan. If it is, it is a crazy plan. They follow a simple model: we wreck everything, we never rebuild, and we extract the resources. That is it.

ED: In other words, it is colonialism, imperialism and capitalism.

Looting After a Disaster

After a natural disaster government authorities usually fail to bring help to people and exercise greater concern about the dissolution of the social order in its more raw expression, which is looting, than about the welfare of the victims. Some looting took place in post-Katrina New Orleans, in Port-au-Prince, Haiti, after the January 12, 2010 earthquake, and in Concepcion, Chile, after the February 27, 2010 magnitude-8.8 earthquake.

Chileans in Conception were in shock, just like the trapped New Orleans residents in 2005 and more than a million Haitians, all of whom felt, for very good reasons, that they had been abandoned by their governments.

They were homeless, thirsty and hungry. Under such circumstances it was absolutely understandable that the social order would quickly break down and that ordinarily law abiding citizens would resort to looting. Yet governments, independently of any geographic considerations or even ideological views, always put the accent on social order and control of people, as opposed to the delivery of necessary help to those they are supposed to protect. This was the case in New Orleans, where the National Guard and Blackwater were dispatched to maintain order. The same applied to Haiti, where the US dispatched a massive number of troops for the same purpose. This was the same direction taken by the left-leaning Chilean government towards its earthquake victims. Chile's President immediately sent 10,000 soldiers to Concepcion to maintain order. "We need food for the population. We are without supplies and if we don't resolve that, we are going to have serious security problems during the night," said Concepcion Mayor Jacqueline Van Rysselberghe.[23]

In such tragic situations, any storeowner in possession of supplies should be required to let the population take what they need, if the storeowner lacks the humanity to do so on a voluntary basis. Instead of sending soldiers brandishing guns to maintain order, a more human form of government would dispatch its soldiers with blankets, bottled water and food to distribute. There is no moral justification that should allow any government to victimize its own people in such a way. In dire circumstances, survival should always supersede social order.

The Slavery of Debt

Predatory global capitalism is running amok on the global economy. In December 2010, several countries of the European Union were on the verge of insolvency. Ireland had to be bailed out by richer EU members and was strong-armed into accepting a budget-austerity plan from the IMF. Later, it was Greece. Financial analysts were predicting that the next victims of disaster capitalism's domino effect would be Portugal and Spain, with Italy as a likely candidate to follow. Britain and France were trying to deal with their own budget deficits and huge national debts by implementing austerity measures, such as raising the retirement age and cutting down social benefits. These measures encountered strong opposition from workers, government employees and Europe's middle class, both in the streets and in the workplaces. Nevertheless, European governments moved ahead and implemented tax increases and spending cuts.

On the other side of the Atlantic, the US went into a completely different direction by betting on tax cuts instead of tax increases, despite the fact that, for every dollar spent by the federal government, 40 cents were borrowed. One thing Americans could count on, after the GOP-controlled House of Representatives was seated in 2010, was a drastic cut in critical federal social services and programs. The same phenomenon had already started at local and state levels. Across the nation, cities and states were cutting down on essential social services for the poor and even on police and firefighters. California, the most populous and one of the so-called richest states in the nation had a budget shortfall of more than $25 billion.[24] California, just like so many states across the US was on the verge of bankruptcy, yet the country was told that the recession was officially over.

During the boom, fueled by the global real-estate bubble of casino capitalism, borrowing was made easy for countries and for individuals both in Europe and the US. In the decade before 2008, many bought houses they could not afford. The banks had persuaded people that the value of their investments would keep increasing. Furthermore, the financial institutions, which had promoted all these loans for properties that they knew were overvalued, also pushed others financial shenanigans, such as equity lines of credit, personal lines of credit and, of course, credit cards on the middle class.

The financial sector had operated like a clever drug dealer: the first few fixes had been free until the buyers were fully hooked. People became addicted to borrowing, took a second loan on their already overvalued properties, and kept three or four credit cards, borrowing on one to pay the other. In other words, Wall Street and other financial markets concentrated wealth at the top while engineering and dumping an insurmountable amount of debt on the middle class and the poor. This highly dysfunctional system came to a halt in late 2008. After this, the banks were no longer eager to lend. Qualification for a loan to buy a house became incredibly difficult, with lenders appraising properties much lower than the market price. Credit-card companies lowered the available credit for most of their customers and stopped seeking new credit addicts like they used to do. In 2015, banks were back at it, and most people were getting hooked again on borrowing money.

Life on $2 a Day: Growth of Inequality and Extreme Poverty

Homelessness in the US is nothing new. This endemic problem was greatly amplified in the 1980s by the policies of the Reagan administration, regarding defunding of mental-health programs. The recession after the financial crash of 2008 compounded the problem to a breaking point. With states and cities nationwide facing major budget deficits, programs for homeless people, such as affordable housing, ended up on the chopping block.

According to a summer 2010 report from the department of Housing and Urban Development (HUD), the total number of people who sought temporary shelter in 2010 grew by more than two percent compared to the previous year, and the upward trend was expected to continue.[25] HUD had wrongly hoped that the $1.5 billion program in the economic stimulus bill would help hundreds of thousands of people to avoid homelessness; instead the funds went to support the working poor.

An even bigger scandal concerning homelessness in the US was the number of veterans in this predicament.[26] According to the Veterans Administration, 107,000 former service men and women were homeless in 2009. Sixty-one percent of homeless veterans were between the ages of 35 and 54. Ninety-six percent of homeless veterans were men, but the number of female Iraq and Afghanistan veterans experiencing homelessness was on the rise, as was the number of homeless veterans with children. Veterans had high rates of Post Traumatic Stress Disorder (PTSD), traumatic brain injury and, sometimes, sexual trauma. All these factors can lead to higher risk of homelessness. About 50 percent of homeless veterans had serious mental illness, and 70 percent have substance abuse problems.

For the overall homeless population, the data from HUD showed that over 42 percent of those who were living in shelters in 2008 had a disabling condition. HUD also noted a sharp nine-percent increase for families with children living in shelters. The number grew from 473,542 in 2007 to 516,721 in 2008; HUD noted that these numbers only accounted for school-age children. "It is likely that the actual number of homeless children may reach as high as 1.3 million," said the HUD report.[26]

Indeed another report released in December 2011 by the National Center on Family Homelessness, found that more than 1.6 million children were homeless in the US. The report titled, "America's youngest outcasts 2010," painted a grim picture, provided a ranking for the 50 US states, and recommended some policy solutions to be implemented both at the federal and state levels.[27] "The recession has been a man-made disaster for vulnerable children. There are more homeless children today than after the natural disasters of hurricanes Katrina and Rita, which caused historic levels of homelessness in 2006. The recession's economic devastation has left one in 45 children homeless, an increase of 38 percent from 2007 to 2010," said Dr. Ellen Bassuk, President and Founder of the National Center on Family Homelessness and associate Professor of Psychiatry at Harvard Medical School.[27]

The report showed that homeless children in the US suffered from hunger, poor physical condition and poor emotional health as well as limited academic proficiency in reading and math. "The constant barrage of stressful and traumatic experiences has profound effects on their development and ability to learn," said the report.[27] The planning and social safety net to protect these vulnerable children was extremely limited. Sixteen states had no planning at all, and only seven states had actively addressed the issue. The states that fared the best were Vermont, Minnesota, Nebraska, North Dakota, Maine, New Hampshire, New Jersey, Massachusetts, Montana and Iowa. At the bottom of the ranking were Georgia, Florida, Nevada, Louisiana, New Mexico, California, Arizona, Arkansas, Mississippi and, at the very bottom, Alabama.

According to the report, 30,000 children became homeless each week, and more than 4,400 each day. "In the face of this man-made disaster, there must be no further cuts in federal and state programs to help homeless children and families. Deeper cuts will only create more homelessness that will cost us more to fix in the long run. We can take specific actions now in areas of housing, child care, education, domestic violence, and employment and training to stabilize vulnerable families and prevent child homelessness," said Bassuk.[27]

Wealth inequality in the US has never been as great as it is today. Throughout the 18th and 19th centuries, wealth inequality increased, with the sharpest rise occurring during the birth of capitalism and the massive industrial revolution in the mid-19th century. The concentration of wealth, or share of it owned by the wealthiest one percent, rose sharply after this period to peak at about 40 percent of the total wealth right before the crash of 1929 and the onset of the Great Depression. Thereafter, wealth inequality gradually decreased until the late 1970s. That era, from the end of World War II to the late 1970s, will be remembered with nostalgia as the golden years of the US middle class. It was a time of optimism, opportunities and expansion, when hard work could legitimately pay off in the form of the middle-class American dream: a breadwinner who could, on a single salary, support an average family of four and provide it, among other things, with a car, and even a modest home with a white picket fence. Those days are long gone.

In the past 35 years, the US has become a study in blatant and obscene contrast between rich and poor. Although FDR's New Deal had helped to lift the country out of the Great Depression and to establish the social and economic policies and standards that created a middle class, the pendulum shifted in 1980. America's social fabric has been eroding ever since. Between 1983 and 1989, the share of wealth held by the wealthiest one percent grew from 33 to about 38 percent. Overall, the most pronounced increase in US wealth inequality occurred between 2001 and 2007, when the wealthiest one percent managed to take a phenomenal 43 percent of the country's total wealth. According to a study released in 2010 by the consulting firm Capgemini, the population of high-net-worth individuals, i.e. people with $1 million or more of investible assets, within the top 10 US metropolitan areas, increased by 17.5 percent in 2009 compared to 2008, which was the highest growth rate for a single year in the previous four years.[28] Simultaneously, the national unemployment rate jumped from 5.8 to 9.3 percent. Most of the gains for the rich were attributable to the stock market. New York City received a greater boost than any other metropolitan area, with the number of high-net-worth individuals growing to 650,000: an 18.7 percent increase in 2009 compared to 2008. This helped to confirm that US taxpayers' bank bailouts had helped those on Wall Street and been a giant swindle to plunder the public treasury for the bank accounts of millionaires. This was socialism in reverse: a transfer of wealth from the public to the private sector. By 2013, only seven percent of the wealth was left to the bottom 80 percent. The middle class had become poor, and the poor had grown destitute.

In September 2013 *Forbes* magazine reported that the 400 wealthiest Americans were worth just over $2 trillion.[29] This was equal to the gross domestic product (GDP) of Russia and represented a doubling of their combined net worth since 2003. So, five years after the financial crisis had bankrupted many in the US and the globe, the rich were getting a lot richer. The average net worth of the billionaires on the *Forbes* 400 list was an astonishing $5 billion: an increase of 800 million in just one year. In fact, the rich had become so wealthy that 61 billionaires had failed to make the cut. They were omitted from *Forbes'* list because, to enter the exclusive club of the super rich in 2013, one's net worth had to exceed $1.3 billion.[29]

Simultaneously with celebrations by *Forbes* and other business magazines about who had regained his place as number one, or who made the top 20 this year but not last year, and which wealthy 83-year-old married his 42-year-old consultant, and what sorts of mansions the super rich favor nowadays, the US House of Representatives announced its intention to cut the food stamps program, also called the Supplemental Nutrition Assistance Program (SNAP), by a whopping 50 percent, i.e. $40 billion. Contrary to the use of food stamps by the needy in the past to supplement assistance programs for those who could not work, many working families were relying on food stamps to survive, because the income from their jobs was keeping them at or below the poverty level. This was especially true for those who worked in the big retail chains. For example, the salary of a Walmart sales associate in 2013 ranged from $7.47 to $10.77 per hour. Consequently those with full-time status, defined as being employed for 34 hours per week for 52 weeks per year, earned only $13,200 to $19,000 a year: a salary that put them well below the poverty level of $23,000 per year for a family of four. Nevertheless, Walmart was fighting all proposals to raise the minimum wage in the US. Given that Walmart was employing 1.2 percent of the US workforce in the private sector in 2013, one could say that a significant part of SNAP was serving to subsidize Walmart. That was not all. Many Walmart employees also relied on Medicaid and other government programs for anything approaching a decent living standard. Indeed, taxpayers were estimated to subsidize Walmart to the tune of $900,000 per store, per year.

By contrast to the dire poverty of those who generated Walmart's wealth, if we put aside *Forbes'* official list of the super rich and did some of our own math, it immediately became evident that number one (Bill Gates) and number two (Warren Buffet) were rather puny compared to Walmart's owners. Specifically: in the *Forbes* gallery of the super rich, Christy, James, Alice, and S. Robson Walton hardly stood out at the seemingly modest rankings of number six through number nine, respectively, but in fact their net worth added to an obscene $136 billion. This was $6 billion more than the fortunes of Gates and Buffet combined! As for the nominal number one: his fortune seemed to defy all physical laws, having grown from $9.35 billion in 1994, when he became a philanthropist, to $72 billion in 2013. Unlike Bill Gates, Warren Buffet had only recently jumped on the bandwagon of tropical-disease eradication. His fortune had merely stayed the same despite his various donations; but being the world's most successful investor, profits would surely flow to Buffet from his pledge to give away his fortune to the Bill & Melinda Gates Foundation. True, it is difficult not to make money when one is a billionaire, given the power and access that money buys. But was this all that had grown the Gates fortune at such a phenomenal rate? How could one fail to make a profit from supposed philanthropy projects to eradicate tropical diseases when one is able to support the development of vaccines, invest in the companies that manufacture them, pressure governments throughout the world into adopting them into their vaccination programs, and control all the publicity about them?[30] [31] After all, one of the most valuable things that money buys is the control of language and information.

In the US, which is home to the *Forbes* 400, households with children are a fast-growing group that lives on $2.00 or less per person per day. This shocking condition is formally labeled extreme poverty by a World Bank metric that gauges poverty "based on the standards of the world's poorest countries." Since poor Americans live in a wealthy country, before 2013 they had been excluded from this official estimate of dire poverty in the world. In a study for the National Poverty Center, H. Luke Shaefer of the University of Michigan and Kathryn Edin of Harvard University applied the World Bank metric to the US for the first time to show that in mid-2011, and based on cash income, about 1.65 million households, with 3.5 million children, lived in extreme poverty.[32] Since the official poverty level was considered to be $17.00 per person per day, this extent of extreme poverty implied that millions of Americans were subsisting on less than 12 percent of the poverty-line income. Contrary to popular perceptions, the authors further found, based on a measure of cash income, that about one half of the extremely poor heads of households were white and almost one half were married. Children suffered most: between 1996 and 2011, their numbers in extreme poverty increased by 156 percent.[32]

How did the social safety nets in the US shrink to allow such a catastrophe? The authors singled out two main factors: the Clinton administration's welfare reform of 1996, combined with the Great Recession of 2008. The 1996 welfare reform ended the only cash entitlement program for poor families with children and replaced it with a program that provides only time-limited cash assistance, with a requirement that able-bodied recipients promptly rejoin the work force. Specifically, a restrictive federal program, called Temporary Assistance for Needy Families (TANF) has come to replace the need-based program, Aid to Families with Dependent Children (AFDC, or welfare). Consequently, cash assistance fell from 12 million recipient families per month in 1996 to 4.5 million families by December 2011. Meanwhile the 2008 recession led the government to expand SNAP from around 25 million recipients per month in 1996 to 47 million in October 2012. In effect, the working poor were assisted, while those who had become chronically unemployed and desperate were left to fend for themselves. It was astonishing that nearly 50 million Americans — mostly children — were depending on food stamps to survive.

Current conditions in the US are worse than they were immediately before the Great Depression, but gone are the days of an FDR, when a US President was not merely a front for corporate interests, and he could persuade his own class to put a brake on its excesses so as to prevent a worker's revolt. Unconcerned that about 16 percent of all Americans required food stamps to keep from starving, the US House of Representatives proposed, as part of the Farm Bill deliberations, to reduce SNAP by $40 billion, i.e. 50 percent, so as to provide subsidies such as free crop insurance, mostly to rich farmers. Although it was unlikely that the US Senate would pass such a deep cut, its discussion had the effect of muting all earlier debates about a cut of less than 10 percent. Much was made of the fact that the food-stamp program had become exceptionally fat in the preceding few years and was presumably in need of a trim. Such arguments almost always omitted any mention that this expansion had been done to alleviate the social impacts of the 2008 recession, compounded by the dismantlement of AFDC in the 1990s. The US House of Representatives further declared that it would only give food assistance to those who worked for more than 20 hours per week: in effect, formalizing poverty for US workers. In the end, in February 2014, Obama signed into law a Farm Bill (H.R. 2642) that reduced SNAP by $8.6 billion.[33] Along with this cut in food stamps, there would be coercive requirements for drug tests. Thus the poor would be infantilized and dehumanized. Unlike the US poor of the past, who were treated with dignity and could dream of a better future for their children, today's poor have no hope at all. Their children will likely not attend college. At best, they might also get a minimum-wage job.

Global disaster capitalism has turned many nations into beggars, but a third-world country is rapidly growing at the heart of the empire. Beyond the cold reality of numbers and statistics, there is nothing abstract about feeling the pain in your guts when you don't have enough to eat; seeking a safe shelter for the night when you are a homeless woman with two kids; and, when you still have a roof over your head, constantly struggling to keep food on the table and pay the bills. A shameful poverty already affected 50 million people in the US, and more families would sink into extreme poverty, and millions more children would go to bed hungry as US politicians run their campaigns around the issues of family values and sanctity of life. Poverty is not an abstraction at all, or a pissing contest like that of the mega-rich who fight to be number one or two. Poverty is an inhuman burden that nobody should have to experience. In the past three decades, in the US, the middle class has become poor, and the poor have become destitute; meanwhile, the disgustingly rich have wallowed in their insatiable greed, making money with money and exploiting their new serfs. How long will the rich be allowed to worm their way through the core of the country even as they present it to the world as an appetizing shiny red apple? A revolution will surely come. A nation cannot function with wealth so concentrated and misery so widespread.

6

Putting Bandages on the Titanic

W HEN HE WAS ELECTED in 2008, President Obama brought a sense of hope for real changes, not only in the US but also abroad. Some people naively hoped that the new US administration could become a catalyst for a peaceful global revolution that would address world problems like poverty, climate change and social justice. The timing could not have been more perfect, considering that global capitalism was in the midst of a collapse. The notion of hope for changes that Obama conveyed was recognized with a Nobel Peace Prize in 2009. During a speech in Cairo that year, Obama eloquently defined our universal common grounds despite cultural and religious differences.[34] Soaring rhetoric was always a key element in the so-called Obama effect. Unfortunately, the great words were never followed by tangible actions.

It is ironic that this cornerstone speech on US foreign policy was delivered in Egypt while Mubarak, a dictator who had been fully supported by all US administrations for the last 30 years, was still ruling that country. Up until about three weeks before, Hosni Mubarak had still been considered by the Obama administration as an important ally and good friend in the region. Even more ironic was the fact that, about a year and half later, Egypt had become a center of protest in the Middle East.

During the crisis in Egypt, American politicians displayed a remarkable show of unity. Ever since World War II, it seems that Democrats and Republicans easily agreed on one thing: preserving US interests. In the context of the still prevalent American exceptionalism, this meant nothing less than defending the empire, controlling worldwide resources, and shoring up vassal regimes and transnational corporations. Mubarak in Egypt and Ben Ali in Tunisia were typical examples of the American empire's vassal structure system that were being challenged by a 2011 political tsunami (under Chapter 20). The Arabs in North Africa and the Middle East wanted to set their own destiny and were redefining the geopolitical landscape. If this movement had bloomed, it might have become the catalyst for fundamental changes where humankind unite to seek better governance on a global scale, to tackle the real problems of our times such as overpopulation and climate change.

Despite a change in Washington's narrative, the political class refused to reconsider some basic parameters. During a press conference in February 2011, Obama talked about his proposed budget and the events unfolding in the Middle East.[35] His goal was to cut the budget deficit by $1 trillion in 10 years. The cuts would affect education and social programs but would largely leave the monstrosity that was the so-called national security budget fully funded. America's ruling class was unable to see that the clear-and-present danger for worldwide peace, prosperity and progress was not coming from pseudo-terrorist threats, but instead from an out-of-control empire set on waging permanent wars. If the US military would pull out from Afghanistan, Iraq, Japan, Germany, South Korea and Africa, $7 trillion could probably be cut from the budget deficit within 10 years.

Obama saw himself as a pragmatic leader who wanted to implement incremental change, but despite his rhetoric he was still trying to shore up the foundations of a crumbling empire. The times called for deep systemic transformations, not window dressing changes. Revolutions have a common meaning: they are all a symptom of a broken system. The system was broken globally, and Obama was putting bandages on the Titanic.

Fifty years from now, historians will probably write about the fall of the US empire, but history is writing itself furiously in the present, accelerated by the revolution of global freedom of information. What would have taken years to gather is accessible to anyone with a few strokes on a computer keyboard. So, never mind the historians of the future, and let us see how reality is shaping up today.

Since 9/11, a chain of events so dire has occurred that it would seem the empire defeated itself by a series of catastrophic mistakes. After that day, the US wanted revenge, and the war in Afghanistan became an easy sell for the Bush administration. The neoconservatives seized the opportunity to push their agenda for the Project for the New American Century (PNAC), and this was precisely the Achilles' heel of the empire.[36]

When the Bush administration attacked Iraq in 2003, a critical element escaped its understanding of the regional and demographic parameters: namely, that by toppling the Sunni regime of Saddam Hussein, they would give the upper hand to the oppressed Shiite Iraqi majority allied with Iran. In other words, the US troops who fought and died in the conflict did so ultimately for the benefit of the Iranian Islamic Republic. The blunders did not stop with geopolitics but were compounded by a catastrophic financial burden.

If the Pentagon had been a corporation, it would have been the largest one in the world. The curiously called, Department of Defense (DOD), has cost American taxpayers, since the ill-advised attacks on Afghanistan and Iraq, around $700 billion a year. If you add up the health care for wounded veterans, and layers of new security administrations such as the Department of Homeland Security, the numbers keep adding up to top $1 trillion a year. Overall, more than 25 percent of the federal budget gets swallowed up in the financial black hole that is the Pentagon. If Americans could do the math, they would quickly understand that the bill for the two wars has crept up to more than $15 trillion. To achieve the neocons' chimera of an everlasting global American empire, money had to be borrowed. For every dollar spent by the federal government, at least 40 cents are borrowed. The US used to borrow money mainly from Japan and Europe, but now it does its main borrowing from China. In a striking reversal of fortune, the poor man of Asia has become the country in the world with the most liquid assets.

Americans have a delusional sense of historic exceptionalism, which they share with most previous empires. After all, the US ascension to a leading role on the world scene is recent. On the losing side of history were Japan, the empire of the sun, and also Britain and France. The Cold War was a fairly predictable era. Beside a few crises such as the flashpoint of the Cuban missile crisis, the two superpowers fought to augment their respective turfs thought proxy wars. Afghanistan came along for the Soviets, however, and the long war made the Soviet Union collapse. Naturally, the US started to act as the only superpower left and the master of the universe. The narratives of Ronald Reagan and his successors, including Barack Obama, are peppered by such elements. All empires have the same distorted vision of themselves. The Romans imposed the Pax Romana on their vassals for a long time, so did Charlemagne and Napoleon for a much shorter time. Power is cyclical and never lasts.

Thanks to *WikiLeaks* and the courage of his founder Julian Assange and Pentagon whistleblower Bradley Manning (under Chapter 17), it became rather obvious that, while Obama had changed the official tone of Washington from the Bush administration, the overall goals of US foreign policy had remained the same: ensure and expand US power and authority over vassal states. This push to establish a new world order under exclusive US authority has been prevalent in all of the US administrations since the end of the Cold War. Obama, whatever his personal convictions, is trapped by a complex nexus of interlocking institutions such as the Pentagon, CIA and State Department, and by powerful interest groups that profit from endless wars. The very same institutions and interest groups have been at the core of every post-1945 imperial presidency. As early as 1946, President Harry Truman wrote: "From Darius I's Persia, Alexander's Greece, Hadrian's Rome, Victoria's Britain, no nation or group of nations has had our responsibilities."[37] Nevertheless, most analysts and foreign-policy experts assume that the 21st century will not be exclusively American and that, in this tectonic power shift under the push of Russia, China and India, the emerging new world order will be plural and decentralized. Americans will have to adapt to a new paradigm where the US loses its status of uncontested leadership.

A Castle Made of Sand

What some economists called the Great Recession officially started in December 2007. The global financial meltdown started a bit later, in the fall of 2008, in the US. To call this massive crash a recession was always an understatement made to avoid a global panic. A more accurate term would have been to call it the Second Great Depression, which almost all financial experts and policymakers failed to diagnose and treat as such.

On June 27, 2008, I wrote an article titled: "Are We Heading for a Worldwide Depression Worse than 1929?" for a news site that is now defunct. At the time, most readers found my forecasts to be alarmist or even disconnected from reality. It turned out that, on the issue of the looming crisis, I was much closer to the mark than most economists or journalists who cover financial topics. In retrospect, what I find most alarming, especially because I don't claim to be a financial expert, is the fact that so few people saw the coming financial crash.

Most Americans, either Republicans or Democrats, are still fervent advocates of the free-market concept of capitalism. "The market knows best" is still their motto and the cornerstone of a crumbling US economy. Americans accept the pathological cycles of boom and bust, which are directly related to the free market, as being as unavoidable as death and taxes. The collapse of late 2008 was a perfect opportunity to reconsider these foolish notions and put on trial this blind and irrational reliance on free-market-is-king.

The Obama administration had failed to address any of the systemic issues at stake in the matter. To make things worse globally, the European Union was on the brink of insolvency, with Greece, Spain, Portugal and Ireland in the lead. In the US, the so-called finance reform bill was not a game changer but mere window-dressing. The bill was passed too late and should have been implemented before a huge bail out was given to Wall Street, with almost no strings attached, unlike most of the Troubled Asset Relief Program (TARP) funds that were supposedly paid back to US taxpayers.[38] This poor timing on the part of the Obama administration and the Democrats in Congress made any real leverage on financial institutions disappear. If nothing else, the financial collapse and the massive bailout from the federal government made those financial institutions that had been deemed too big to fail even bigger. Before and during the collapse, Bank of America bought Countrywide; Morgan Chase took over Washington Mutual, and Wells Fargo bought Wachovia. And of course, bigger banks translate into fewer options for consumers, less competition and tighter credit.

Of the last three big banks still standing, i.e. Bank of America, Chase and Wells Fargo, Chase was the one with the most dubious practices. It was facing several Class-A legal actions for being uncooperative and even deceptive in working with distressed homeowners to restructure their loans. It did not return calls, shuffled people around from one division to another and, last but not least, lost loan documents as a policy in what amounted to a financial version of Kafka's *The Castle*. On the credit side, Chase had relentlessly put the squeeze on consumers. For example, until August 2009 some lines of credit with Chase were at high as $40,000. The first thing Chase did was to double minimum payments and lower, by increments, the credit lines down to 50 percent.

Some people wondered why Wall Street's recovery had not translated into a recovery for Main Street, but the reasons were rather simple: banks were not eager to lend, and corporations, which were doing well and showing large quarterly profits, were not hiring. Instead, both banks and corporations focused on accumulating large cash reserves. The boom in the US economy that ended in 2007 had been fueled by speculation on real-estate values and consumer spending. After this, in the grim new economy, as defined by the proponents of jungle-free-market capitalism, we were all supposed to show restraint and tighten our belts. Just like the banks and corporations, wealthy Americans were sitting on their considerable assets and being ruled by fear. Meanwhile, the middle class was dwindling and quickly becoming insolvent, with almost no midsection and certainly unable to tighten its belt.

If the US had been a person, it would probably have been diagnosed as suffering from untreated bipolar disorder, with the boom parts of the cycle as manic episodes and the bust as depression. From the late 1990s until

2007, the euphoria of mania was running the psyche of most Americans. Within just three years, the US global consciousness hit rock bottom, with constant anxiety, as if fear and a deep sense of loss, like the sword of Damocles, hanged over the heads of Americans. Yet the advocates of free-market capitalism still view the manic-depressive cycles of boom and bust as a normal and almost natural phenomenon. The therapy to heal America's psyche might have to be a long-term undertaking, but the alternative of disaster capitalism is not working. To get on track to a sustainable economic recovery, we must first put in question the sacrosanct dogma of the free market and its manic-depressive manifestations of boom and bust cycles.

After the US election charade of 2012, Wall Street apparently had mixed feelings about either the results or the general health of the global financial market. The Dow Jones index had dropped by 312 points on November 7. Some mentioned increased concerns about Europe's financial crisis, but the discourse in Washington, from both Republicans and Democrats, was about a looming fiscal cliff from which they would fall in January 2013, when a new budget needed to be passed. The word recession began to reappear in the lexicon of politicians. As the discussion raged in Washington concerning the deficit and the US debt ceiling, it became obvious that a backroom deal would be made between the GOP-controlled House of Representatives and the Obama administration. Tackling the deficit would entail not only spending cuts, which were the agenda of Republicans, but also higher taxes across the board, which was a notion pushed by Democrats. Among other things, the election cycle had served to distract the public from the financial tsunami building on the horizon. Ordinary Americans learned that they would pick up the tab by getting the critical social programs standing between them and dire poverty drastically cut. The social safety net was already one of the worst in the industrialized world and what could remain of it would put the US on a par with developing countries and banana republics.

Most Americans have refused to connect the dots between the two wars charged on the national credit card and the financial crash. Neither the Bush administration nor the Obama administration had raised taxes to pay for the wars and, as matter of fact, both US administrations had lowered taxes on the rich. The austerity measures, promoted by Republicans and Democrats alike, were directly connected to this insane war spending. People did not understand that they could not have both bread and guns, and the cost of wars is real even if the bulk of the burden is deferred to future generations.

The US federal debt reached more than $16.4 trillion by the end of fiscal year 2012, and the budget deficit reached more than $17 trillion by the end of fiscal year 2013. Capitalists pretend that financial markets know best. Financiers know a few things, but usually that information is not disclosed to the public until it is too late. The global financial crisis of 2008, generated by the US real-estate bubble, produced a global recession. With the US and European financial situations currently being held by strings, rubber bands and duct tape, the combined fiscal cliff could easily become a global financial crash to make 2008, and even 1929, look like a walk in the park. The gathering storm coming will make calling a cat a cat unavoidable even for the staunchest proponents of justifications to shore up disaster capitalism.

People close to the Federal Reserve Chairman, Ben Bernanke, announced on October 23, 2012 that he would "most likely step down from his position in January 2014, even if President Obama is reelected for a 2nd term."[39] Bernanke did leave his post on January 31, 2014, although he never confirmed or denied the information that was leaked in 2012.[40] His desire to retire was understandable: after all, it must get pretty tiresome to print money around the clock. Chairman Bernanke and the Obama administration used highly academic and purposefully cryptic terms to define their massive money-printing operation. Bernanke described it alternatively as monetary stimulus, the more obvious name, or quantitative easing, the more cryptic one. Both consisted of injecting large amounts of money into the financial system following a Keynesian economic model. US economic academics, with Nobel Prize Winner Paul Krugman in the lead, were proponents of this approach.

On the other side of the Atlantic, Germany, Europe's healthiest economy, as well as the UK leadership were against this Keynesian approach and favored fiscal responsibility in the form of austerity measures, which they were trying to impose on European countries in a fiscal hole such as Greece, Spain, Portugal and, to a lesser extent, Italy. German Chancellor Angela Merkel viewed the US policy of extensive monetary stimulus as being reckless for the global economy. Merkel was born in what was at the time East Germany. She was not old enough to have directly experienced the impact of the 1929 great depression, but like all Germans, it was likely to be in the back of her mind. In Germany, the late 1920s' financial crash brought Adolf Hitler to power. Germans were defeated and humiliated by the Treaty of Versailles, post World War I, and had to pay reparations to France. This, combined with the global financial crash of 1929 shortly thereafter, made the Deutschmark collapse. In 1932, Germans needed a wheelbarrow full of Deutschmarks to buy a kilogram of butter because the German currency had become worthless.

Another factor to input in the fractured equation of global finance was the large amount of US Treasury bonds held by foreign nations. The US could posture as much as it wanted, but in reality, especially in the cases of China and Japan, the US government had a massive financial canon right up to its head. According to the US Treasury, China's holding in bonds was

$1.27 trillion in August 2015; Japan held $1.20 trillion. Smaller bonds holders such as Brazil, Switzerland, the UK, Russia and others, all combined, held about another $3.6 trillion.[41] Overall, we were talking about $6.1 trillion, and this did not include the holders from transnational corporate entities.

A fire sale of US Treasury bonds could, on its own, collapse the castle made of sand. In 2012, when the amount already exceeded $3 trillion, if you combined this with an attack on Iran, which the US was threatening, and oil prices more than doubling, we would have had a recipe for the mother of all great depressions. During tropical storm Sandy, people in New York and New Jersey were briefly exposed to the misery of fighting natural forces with little help from a broken government. The massive financial cyclones that were about to sweep the planet from West to East and North to South would not spare anyone. All of us were in the same boat, and it was looking more and more like the Titanic right before hitting the iceberg.

Not only is the US in deep financial trouble federally, it is also in dire shape at the state and local levels. United States policymakers have had to tackle dreadful fiscal challenges. The 2008 recession caused the sharpest decline in state tax revenue on record, with tax collections dropping 12 percent below their pre-recession levels by 2011, even as the need for state-funded services was increasing. After deep budget cuts, especially in social services, the states still faced what seemed to be insurmountable budget gaps. For the 2012 fiscal year, for example, 44 states and the District of Columbia projected budget gaps totaling $125 billion.[42] In New York, Governor Andrew Cuomo declared the state to be functionally bankrupt on February 1, 2011. Cuomo proposed a $132.9 billion budget that would fall short by $9 billion despite $2.85 billion cuts in education and health-care programs. In California, Governor Jerry Brown was running out of ways to make budget cuts; he wanted to raise taxes to balance the budget and planned to take the issue directly to the voters. Historically, one had to go back to the US Civil War to find an instance when several states had defaulted on their debt obligations. Even during the Great Recession, only Arkansas had defaulted.

Despite these dreadful realities, the Center on Budget and Policy Priorities (CBPP) challenged the discussions of state debt as being alarmist.[43] The CBPP said that the fiscal problems due to the recession had been wrongly lumped together with long-term structural problems, such as debts in relation to pension and retirement obligations. Some policymakers suggested that federal laws should be enacted to allow states to declare bankruptcy so that they could default on their bonds, pay vendors less than they are owed, and modify, or even cancel union contracts. The CBPP, however, cautioned that such a move "could push up the cost of borrowing for all states, undermining efforts to invest in infrastructure."[43]

At the national level, the US debt had passed $14 trillion by early 2011. For each dollar spent by the federal government almost 50 percent was borrowed. So technically, the US was already bankrupt because it had a debt almost four times larger than its economy. Lawmakers in Congress were saying that their major priority was to tackle and find ways to reduce the national debt, yet they were unwilling to admit that the only way to avoid fiscal insolvency was to cut spending, on one hand, and increase taxation on the other. Short of this, the US would never get out of the giant hole that it has dug for itself. During his 2011 State of the Union Address, Obama said that the US needed a new Sputnik moment.[44] If and when this moment comes, it is the time when the US will make drastic cuts in its military spending by getting out of Afghanistan, Iraq, Germany, Japan and South Korea.

The declining empire's debtors are legitimately getting increasingly worried about America's appetite to print money, and ultimately the country's increasing chance of defaulting on its astronomical debt. When will China, Germany, Japan and Brazil, which are holding more than $4 trillions in US assets, say enough is enough and pull the plug on their US Treasury Bonds in a fire sale? The calculus of America's political and financial class, one being interchangeable with the other, is to gamble that foreign debtors will not use this kind of financial weapon as leverage on Washington, because it would make their own economies collapse. So the global financial insanity, with the US in the lead, continues unchecked.

Four main factors can be identified as key components in the US ballooning debt: war costs, financial sector recklessness, the Bush-era tax cuts, and rising health-care costs. The stock market crash of 2008 wiped out trillions in savings and put millions of Americans out of a job, yet by 2011 Wall Street was back up, in appearance stronger than ever, at the expense of Main Street; however, the health of the stock market is, as usual, built on quicksand and could cave in at any time. In 2008 and 2009, the financial sector was deemed too big to fail by both the Bush and Obama administrations. The American people were told that, to prevent a complete collapse, Wall Street needed hundreds of billions of federal dollars, or the rest of the economy would go down with it. The taxpayers' billions were sucked in by the parasitic banks, which, as a payback for the taxpayers' generosity, promptly shut down access to money for ordinary Americans in order to fill the pockets of their top executives.

Some organizations, such as the Roosevelt Institute, have come up with some creative solutions to rein in Wall Street and also expand access to capital for ordinary Americans. The Roosevelt Institute's "Budget for the Millennial America" proposed a 25-percent activities tax on financial institutions having more than $200 billions in assets.[45] This too-big-to-fail tax would affect the top 12 largest US banks and force them to split up their activities into smaller companies that would pose significantly less risk to the global financial system.

In the European Union, the global financial sector, the World Bank, and the IMF used the same scare tactics as those they had used in the US. The debt crisis was painted as the ultimate scarecrow, the end of the world as we know it, while in reality it was only a threat to the world's financial leeches. After the austerity measures in Greece, Portugal and Ireland, it was the turn of Italy, which had $2.2 trillion of debt. Financial analysts were concerned that Italy, Europe's third largest economy, would be the next domino to fall from the push of disaster capitalism. On July 12, 2011, Isabella Bufacchi, a journalist with the Italian newspaper *Il Sole 24 Ore,* said: "We are too big to fail. But we must also remember that Italy has got a big GDP, it is a big country. However, there is a contagion now coming from Greece, Ireland, and Portugal, which are countries that were in a condition not to be able to repay their debt."[46] Ms. Bufacchi might have been too optimistic about her country.

The question for the southern part of Europe with its debt crisis is how long Germany and France, the healthiest economies in the EU, will be willing or even able to pick up the tab and bail out the weakest countries in the union? In a context wider than Europe's debt crisis, how long will the stronger economies worldwide, with China in the lead, be willing to tolerate the US' inexorable race towards more debt? For heavily indebted nations, the solutions proposed by the slave masters of global capitalism are always the same: more austerity for the people simultaneously with greater productivity. In other words, slave away as a country or an individual to service the debt for the benefit of the financial sector.

The following tale has gained some traction in some political and financial circles:

> A Chinese man, a Frenchman, an Indian, and an American were shipwrecked on an island. To survive, everyone was given his own job. The Chinese man had to catch fish, the Indian had to collect vegetables and fruits, the Frenchman had to cook the meals, and the American had only to eat as much as he could, leaving only some crumbs and fish heads to the other three. The American said he had the most important job of all, because if he didn't eat so much, and if the Chinese man, the Indian and the Frenchman did not have to respectively fish, gather and cook, they would be unemployed. The skinnier men went along with this until one of them had an epiphany. They kicked the American off the island and discovered that suddenly they had 10 times as much to eat and only had to work half as hard.

Of course the villain in this story is not an ordinary American but an American banker. If the US is quickly rising again as the main global financial liability, the rot at the core of this is much more a moral issue than an economic one. What the US ruling class is telling the huge majority of the population, loud and clear, is a simple message: if you are sick or old, unless you are rich, you are on your own. It is the old and simplistic American notion of picking yourself up by your own bootstraps, but as MLK often pointed out, it is impossible to do this when you don't have any shoes. How can you do this in a system where incarceration costs exceed the public education budget by six to one? How can you do this in a society that spends more than a third of its taxpayers' money on the military but still lacks universal healthcare?

The looming US bankruptcy is merely a reflection of a deep moral and ethical crisis decades in the making. When a society becomes so corrupt and amoral that it stops to care for and protect the weak, the sick, and the poor, it should and will eventually collapse. Lasting social structures are based on very few key principles, the main one being that the majority of the people, as opposed to just a few, must share any progress or benefit. Systems that are built primarily on inequality eventually implode. The US is almost at this systemic breaking point where the exploited and oppressed are finally seeing the myth of the American dream as the ultimate charade to keep them slaving away for the sole benefit of about one percent of the population.

Washington's political class belongs to and does the bidding for this one percent of Americans for whom the American dream is a reality but, from time to time, some politicians strike a populist tone and pretend to be on the side of the little guy. On July 26, 2011, House Minority Leader Nancy Pelosi told a crowd of union workers on Capitol Hill: "The budget deficit is an excuse for the Republicans to undermine government plain and simple. They don't just want to make cuts, they want to destroy. They want to destroy food safety, clean air, clean water, the department of education. They want to destroy your rights."[47] She concluded that the GOP and the president have a different vision of America: "Quite different.... We get the sacrifice, they get the wealth," Pelosi said. Pelosi's conclusion, which sounded almost like a revolutionary call to the barricades, was quite disingenuous. Had she been perfectly honest, she would have instead said: "You get the sacrifice, we get the wealth." Nevertheless, her call to the barricades was fully justified. We could be near the boiling point where a real American revolution might explode by force to change a system that is morally bankrupt and lacks the intelligence or ability to reform itself.

III. War Is Peace

7

Empire of the US Military-Industrial Complex

SINCE THE US ENTERED World War II, its economy has been arguably a war economy. The initiation and propagation of wars became, independently of geopolitical reasons, a good business proposition. The early 1940s marked the start of the era of systematic wars for profit. War became the ultimate capitalist enterprise. The extraordinary war efforts of World War II turned the US into a giant global arms factory for the war in Europe and the Pacific. Manufacture for war has even been cynically credited with ending the Great Depression that started in 1929. The war enterprise continued at a slower pace, but without any real interruption, with the Korean War in the early 1950s, the Vietnam War in the 1960s and early 1970s, and various proxy wars worldwide against the Soviet Union, including Afghanistan in the 1980s.

The events of September 11, 2001, i.e. 9/11, gave American politicians the unique opportunity to start the perfect war on behalf of their friends and patrons of the military-industrial complex: the endless war on terror, without geographic boundaries, or even a well-defined enemy. This permanent war business proposition is criminal in nature but absolutely fool proof in terms of maximum return on investments. The bloodthirsty machine that is the US military-industrial complex makes billions at three phases of the war industry process: the manufacture of ever more lethal and complex weapons systems, the killing and destruction stage, and finally the occupation and rebuilding phase in countries such as Germany, Japan, Korea with programs like the Marshall Plan, and more recently the reconstructions of Iraq and Afghanistan. War Inc. and its political associates always need new conflicts. The US is the uncontested juggernaut of the war business, or war for profit; its economy is defined by permanent war.

According to a report released by the Congressional Research Service (CRS) in summer 2012, business has been booming for the military-industrial complex.[1] The US had become, by far, the largest arms dealer of the planet, with 78.1 percent of the overall market. The CRS report put Russia as a very distant second at $8.7 billion and Britain third at $3 billion. Between 2010 and 2011 alone, the export of US weapons more than tripled, from $21.4 billion to $66.3 billion: the largest increase for a single year in the history of US arms export.[1] The leading buyers of US weapons between 2004 to 2011 were Saudi Arabia at $75.7 billion, India at $46.6 billion, the United Arab Emirates (UAE) at $20.3 billion, Egypt at $14.3 billion, and Pakistan at $13.2 billion.[1]

The accumulation of US weapons in the Middle East via Saudi Arabia and the UAE, with Israel's blessings, is unquestionably a preparation for what might be the next big profitable venture for the military-industrial complex: a war with Iran. The accomplices to the crimes of War Inc. are not limited to the politicians who declare the wars or the soldiers who pull the triggers; they are also the engineers who design the weapons systems, the workers who make them, the stockholders who buy the shares of publicly-traded companies of the military-industrial complex and, of course, the ultimate war profiteers: the merchants of death from Wall Street.

In the recession that started in December 2007, the burst of the real estate bubble was more a symptom than the root cause of the systemic problems. The real problems were two-fold: firstly, there was the out-of-control increase of the defense and security budget which, including the cost of the wars in Iraq and Afghanistan, represented about 25 percent of the overall federal budget; secondly, there was the broadened income gap between the very rich and everyone else.

The Center on Budget and Policy Priorities (CBPP) published data in the fall of 2010 showing that the income gap between the very rich and everyone else had more than tripled in about 30 years.[2] "The gaps in after-tax income between the richest 1 percent of Americans and the middle poorest fifths has more than tripled between 1979 and 2007. Taken together with prior research, the new data suggest greater income concentration at the top of the income scale than at any time since 1928," wrote Arloc Sherman and Chad Stone, the authors of the report.[2] Between 1979 and 2007, average after-tax incomes for the top 1 percent rose by a stunning 281 percent. After adjusting for inflation, this represented an increase in income of $973,100 per household. By comparison, the increases in income were a modest 25 percent ($11,200 per household) for the middle fifth of households, and a meager 16 percent ($2,400 per household) for the bottom fifth. Additionally, in 2007, the average household in the top 1 percent had an income of $1.3 million, up $88,800 just from the previous year; this gain alone was well above the total 2007 income of the average middle-income household, which was $55,300.[2]

In Washington, the talk of the town immediately before tax day 2010 was the ballooning budget deficit and possible ways to cut it. Nevertheless, since 99 percent of America's political class, Democrats and Republicans alike, were unwilling to address the real issues behind the disarray of the US economy, the more than 1-trillion pound gorilla in the room, which represented war and security spending would keep running amok. The black hole that is the military-industrial complex was swallowing a large portion of the US debt.

For fiscal year 2010, the federal government spent $3.6 trillion. Federal tax revenues supplied $2.2 trillion of the budget. The remaining $1.4 trillion were borrowed, and future taxpayers would ultimately pay this deficit. In other words, American children and their future children would pick up the tab for the wars in Iraq and Afghanistan. In 2010, the defense and security expenditures represented about 20 percent of the overall federal budget, or $715 billion, even without including indirect defense expenditures; if these were included, defense spending would amount to about 35 percent of the total budget. About 3.5 percent of the budget provided care and benefits for war veterans; by contrast, only 3 percent was spent on education. Meanwhile, the interest on the debt had already skyrocketed to 6 percent of the budget. The huge national debt, which reached more than $9 trillion by the end of fiscal 2010, would claim $209 billion of the budget in interest.

According to the US Congressional Budget Office, between 2000 and 2008, defense spending exploded, with an increase of about 9 percent annually.[3] Even when costs for Iraq, Afghanistan and the supposed global war on terror were excluded, funding for the DOD more than doubled during this period and dwarfed the growth rates for all parts of the domestic budget combined. In fiscal year 2010, DOD expenditures took up 28 percent of all federal tax revenues and amounted to 5 percent of the country's GDP. Despite this, in 2011 the DOD requested a 6 percent increase over its 2010 budget. Officially, the total amount included the so-called base budget request, which was $549 billion in 2011 (compared to the approved $528 billion in 2010), plus $159 billion in Overseas Contingency Operations (OCO), or war spending. The real cost, however, would be more than double the DOD funds, if one included veterans' benefits, energy costs of the war, and other security expenses. The overall US budget deficit was skyrocketing, but Obama had already indicated in his State of the

Union address that he would not cut the defense budget. Americans did not question much at all the absurd logic of borrowing more money and committing yet another large portion of their taxes to the black hole of military spending.

To justify a larger 2011 budget, the Pentagon added a $9.6-billion item that included modernizing its helicopter fleet for the wars in Iraq and Afghanistan, training more pilots to add two extra army combat aviation brigades, buying more drones for use in Afghanistan, Yemen and Pakistan, and expanding the special operations forces by 6 percent. "We are adding 2,800 people to the special operations command in fiscal 2011, and through fiscal 2015 about 10,000 military and civilian will be added overall. Special operations forces are particularly important in irregular warfare such as we see in Iraq and Afghanistan," said DOD controller Robert F. Hale.[4] The padded 2011 budget also allowed for what the Pentagon called the next-generation bomber. "Over the next five years, we are spending more than $4 billion in long range strike. Part in the next generation bomber, but we are also upgrading our existing bombers, the B-2 and the B-52. We are also looking at a prompt global strike capability, possibly a missile," said Hale, who added that he was confident that the DOD was "beginning to strike the right balance between funding today's wars and funding the forces needed for the future."[4] In the end, the budget was not cut, which was what the Pentagon had wanted. This was great news for the military-industrial complex and terrible news for peace, fiscal responsibility, or even rationality. These military expenditures were completely unsustainable and would sooner or later bankrupt the US economy.

By 2012, to maintain the empire, kill people in Afghanistan, Pakistan, Iraq, Libya and elsewhere, and give American citizens a false sense of security at home, the overall defense and security expenditures were between $1.03 and $1.50 trillion. The DOD's base budget plus the OCO amounted to $645.5 billion; the FBI counter-terrorism costs reached $2.7 billion; the Energy Department's defense-related spending climbed to $21.8 billion; veterans' affairs cost taxpayers $70 billion, and veterans' pensions $54.6 billion. Last but not least, the interest on debt incurred in past wars reached around $300 billion. Between 2013 and 2015, the overall budget remained in the trillion-dollar range, but defense expenditures were projected to grow again between 2016 and 2019 by drumming up threats from Russia, China, and the Islamic State in Iraq and Syria (ISIS, also called Islamic State in Iraq and the Levant, ISIL).

Despite the fact that ISIS was originally the foster child of Saudi Arabia and Qatar, with Uncle Sam for its godfather, it has become labeled enemy number one and is a dream come true to make the war on terror global, permanent and yet more destructive. The Islamic state foreign legion is the perfect enemy: one that can justify a permanent war without borders, help finish the job of wrecking the Middle East in preparation for the greater Israel project, create a clash-of-civilizations discourse in Europe to make people accept a full-blown police state and, finally, allow the US military and its NATO surrogate to invade and occupy more countries.

On February 11, 2015, Obama officially requested in a letter that the US Congress pass an Authorization for the Use of Military Force (AUMF) against ISIS.[5] The letter explained the plan to use convenient regional surrogates on the frontline of the empire's new war: "Local forces, rather than the US military should be deployed to conduct such operations. The authorization I propose would provide the flexibility (for the US military) to conduct ground combat operations...."[5] The timing of the AUMF, a few months after a full-scale operation against ISIS had started without it, had to do with the DOD budget for fiscal year 2016.[6] Added to a base defense budget of $534 billion, the Pentagon asked for $51 billion to pay for "the war on ISIL in Iraq and Syria," $168 million to "counter Russian aggressive acts" (with $117 million for Ukraine and $51 million for Moldova and Georgia), plus $789 million to bolster NATO in the EU.[6] The colossal war machine's direct and indirect beneficiaries, namely Wall Street and the political class, were thrilled with the prospect of more profit from permanent war. The debt, of course, would continue to balloon.

For years, the US has spent more money on its military than the rest of the world combined. Between 66 and 75 percent of worldwide military spending is now due to the US share, which is six times higher than China's military budget. To talk about fiscal responsibility without addressing the madness of runaway war and security expenditures is a farce played at the expense of the American people. The US political class cannot be taken seriously on the budget-deficit issue until it reconsiders the imperialist policies that have been bleeding the US treasury dry. The more than $1-trillion-a-year monstrosity created to maintain the empire and sold to US citizens as being necessary to keep America safe only benefits the military-industrial complex. Citizens should demand from their elected officials that they rethink this road to perdition and withdraw the US military from Afghanistan, Iraq, Pakistan, Japan, Germany, and South Korea. Else, the US will disintegrate from within, go bankrupt and eventually collapse.

The Uninvited Guest Who Never Leaves

When President Obama addressed the nation on August 31, 2010 from the oval office to praise the sacrifice made by the US military in Iraq and claim that the US combat operations in Iraq were over, the reality of Iraq and the US presence there were quite different.[7] About 50,000 US troops would still be stationed in Iraq for so-called training purposes, as well as more than 100,000 contractors who were hired guns for either the State Department or private US or international corporations. The 50,000 remaining troops were supposed to leave in 2011, but the Obama administration had already indicated that they might stay longer at the request of the Iraqi government.

Despite all the claims of progress made in Iraq, the country was broken. Almost half year after the supposed elections, Iraq still lacked a new government. A few hours before Vice President Joe Biden's arrival in Baghdad to commemorate this government officially, mortars landed on the fortified American-controlled Green Zone. The Obama administration could spin the reality of Iraq however it wanted, but this did not mean that the war was over for Iraqis. Bomb attacks were a constant threat; more than three million Iraqis were refugees in Jordan, Syria or Europe, and the conflict between Sunnis, Shiites and Kurds had not been resolved. The US invasion had not turned Iraq into a functioning democracy at all. The country was unstable, and a full-blown sectarian civil war between the three communities could have restarted at any moment.

It was hard to reduce the tragic mistake that was the Iraq war to numbers, but in August 2010, when the war was supposedly over, the US military newspaper *Stars and Stripes* reported the somewhat rosy estimate of: 4,414 US troops killed; 31,897 US troops wounded in action; 1,135 US-troop amputees; 113,166 Iraqi civilian deaths; $747.6 billion for the war's operating costs, or $2,435 per US citizen.[8] The estimated total cost of the Iraq war stood at $3 trillion, plus an additional 500 million for medical care and disability compensation for veterans.

By May 2011, Prime Minister Nouri al-Maliki, Washington's man in Baghdad, was pushing, in conjunction with the Obama administration, to keep some US troops in Iraq after 2011, although he had been elected on the premise that all American occupying troops would be out of the country by the end of December. At a press conference, Maliki said: "We won't get unanimous agreement on this issue, but if we get 70 or 80 percent, isn't that the will of the people?"[9] Maliki and officials within the US military were trying to change the narrative. US troops would not be called combat troops anymore, or even military advisers; instead, Baghdad and Washington would call them technical experts. Despite the name change, for a majority of Iraqis the 20,000 US troops would remain, de facto, the occupiers.

A big problem for Maliki was that, in order to get elected Prime Minister in the first place, he had made deals with people like cleric Muqtada al-Sadr. The key element of the alliance between Maliki and Sadr was that all US troops would leave by the December 2011 deadline. Sadr had no intention to let Maliki break his commitment on this issue. Tens of thousands of Sadr supporters took to the streets of Baghdad in May 2011 to demand that every American soldier be gone by the year's end. In an interview with the *BBC,* Sadr threatened to reactivate his militia, the Mahdi army, if the US troops stayed.[10]

Most analysts in Iraq said that a new agreement between Iraq and the US to authorize around 20,000 American troops to stay beyond December was likely. If the US had decided to keep troops in Iraq, the next time the Mahdi army marched in Baghdad, they would have likely been carrying guns. Attacks against American interests had already increased. In the end, the last US troops did leave Iraq on December 17, 2011. Nevertheless, the country's occupation continued. American mainstream media trumpeted that the war in Iraq was over, but the war had become a pacification process. The mission to control US interests in Iraq had fallen from the Pentagon onto the lap of the State Department.

On December 18, 2011, millions of Americans received a pseudo-personal e-mail message from President Barack Obama: John Doe, "Early this morning the last of our troops left Iraq. As we honor and reflect on the sacrifices that millions of men and women made for this war, I wanted to make sure you heard the news. Bringing the war to a responsible end was a cause that sparked many Americans to get involved in the political process for the first time. Today's outcome is a reminder that we all have a stake in our country's future, and a say in the direction we choose. Thank you. Barack."

The US would leave in Iraq its largest embassy in the world. According to official figures, 20,000 people would work for the State Department at the embassy in Baghdad's Green Zone and US consulates elsewhere in Iraq. Between 7,000 and 16,000 of the Americans who remained in Iraq would be private security contractors or, to call them by a more accurate name, the mercenaries of Blackwater (aka Academi, aka Xe). Some Blackwater mercenaries would stay on the payroll of big oil companies to protect their assets. This new supposed civilian operation in Iraq would cost US taxpayers more than $3.5 billion a year.

Some legislators questioned the scale of this so-called diplomatic presence. Senator Patrick Leahy from Vermont called the embassy "a behemoth... that costs more than US missions to key allies and trading partners."[11] Blackwater would provide the muscle for this new phase of the Iraq pacification, and Halliburton would keep its contract with the State Department for logistical support, such as the provision of food, dining facilities, construction, and delivery of water and fuel. Some were concerned, as they should have been, about the oversight on the sums that would flow into the coffers of Blackwater and Halliburton. For example, to get a meal in the Green Zone, visitors or State Department employees were issued coupons. A coupon for a basic meal, such as burger and fries, had a face value of $37.00. Such ridiculous sums were being paid by the State Department to Halliburton.

Undersecretary for management Pat Kennedy, at the State Department, put an optimistic spin on this new phase of the US occupation.[11] "The US-

Iraq relationship is incredibly important. This is a democracy in the Middle East. Is it perfect? No. A lot of people think our system is not perfect either. But this is a major oil producer, a friend of the United States, a potential market for American goods and now, I think, a very important symbol in the Middle East of what democracy in the region could be," said Kennedy.[11] The cost of the Iraq war, estimated at $3.5 trillion by December 2011, continued to grow for American taxpayers without any end in sight, while Blackwater and Halliburton made a killing.

It is extremely naive to believe that US troops and mercenaries will completely leave Iraq and Afghanistan any time soon. The situation is actually murkier than just wars over resources such as oil in Iraq and lithium in Afghanistan; it is also about the US strategy of placing substantial military assets on Iran's borders. The very same imperialist logic has kept US troops in Germany and Japan since World War II. In Germany, this was started in the context of the Cold War with the Soviet Union; in Japan today, this has to do with counterbalancing the growing military power of China. After the war, Germany and Japan were not rebuilt as free national entities but as occupied vassals. The two parts of Germany, east and west, were rebuilt from a wreckage in the image of their new respective masters, with the Marshall Plan being the prescribed remedy for West Germany's ruins. In Japan, General MacArthur took charge of the mass murder, demolition and later reconstruction for the US empire. Seventy years after the war, more than 40,000 US troops remain in Germany and about 60,000 occupy Japan. Let us not kid ourselves: if the US military is still in Germany and Japan, it also intends to stay in Iraq and Afghanistan for decades to come.

8

Cold War Redux

THERE IS A VAGUE NOSTALGIA for the Cold War era, which spanned from almost immediately after World War II in 1945 to the collapse of the Soviet Union in December 1991. It was arguably a period marked, if not by peace and stability, then at least by a sense of predictability that emanated from a balancing act between the two superpowers. For 46 years, world geopolitics was rather simple as countries aligned themselves with one block or the other. The conflicts between the two empires were mostly limited to proxy wars. A weak attempt to challenge the bipolar world order of the Cold War was a timid creation by six countries of the European Economic Community (EEC) in 1957. It took another 36 years for the European Union (EU) to become formally established by the Maastricht Treaty of 1993.[12] With most of its big members belonging to NATO, the EU always lacked the political will to break away from the US. Twenty-two years after Maastricht, the 28 members, even the biggest ones, are more than ever the vassals of Uncle Sam.

An association of Brazil, Russia, India, and China was formed in 2008 as BRIC, and it became BRICS after South Africa joined it in 2010.[13] This formidable group of so-called emerging economies represents the first challenge to the unipolar world, which had been under de facto US rule politically, economically and especially militarily since 1991. Originally,

BRICS seemed concerned only with economic issues, but there were already signs, in late 2013, that the group wanted to handle global affairs. On foreign-policy issues, BRICS countries supported a central role for the UN and were, in principle, against foreign interventions in the affairs of other states.

An official declaration from BRICS at an April 2011 Chinese summit was that "BRICS members are deeply concerned with the turbulence in the Middle East, the North African and West African regions and the self determination of its people. Further, members also share the principle that the use of force should be avoided."[14] BRICS is so eclectic, vast and diverse that its members' political interests can and have clashed on some critical international issues. For example, Russia and China abstained from voting on UN Security Council (UNSC) Resolution 1970 on armed intervention in Libya, whereas Brazil supported it. South Africa supported UNSC Resolution 1973, opening the way for a NATO attack on Libya, while Brazil, India, China and Russia abstained.

Considering how new the BRICS grouping of countries is, its creation has unquestionably been a geopolitical game changer, and the repercussions are already significant. Gone are the days of the mid 1990s, when a weak and crumbling Russia would let NATO bomb its historical ally Serbia and let the West impose its will in the dismantlement of Yugoslavia. The coming of age, as a major international player, for BRICS was to win the showdown with the West over the Syrian crisis at the end of 2013, and by doing so perhaps to have defused World War III (under Chapter 11). At the peak of the crisis, BRICS became more coherent, and the four other partners fully backed Russian President Vladimir Putin's uncompromising stance. The turning point was during a G20 summit in early September 2013 in Saint Petersburg. BRICS drew a line in the sand: the US imperialist follies in Afghanistan, Iraq, and Libya would not be allowed a repeat in Syria or Iran. It had to be done. The days of American exceptionalism had come to an end. Under the impulse and leadership of Putin, BRICS came down resolutely and unanimously against a US-NATO military intervention in Syria. The members stressed, in common, the cornerstone of their foreign-policy principle: force against a sovereign state may be used only in self defense, and such a decision can only take place with the approval of the UNSC. Syria did not attack the US; therefore a NATO attack was illegal and would provoke BRICS' retaliation.

President Putin, in principle, did not view BRICS as an opposing force to the West. For him "BRICS is a key element of an emerging multipolar world" without empires.[15] In an interview with *ITAR-TASS Agency* in late March 2013, before the BRICS summit in Durban, South Africa, Putin said: "The group of five has repeatedly affirmed its commitment to the fundamental principles of international law and contributed to strengthen the UN central role. Our countries do not accept power politics or violation of other countries sovereignty. We share approaches to the pressing international issues, including the Syria crisis, the situation around Iran and the Middle-East settlements."[15]

There were, however, quite a few contradictions in this overall agenda. For example, how could you advocate respect for national sovereignty on one hand, and a greater role for the UN, especially its Security Council, on the other? One could wonder how India and Brazil regard not having a seat on the Security Council while Russia and China do. Presently, the UN is a tool for imperialism — certainly not a vector for a multipolar world. Another factor that greatly differentiates the five BRICS members is history. If Brazil, India and South Africa have been, in their own rights, victims of colonialism and imperialism, this was never the case for Russia and China. As matter of fact, it was the opposite for BRICS' two heavyweights. China and Russia have had empires, and the nostalgia of imperialism occasionally still shows its ugly mug in them. China's imperialism brought it to Tibet, and the logic of empire keeps Tibetans under Chinese boots. Along the same lines, some of the events taking place in the former Soviet satellites are troubling, to say the least. In the case of Ukraine, it does not seem that either the West or Russia has Ukraine's best interest or national sovereignty in mind by interfering in its affairs. Ukraine and Syria are pawns in a massive new geopolitical game that opposes the US-EU against the mighty BRICS.

A few months after BRICS defused the major international conflict over Syria, the world was on the verge of another, potentially more dangerous, crisis in the aftermath of the so-called Ukrainian revolution. The coup in Ukraine was as much about freedom and democracy as were the invasions of Iraq, Afghanistan and the sponsored attempt to topple Syria's Bashar al-Assad. In the prevailing Orwellian climate, news outlets became propaganda machines that presented a group of neo-Nazis in Ukraine as being revolutionaries. In fact, the crisis was not about Ukraine at all, but rather about putting the squeeze on Russia. It also served as yet another distraction to switch people's focus from one fabricated crisis to another, and to prevent any sustained examination of the looming systemic failure of global capitalism. The destabilizations of both Syria and Ukraine had been triggered and financed by the West, and in both instances Russia reacted more strongly than had been expected. In Crimea and Eastern Ukraine Russia and Russian nationals immediately began to flex their military and militia muscles. Even if the West's foreign policy acumen was low, it should have expected a forceful reaction from Putin. Nobody could be so dumb or so oblivious of recent history like the Cuban missile crisis of October 1962 or Czechoslovakia circa 1968.

During the Cuban missile crisis, which lasted for 13 tense days, the Soviet Union and Cuba on one side, and the US on the other, almost came to a direct confrontation involving nuclear weapons, over the installation of nuclear missiles by the Soviets in Cuba. The Russian move was meant to prevent the US from toppling its ally Fidel Castro; it was also retaliation against the threats posed by US nuclear missiles in Turkey and Italy, aimed at the Soviet Union. The Cuban missile crisis was rightly considered to be the moment when the Cold War could have erupted into a full-blown nuclear conflict. This was defused when Nikita Khrushchev accepted to withdraw the missiles. Back then, the US presidency, in John F. Kennedy, still held enough real power to resist the growing influence of warmongers.

As the rhetoric for sanctions against Russia heated up in Washington and the crisis in Ukraine amplified in early March 2014, some Western Europeans said jokingly that at least winter was almost over, and if Putin shuts off the gas, they would not have to be cold for long. But their laughter was short lived. If the EU had not behaved as a doormat for Washington's neocons to wipe their feet on, the crisis would not have been engineered. What was the mock-up EU leadership thinking, if anything at all? What could the EU gain from forcing Putin's back against a wall? Further, what could the EU offer to Ukraine at that juncture besides a belt-tightening austerity program similar to the Greek model? It was still cold in Europe, but a new Cold War was heating up.

A Ukrainian aid package was discussed, but Ukraine had not yet seen a penny either from the IMF, the EU, or the US. The US had only pledged $1 billion of loan guarantees. The money would be coughed up mainly by the EU, and it was clear that once Ukraine was on the hook with the IMF, there would be cuts in all social services, pensions, etc., and the neoliberal capitalist model that had ravaged Detroit and Greece would be applied to Ukraine. The aim was to create a failed state. The director of the CIA, John Brennan, visited Kiev in mid-April 2014 and instructed the coup government to do certain types of actions, but the Ukrainian military was falling apart, and there was no chain of command. Ukraine was fragmented, and Kiev had lost grasp on what was going on in East Ukraine. Putin said that Ukraine was on the brink of a civil war. The Western media, not only in the US but also in the EU, began to compare Putin to Adolf Hitler and to turn the Russian head of state into the ultimate bogeyman. As the situation turned into an Orwellian reality, there grew the real fear that the US would draw Russia into a proxy war in neighboring Ukraine.

Europeans should have been concerned about the implications of the economic sanctions that Washington was pushing against Russia. Russia's not so secret weapon in Ukraine's crisis was gas, and this economic weapon could be aimed both at an unruly West Ukraine and the EU. In effect, 30 percent of the natural gas used by the EU was Russian, and 60 percent of it transited in a pipeline through Ukraine. Ukraine itself imported 60 percent of its gas from Russia. With the powerful gas-supply issue, Russia could easily put the squeeze on the 28 EU members. While only 15 percent of the gas used in France was Russian, in Baltic countries it was 100 percent and something to think about before getting tough on Russia.

The financial sector actively attacked Russia. On March 3, 2014, the ruble fell by 2 percent against the dollar, and $55 billion were lost in one day from the Russian stock exchange. The banksters were pulling their money out of Russia. The value of Gazprom, Russia's energy giant, whose exports to Europe transited via Ukraine, fell by $12 billion. Some in Washington's neocon think tanks were recommending drastic measures to punish Russia, such as: rejecting visas across the board for Russian citizens to visit Western countries; immediately putting Ukraine under NATO's umbrella; and artificially driving down the price of oil, a prime source of revenue for Russia, by dumping on the global market some of the 700 million barrels from the US Strategic Petroleum Reserve.

For some suits of the global corporate empire, regime change in Ukraine was a steppingstone to the real goal of removing Putin from power in Russia. Ukraine's independence from Russia is recent: about 20 years. Before this, Ukraine had been part of the czars' empire for almost 300 years and then a Soviet republic during the communist era post World War II. In the context of the Soviet Union in 1954, Nikita Khrushchev transferred Crimea to Ukraine, which had a 60-percent ethnic-Russian majority. Further, in East Ukraine the population was 45 percent ethnic Russian. So Kiev's affairs and policies closely involved Moscow. For some perspective, US citizens should reflect on what their reactions would be if Russia or China had sponsored a communist regime change in, let us say, Puerto Rico.

Germany is often described as an economic giant but political dwarf. In early spring 2014, this complete lack of political backbone or even basic dignity appeared to have spread to the rest of Europe. The national spokespeople of global corporate imperialism let the US National Security Agency (NSA) spy on them without retaliation. Later the likes of Angela Merkel and François Hollande showed their subordination to Uncle Sam by letting Victoria Nuland, a US official, insult them without demanding her resignation. Ms. Nuland was married to top neocon Robert Kagan, the co-founder of PNAC, and was the Assistant Secretary of State for European and Eurasian Affairs at the US State Department. She summarized the EU's lack of political will crudely but honestly when she said: "F@#k the EU."[16] F@#k the EU indeed, but mainly Ukraine's population. People like Kagan and his powerful friends were pouring gasoline on an open flame that could light up a world war.

An involvement of BRICS, and especially its member with the biggest military might, China, to consider retaliations against the West like the threat of a fire sale of US Treasury Bonds, would have helped to avoid the crescendo of tensions and sanctions that looked as if they might escalate to World War III over Ukraine. For Ukraine itself, unfortunately, the only peaceful outcome appeared to be a partition of west, from east plus Crimea. West Ukraine would then become EU's newest poor member, crippled with debt to the IMF and perhaps with a far-right dominated government. The richer East Ukraine, for its part, would become a Russian satellite state with all of the benefits and inconveniences.

In Orwellian Times, Revolution Is Imperialism

We live in a time that George Orwell predicted in his groundbreaking novel *1984*.[17] A time of deception, where nothing is what it seems to be. Lost in a deep fog of propaganda that passes for information, we must decipher our way through conflicting narratives, where stories are planted to hide other stories. In this fictional conundrum, reality has become surreal, and words have lost their meaning. In our Orwellian lexicon, a pro-capitalist and neo-colonialist such as French President François Hollande is called a socialist. Violent imperialist interventions by the US and its allies, or even the UN, worldwide are called humanitarian or peacekeeping missions. Policies of regime change, already conducted in Iraq and Libya, and underway in Ukraine, Syria and Venezuela, are called promoting democracy or strengthening civil society. In Orwellian times, a phony revolution in Kiev is concocted by neocons in Washington DC, with help from so-called humanitarian NGOs. In Orwellian times, a big lie often repeated becomes the truth. When policymakers are spin masters, truth is the first casualty.

Public policy with the welfare of millions at stake should be a serious matter. But this has been treated with contempt by the supposed public servants who should take it most to heart. Politicians, especially the heads of state, are marketed to the public like big-ticket items. Citizens are the consumers of political products. As in advertising, political campaigns are tested on focus groups. Once a political brand is established, consumers develop a relationship to the brand, either of trust and fidelity, or hostility. In the US, Bush, Clinton and Kennedy are well-known political brands. In France, Le Pen has become a strong brand. The symbiosis of politics and marketing is symptomatic of this age. Once addicted to a brand, the political consumer will keep buying it, i.e. voting for it. In Orwellian times, branding is king.

Before the referendum in Crimea on March 16, 2014 attached the peninsula to the Russian federation, Hillary Clinton compared Vladimir Putin's actions to those of Adolf Hitler in the buildup to World War II.[18] Historically, this was a grossly inaccurate comparison, but to the average

Clinton consumer, it conveyed the simple equation: Putin = Hitler. The West always needs a bogeyman. Russian President Vladimir Putin, the current popular leader of the former evil empire could not have been a better candidate for enemy number one. To stay on message, the sycophant Western mainstream media hinted that Putin's hidden agenda is to restore the Soviet Union, and that the neo-Nazis in Ukraine and jihadists in Syria are revolutionaries. In Orwellian times, information is mostly propaganda and conventions such as calling the US president the leader of the free world are as oxymoronic as the coal industry's advertisements of clean coal. When NATO declares that it wants to promote stability in Eastern Europe, it does exactly the opposite by provoking Moscow.

NATO has received a big boost from the Ukrainian crisis: a reclaimed raison d'être, and it might recruit new members such as Sweden and Finland. The military alliance plans to reinforce its ties with Armenia, Moldova and Azerbaijan as well as present a stronger presence in the Baltic States. The US stationed six F15 in Lithuania and planned to send 16 F16 and four C-130 to Poland.[19] More surveillance flights with Airborne Warning and Control System (AWACS) and a stronger presence in the Eastern Baltic Sea, regular air patrol over Baltic States, and a boost of the number of troops in Romania were also on NATO's agenda. Russia viewed NATO's actions as a strategy of encirclement.

At the end of the Soviet Union in 1991, US President George Bush Sr., German Chancellor Helmut Khol and US Secretary of State James Baker gave the Soviet Premier, Mikhail Gorbachev, a formal guarantee that there would never be an eastern expansion of NATO to include former members of the Warsaw Pact. But under Vladimir Putin, Russia has been investing in its military, and Western analysts, including the powerful puppet masters of the Council on Foreign Relations (CFR) took notice and were impressed by the Russian troops' performance in Crimea.[20] The 1991 agreement between Gorbachev and the West was never respected by any US administration, and it is the major issue with regard to Ukraine.

Since 1945, and even more so since the collapse of the Soviet Union, the US has behaved as a bully, even as it has presented itself as the voice and conscience of the international community. If NATO is not stopped, its eastward expansion might continue, to include Montenegro, Macedonia, and Bosnia. Importantly, the tension with Russia will serve as a pretext to continue to base US ballistic nuclear weapons in Germany, the Netherlands, Belgium, Italy and Turkey for a long time. This revisited Cold War provides a unique opportunity to justify a boost in military spending everywhere: especially in the US and Russia. It is also a way for the US to legitimize and expand, 70 years after the end of World War II, the occupation by its troops of more than 150 countries, with 900 US military bases. While tensions rise in Europe over Ukraine, the top five arms manufacturing and exporting countries, which are the US, Russia, Germany, France and China, will benefit most, as their merchants of death justify a boost of military budgets by the new arms race, especially between the US, Russia and China.[21]

Phase one of the Ukraine crisis was the Western-sponsored Maidan pseudo revolution, and phase two was the referendum that attached Crimea to the Russian federation. As ethnic Russians and pro-Russians have armed themselves, taken over official buildings in Donetsk and demanded independence from Kiev, Ukraine's crisis entered a third phase. On April 12, 2014, coal miners joined the protesters in Donetsk behind barricades made of stack tires and barbed wire. The support of the coalminers, a work force of about 100,000, might become a tipping point for a push at either a full-on partition of Ukraine or a federation with considerable autonomy. Donetsk is the center of Eastern Ukraine's coal-mining area; it is historically called the Donbass and 75 percent of the population speaks Russian. The pro-Russian secession protest was gaining momentum as the armed separatists took over official buildings in the smaller towns of Slaviansk and Kramatorsk. Meanwhile the benefactors of the Euromaidan coup in Kiev were threatening to crack down on the protesters in Eastern Ukraine, whom they called terrorists: a surreal irony from an illegitimate government.

While it was unlikely that NATO would intervene and seek a direct military confrontation with Russia over Ukraine, even before the spring 2014 referendum on Crimea, the US and EU were already cooking some broad and unwise economic sanctions with which to punish Russia. For its part, Russia had at its disposal some economic weapons for retaliation. The pain from this tit for tat of sanctions would be mostly inflicted on the EU. Because of the interconnections between all economies and financial markets, mutual economic sanctions could drive a still fragile world economy to a financial crash. The West, acting as if it solely and arrogantly represented the international community, had formulated a hazardous policy to isolate Russia. This ill-advised strategy was extremely shortsighted on all levels. Unlike Iran, Russia was fully integrated into the global economy.

The Ukraine crisis was, after Syria, another major test of BRICS' geopolitical validity as an economic group, political force and potential military alliance. China, Russia's biggest partner in BRICS, was strangely muted about Ukraine and the Crimea referendum, urging restraint on all sides and pushing for a political solution. During an emergency meeting of the UNSC on March 15, 2014, on a resolution to declare Crimea's referendum illegal, China did not side with Russia by using its veto power but instead abstained from voting.[22] China's abstention did not fare well for the future of BRICS, as it played into the strategy of the US and its EU partner to isolate Russia. China, by its abstention from the UN vote, and India, Brazil and South Africa, by their subdued responses, had played into the hands of the US and its European allies. Would China and other BRICS members step in forcefully to stop the madness of multilateral economic sanctions?

Russia, to prevent the announced freeze of its assets in the US, liquidated more than $100 billion of its holdings in US Treasury Bonds. The bonds, which represented about 80 percent of Russia's holding in US T-Bonds, were transferred out of the US Central Bank. The US Central Bank revealed the withdrawal when it announced that its holdings in T-Bonds dropped by $105 billion for the week ending March 12, 2014, from $2.96 trillion to $2.85 trillion. This abrupt sale was three times higher than any weekly sale was at the peak of the 2008 financial crisis.

Of all countries, China had the means to diffuse the potential economic crisis by also threatening to dump US T-Bonds. China owned an estimated $1.3 trillion in US T-Bonds and was the number one investor amongst foreign governments. BRICS members Brazil and India owned respectively $250 billion and $64 billion in T-Bonds. Consequently, the threat by BRICS of a coordinated fire sale would have represented more than $1.6 trillion in T-Bonds. This would have been powerful enough to crash Wall Street, the US dollar, and by a ripple effect, the European financial markets.

China had warned that drastic economic sanctions against Russia, and Russia's subsequent retaliation, could make the global economy spiral into chaos. Sanctions on Russian exports would greatly expose the EU. Europe imported 30 percent of its gas from the Russian state-owned company Gazprom. Russia was also Europe's biggest customer. The EU was, by far, Russia's leading trade partner and accounted for about 50 percent of all Russian exports and imports. In 2014, EU-Russia overall trade stood at around €360 billion per year. Russia's total export to the EU, which was principally raw materials such as gas and oil, stood at around €230 billion, while Russia's imports from the EU amounted to around €130 billion of mainly manufactured products as well as foodstuff. The EU was also the largest investor in the Russian economy and accounted for 75 percent of all foreign investments in Russia.

Russian lawmakers announced that, in event of Western economic sanctions, they would pass a bill to freeze the assets of European and American companies that operate in Russia. On the other side, the EU allegedly targeted more than 100 Russian businessmen and politicians for a freeze of their European assets. Besides Alexey Miller, head of the state-owned Gazprom, the CEO of Rosneft, Igor Sechin, was also apparently on the sanction hit list. Rosneft is the largest listed oil company in the world and, as such, has partners worldwide, including in the West. For example, the US-based company Exxon-Mobil had a $500 million oil-exploration project with Rosneft in Siberia, and Exxon-Mobil was already in partnership with the Russian giant oil company to exploit Black Sea oil reserves.

The US' booming fracking business and its lobbyists in Washington viewed Ukraine's crisis as an opportunity to expand into new markets. They argued that the US could provide Europe with all its gas needs and, by doing so, make obsolete Russia's main economic weapon of shutting off the EU's main gas supply. Needless to say, this would harm the Russian economy by cutting off one of its key sources of revenue, which amounted to $230 billion a year of export to the EU.

On paper and in theory, the plan to supply the EU with natural gas from fracking sounded manageable. Fortunately, for the sake of the environment, the idea to provide Europe with gas proudly made in the USA was a pie in the sky. Fracking has been singled out as being perhaps the most damaging way to extract energy, due to its pollution of water, release of the extremely strong greenhouse gas methane, and potential to cause earthquakes. Realistically, it would take at least three years to sort out the issues of transport, storage and distribution of the US-derived natural gas for Europe. Europeans had a choice: either stick to Gazprom's cheap and reliable gas or rely on Uncle Sam's pipe dream for their energy needs.

Between August 2014 and January 2015, prices of gas at the pumps in the US declined by a remarkable 42 percent. This acute drop in gasoline prices was the consequence of a crash in the value of crude oil traded on the global market. Specifically, in early August 2014, crude oil was trading on financial markets for about $106 a barrel, and by January 28, 2015, oil was trading at $49 a barrel.[23] This constituted a sharp and unpredictable drop by an astronomical 54 percent, for no apparent market-based reason such as a global economic contraction. Under normal circumstances, this might have indicated a weak demand for energy due to a severe global recession, but this was not the case. How could such a price drop be explained?

In terms of basic so-called free-market capitalist supply-and-demand analysis, the gasoline price drop was an indication that the global energy markets for oil and natural gas had been flooded by doubling the oil supplies. All fingers should have pointed to the US, Canada, Saudi Arabia and other Gulf States such as Qatar and the UAE as being the culprits in this gigantic market manipulation. This energy warfare could only have been viewed as a concerted and deliberate effort to attack the Russian, Iranian and Venezuelan economies. This was a brutal retaliation against Russia's government, with oil and gas prices being used as the weapons of choice, and with the original trigger being the Ukrainian crisis. To isolate Russia quickly was not good enough. Why not try to crush, once again, the old evil empire as defined by Ronald Reagan in the 1980s. Why not deliver a blow to Russia by turning its thriving economy into worthless rubles and its financial market into junk bonds?

The main political target of this global energy war, started by the West and its Arabian Gulf-State accomplices, was Vladimir Putin. The logic seemed simple and straightforward to the policymakers in Washington, even though it was rather shortsighted and simplistic. A crash of Russia's economy would weaken Putin domestically, and this in turn might create fertile ground for regime change in Russia. So far this has not worked as planned, and despite some major economic and currency setbacks in Russia, Putin has managed to ride out the energy-war storm with little damage to his political clout, not only in his own country but also within the BRICS alliance. The energy war was a major existential test for BRICS. Members China and India were both insatiable energy consumers, and in many ways cheap oil and low gas prices suited their economic needs.

If the transnational global corporate empire's strategy of energy war had managed to weaken Putin, who was the most significant strong nationalist leader left in the world, then the domino effect might rapidly have taken down Iran and Venezuela's governments. Iran's economy had been severely damaged by years of Western economic sanctions. In Venezuela, President Nicolas Maduro's position had become extremely precarious. Venezuela's oil revenues represented 95 percent of the country's export earnings, and the 50-percent drop in revenue had already crippled the country's economy.

Since the crisis in Ukraine, largely engineered by the US and its compliant EU allies, the economic Cold War against Russia had been the number one priority on Washington's foreign-policy agenda. This priority, combined with the boom in fracking and shale oil and gas extraction, primarily in the US and Canada, had given Western corporate policymakers an opportunity too hard to resist: the chance to try to crash, or substantially weaken the governments of Russia, Iran and Venezuela. The secret policy goal of this oil-war hubris was regime change in all three countries, which relied mainly on exports of oil and gas for their revenues. This orchestrated manipulation of oil and natural gas prices by the West was having disastrous consequences for the three countries' respective economies, including a rapid decline of their currencies. This Manichean plan could only have been realized with the full complicity of the largest oil producer worldwide: Saudi Arabia. It was unlikely that, for this top oil producer, a deliberate crash of oil prices would have been an option for Washington if the recently deceased King Abdullah had been more than just officially in power for the previous two years. The late Saudi king was elderly and sick, just like his successor, King Salman, who is alleged to suffer from Alzheimer's disease.

Since 1973, the price of oil had been dictated by the Organization of the Petroleum Exporting Countries (OPEC). During these more than four decades, the biggest player in OPEC was the country with the largest oil reserves: Saudi Arabia. Saudi oil-production capacity gave the country final say on oil output to the market, with the great geopolitical power of being able to shut off the valve that fueled the global economy. This might have changed completely in the middle of 2014. By agreeing to let oil prices crash, the Saudis effectively shot themselves in the foot. A power struggle had been going on within the kingdom since 2013. Until April 2014, when he got pushed aside, Prince Bandar bin Sultan, aka Bandar Bush due to his long friendships with George Bush Sr. and Jr., was the go-to guy for the West in Saudi Arabia. Bandar was, de facto, setting the foreign policy of the kingdom. One of his dossiers was Syria, where his goal had been to topple Bashar al-Assad. Prince Bandar had been the brain behind the formation of ISIS. The fact that the jihadists turned rogue on him brought his political disgrace.

One important sign of the kingdom's political weakness in 2015 was something symbolic that happened at the late King Abdullah's funeral: First Lady Michelle Obama, who was part of the US delegation, appeared without hair covering at the formal tribute to honor the dead king. This pseudo-feminist gesture sent to the 1,000 or so Saudi princes who were jockeying for power the clear message: we Americans can do as we please in your kingdom, just as we do in most countries in the world.

Like for Wall Street, where plans are often limited to short-term quarterly analyses, whoever came up with the idea to crash the oil market to make economic casualties of Russia and its allies forgot to include several key parameters in their twisted calculus. The engineered brutal fall of oil prices, which was allowed to happen by a weak Saudi Arabia that refused to cut down production at the request of others major OPEC members, such as Russia and Venezuela, was an act of war against Russia that had been decided in Washington in July 2014. The sharp drop in oil prices could not be explained only by a sudden rise in the output of US and Canadian oil extracted by fracking and the exploitation of shale oil. Something more sinister might have happened to trigger the crash: the dumping of a large fraction of the estimated 727 million barrels held by the US Strategic Petroleum Reserve.[24]

The economic sanctions against Russia enacted by the US and EU since mid-2014, with the energy war being at the forefront, were threatening to drag the global economy into a deep recession. In a world where all the financial markets were interconnected, nobody would be able to seal off their economy from the ripple effects. The main financial side effect of the stress deliberately put by the West on Russia's economy was a sharp rise of the US dollar. This, in turn, was taking a toll on the export revenues of US corporations. The last, but perhaps most serious collateral damage of the oil war was the environment. Cheap oil meant no incentive whatsoever to accelerate the adoption of renewable energies, including solar and wind power. If the oil market continued to get flooded, people, not only in the US and Canada but also elsewhere in the world where gasoline is minimally taxed at the pump, would revert to their awful habit of buying gas-guzzling vehicles. After all, why not drive a car with an eight-cylinder engine when gas is so cheap? The oil Cold War had been designed to take down Vladimir Putin, the last main hurdle in the way of the US neocons' PNAC; this goal of a new century of US hegemony took precedence over any potential negative consequences. The ramifications of the crash in oil prices had obviously not been thought out at all, unless they had been meant to create turmoil, in an inept and borderline-insane strategy of controlled chaos.

Will We Ever Overcome the Collective Madness of War?

On the 11th hour of the 11th day of the 11th month of 1918, World War I officially ended. That day marked the end of a four-year massive slaughter that killed more than seven million French, German, British, Russian and Austro-Hungarian soldiers, and killed or wounded millions more civilians. The US stayed on the sidelines of the conflict to enter it only in its last 19 months. Nevertheless, during World War I, 116,000 US soldiers were killed in action, making this a conflict twice as deadly as Vietnam was for the US military.

World War I, at its inception, was rationalized as the war to end all wars. The soldiers who fought the first modern war were under the illusion that they would be the last ones to die in the name of the human collective psychosis that is warfare. A story that deeply affected my own family is worth telling here. In every single town and village in France, there is a monument with many names to honor the local men killed in World War I. Just like any French family, mine was strongly impacted by the conflict, and, even though France, which carried the heaviest death toll on the allied side, technically won the war against Germany, French people across the board lost. My maternal grandmothers' older brother was a young French officer who fought the Ottoman Empire, an ally of Germany, at the border between Syria and Lebanon. He was a bright young man and, if he had survived the war, he would have taken over the thriving family business from his father. Two days after the war was officially over, he was shot and killed by Ottoman troops, as neither side had been informed that the war had ended. The cruelty and absurdity of it all made my great grandfather fall into a deep depression that eventually compromised his health and the family business.

The war to end all wars did not work out as planned. During the Peace Treaty of Versailles to settle World War I, France still sought revenge against Germany. The French imposed on Germany an incredibly harsh punishment. France's lack of realism and flexibility, combined with the global economic crisis of 1929, contributed to the rise of Adolf Hitler. So 21 years after World War I, Europe and the world were once again engulfed in a collective psychotic episode on an even bigger scale. About 80 million people died globally during World War II, and every country worldwide was affected in what remains today the most brutal and insane conflict in human history.

Since then, the world has known few periods of sanity, despite the creation of the UN to offer peaceful resolution to keep conflicts and disputes between nations from degenerating into wars. The idea, based on the Universal Declaration of Human Rights, was absolutely the right one, but, unfortunately, at least so far, it has failed.[25] After World War II, proxy wars unfolded almost immediately between the US and the Soviet Union. War was in Korea in 1950, and shortly thereafter France was trying to preserve its fading empire in Indochina. The insane logic of war seems always to have the upper hand over peaceful solutions between nations. For centuries politicians and generals have made arguments to justify warfare. One of the versions currently proffered by the defenders of military action in the US, is the convoluted and disingenuous distinction between wars of choice and wars of necessity.[26] One could argue that the last war of necessity fought by the US was World War II. In effect, the US was attacked by Japan in Hawaii and German U-boats in the Atlantic, and had the right to defend itself. After this, the wars fought by the two new superpowers were wars either to maintain or expand their respective empires. This was the case for the Korean and Vietnam wars, both fought on the ideological ground of preventing the so-called domino effect of communism.

The US and its subservient NATO allies are waging wars across the globe today. The never-ending war in Iraq is almost unanimously identified as being a war of choice, while the conflict in Afghanistan is too often called a war of necessity. Some have even pushed the barbaric logic of this definition by calling it the good war. For the US, war is not the solution of last resort anymore; it has instead become a pathological way to assert dominance and conduct world affairs. It is also, and mainly, a crucial part of the economy.

In a book titled *Washington Rules: America's Path to Permanent War,* Andrew Bacevich, a retired US Army Colonel, offers one of the most drastic and insightful critiques of America's military and foreign policies since World War II. Bacevich wrote in his book:

> By the midpoint of the 20th century, the Pentagon had become Leviathan, its actions veiled in secrecy, its reach extending around the world. Yet, while the concentration of power in Wall Street had once evoked deep fear and suspicions, Americans by and large saw the concentration of power in the Pentagon as benign. Most found it reassuring.[27]

Seventy years after the end of World War II, we live in a world at war, as if no lessons have been learned. The logic of capitalism's global war economy dictates US foreign policy. There are no more wars of necessity or even choice. The wars are for profit, and they feed the infinite appetite of the military-industrial complex and its Wall Street stockholders. It does not matter that Libya, Iraq, Syria, Afghanistan and Yemen have been turned into permanent killing fields. Unless the edifice that manufactures ruins, death and misery either collapses or is taken down, the permanent wars for profit of America Empire Inc. will indefinitely continue.

As a species, we have come a long way in terms of technology, science, and communication, but if you scratch the skin of modern man, there is still a brutal Neanderthal lurking in the darkness of our psyche: one who can kill, rape, and commit the most gruesome atrocities. War is our collective sickness, and in this regard we are no better than our ruthless predatory ancestors. Our collective psychology is still stuck into resolving conflict with incredible violence, and, so far, we have not found the cure for this madness.

IV. Engineering Failed States

9

The Strategy of Global Corporate Imperialism

IMPERIALISM HAS LONG BEEN a disease for humanity, but in its current perverse capitalist incarnation, imperialism's methods have become more brutal and ruthless. If the physical destruction of a country's infrastructure is still in the foreground, this is used in conjunction with the instigation of civil wars and bloody sectarian conflicts in previously stable national entities. The few remaining sovereign nations are the final obstacles to the looming threat of a global transnational corporate coup. Consequently, corporatism aims to break the national spirit. This kind of imperialism is on a permanent quest to maximize profit, and its only concern is the bottom line. Unlike the old-fashioned imperialist adventures, corporatism is not about bringing the supposed gift of civilization to so-called savages. Why bother to rebuild the shattered countries when the only goal is to plunder resources, either natural or human? Public resources are allocated to reconstruction, but these resources usually disappear in a vortex of corporate war profiteers like Halliburton. The wrecked countries are never rebuilt because they are easier to exploit while they are in a shambles.

The model for transnational corporate imperialism was set up in Iraq and later applied to Libya. This global imperialist strategy is in the works in

Syria, Ukraine, Mali, the Central African Republic, and Venezuela. NATO usually acts as the armed fist for this process, but sponsored proxy agents such as jihadists in Syria or fascists in Ukraine and Venezuela are also used to destabilize governments. In Venezuela on February 7, 2014, before the not-so-spontaneous protests started, Japanese car giant Toyota abruptly announced it was closing a plant that employed 1,700 people.[1] Was this a coincidence or part of a ploy to crash Venezuela's economy? There is a saying in Lebanon, that the country is "always five minutes away from civil war." This tragic Lebanese reality has spread to the entire Middle East, Africa, and it is gaining ground in Eastern Europe. The old imperialist adage, divide and rule, has become obsolete. The new motto seems to be: divide and steal. The strategy is to fuel ethnic or sectarian conflicts as much and as long as possible, and ideally maintain a permanent state of low-intensity civil war. In the Central African Republic, the clashes between the majority Christian population and the 15 percent Muslims gave France the perfect opportunity to send 2,000 troops.[2] French troops are still in Mali to protect mining interests. In Iraq, the low-level sectarian warfare is a disaster for Iraqis but has worked well for corporate interests. The oil is flowing, and of course, just like in Syria, weapons dealers, mercenaries, and reconstruction contractors are making a killing.

Should the TPP and the Transatlantic Trade and Investment Partnership (TTIP) become ratified, they would provide a legal framework for the global corporate empire. When top elected officials travel abroad, they are supposed to represent and defend the national interests of their people; however, they function mostly as sales representatives of mega-corporations. For example, French President François Hollande travelled to Qatar, Saudi Arabia, Egypt and Brazil to sell the fighter jets Rafale.[3] One of the main goals of a 2014 trip to the US was to indicate to top Silicon Valley technology executives that, despite the misleading socialist label and such, France's best friends are corporations, not people.[4]

Opponents of the TPP have called the agreement NAFTA on steroids, but they rarely talk about its Atlantic counterpart, the TTIP.[5] If the agreements ever see the light of day, most people would end up working for slave wages. Like the wealth of ancient empires that was built on slavery, the fortunes of today's masters of transnational corporatism are made principally on the backs of people who work for slave wages. The princes of Qatar are building their World Cup stadiums with slave labor from Nepal. Global corporate imperialism not only aims to dismantle the few sovereign nations that are left but also to cripple regions and towns. A microcosm of this is Detroit, Michigan. The Motor City is in ruins, a failed town, and a symbol of what corporatism can do. With the TPP and the TTIP in place, we will have hundreds of Detroits. Large sections of Detroit have become ghost towns. In 1984, the independent non-aligned nation of Yugoslavia was able to organize Olympic games in Sarajevo. Thirty-one years later, and after the dismantlement of Yugoslavia by Clinton and his Western vassals in the mid 1990s, more than 40 percent of Bosnians are unemployed.

At the peak of the Syrian crisis in 2013, Russian president Vladimir Putin stood his ground and got NATO to back off from attacking Bashar al-Assad. Many awful things have been said about the former KGB Colonel, but nobody can claim that he is not the man at the helm of Russia. Like it or not, Putin is clearly in charge of his country, which, if nothing else, at least gives people a sense of clarity. Unlike the so-called leader of the free world, there are no puppet masters behind Putin. Fidel Castro was the same, although he ruled a smaller island state. Putin also understood, that in order to maintain Russia's national sovereignty against US and EU domination, he had to forge strategic and economic alliances, especially with China. The BRICS group was created in this context and for this reason. The engineering of a failed state in Ukraine cannot be allowed to happen. Likewise, BRICS' member Brazil must also closely monitor the situation in Venezuela. President Nicolas Maduro is less charismatic than his predecessor, the late Hugo Chavez, and what global corporate imperialism abhors the most is resource nationalism, i.e. the nationalization of prime resources such as oil by sovereign states, as is currently the case in Venezuela. Sovereignty is not entirely about nationalism; it is mainly an expression of cultural identity. National and cultural specificity are getting in the way of the end game of corporatism. We must, as diverse people, unite and fight to stop this abomination. The UN is a failed institution at best, but it could be worse if it should ever become the United Corporations.

NATO: Armed Fist of the Global Police State

NATO was created in 1949, strictly in the context of the Cold War, in response to what was perceived as the threat of expansion by the Soviets into Western Europe. After the collapse of the Soviet Union, it would have been logical to dismantle a military alliance that had become obsolete by losing its enemy; however, NATO not only survived but also thrived in the context of the post Cold-War era. Today, NATO is still expanding its global reach under the strict leadership of the Pentagon. To justify NATO's continued existence, new global security threats are invented, amplified, or generously recycled. The perfect example is, of course, the so-called war on terror, which is an opportunity for increased militarization and global policing at the expense of the most basic rights of democracies. All NATO member states are under strict obedience to the decisions made by the mother ship: the Pentagon. Since the inception of NATO, the only world leader who has had the courage and foresight to oppose the alliance and see its dangers was General Charles de Gaulle. The fiercely independent French leader had no intention of becoming the vassal of the US. Some of the most tragic consequences of the growth of the monstrous Leviathan that is NATO are: systematic militarization of member states; strengthening of military work in conjunction with paramilitary police; systematic use of war to control resources such as energy, water, and minerals, and their transport routes; growing expansion of the area of interventions.

In a NATO summit in Portugal, on November 20, 2010, the main topics on the agenda were the adoption of a new strategic concept for the alliance and a decision on the fate of Afghanistan. The war was unpopular in Europe, and governments were under increased pressure to pull their troops out of NATO, especially in the context of austerity programs started in response to the global recession. Thousands of people marched in a peaceful anti-NATO demonstration. The showing was small compared to the protest at the 2009 summit in Strasbourg, where demonstrators had clashed with police. A heavier presence of armed riot police in Lisbon prevented the peace activists from approaching the cordoned-off summit site.

Former enemy Russia was courted to get more involved with NATO and give it logistic assistance in the Afghan conflict. The leaders of the countries with troops in Afghanistan endorsed a plan to exit the Afghan conflict by 2014. The 2014 date was meaningless because NATO had planned to stay afterwards, without an end date, in an undefined supporting role. Washington's man in Kabul, Hamid Karzai, signed the deal along with UN Secretary General Ban Ki-moon and NATO Secretary General Anders Fogh Rasmussen. "We have launched the process by which the Afghan people will once again become masters in their own house. The direction starting today is clear towards Afghan leadership and Afghan ownership. That is the vision President Karzai has set out. It is a vision we share, and we will make it a reality starting early next year," Rasmussen told a press conference in Lisbon.[6] Rasmussen only listened to Karzai when he went along with the overall agenda. One of Karzai's best initiatives to end the conflict, which was an attempt to negotiate with the Taliban and bring them to the political process, was barely mentioned at the Lisbon summit after being endorsed by previous international conferences in London and The Hague.

Rick Rozoff of *Global Research Canada,* an anti-globalization web site, argued that after the Lisbon NATO summit, the US would intensify its military drive into Asia. He explained that Europe had become a pawn in the game, a vassal of the first global empire, and he called US President Obama the empire's latest rotating emperor. Rozoff wrote:

> So uncritically and unquestioningly compliant has Europe been in the above regards that Obama and the governing elites in the imperial metropolis as a whole have already looked beyond the continent for additional military partners. With the exception of fellow members of the NATO Quint — Britain, Germany, France and Italy (Britain more and

Italy less than the others) — alliance partners are accorded the same status and assigned the same functions as American territories like Puerto Rico, Guam, etc.: geopolitically convenient locations for live-fire military training and for troop, warplane and warship deployments. Two millennia ago the Pax Romana of Augustus brought roads and ports, aqueducts and irrigation, amphitheaters and libraries, and Greek writers from Aristotle to Aeschylus to occupied territories. Bellum Americanum burdens its vassals and tributaries with military bases, interceptor missile batteries, McDonald's and Lady Gaga.[7]

Praetorian Guard of the Orwellian Empire

Since the collapse of the Soviet Union in 1991, the US has positioned itself, one administration after another, as a global supercop guarantor of world peace. Indeed, since the end of World War II, even as the US has projected its power worldwide through military might, its clever ideologues have managed to convince a large portion of their public that their ambitions for global hegemony are altruistic and benevolent. This dichotomy between the fictional discourse and the brutal reality of US imperialism, applied globally since 1945, is more blatant than George Orwell's worst fears expressed in his book *1984*. In this war-is-peace construct, nothing is what it appears to be, and imperialist wars are sold to a gullible citizenry as being humanitarian. Despite the disinformation propagated by the think tanks and Western mainstream media outlets, factual evidence shows that currently, the clear-and-present dangers to world peace are not ISIS, Russia's supposed aggressive acts, or the Ebola virus but, rather, the US military and NATO.

The justification for the 2003 invasion of Iraq, given by the spin masters of Orwellian imperialism, was to spread freedom and democracy to the Middle East. Twelve years later, what have spread in Iraq, Libya and Syria are not freedom and democracy, but ashes, ruins, blood baths and despair. The new world order that the empire's ideologues are striving to impose globally under the cover of fake revolutions, at least until everyone is beaten into submission, is actually controlled chaos. The destructive empire has several wrecking balls at its disposal, but its tools of predilection are the US military, the troops of its dependable and mostly occupied vassals in NATO, and the Israel Defense Forces (IDF). The creation of controlled chaos works as a tactic to mold the collective psyche of the citizenry, because people usually strive for stability, security and order, even at the expense of their personal liberty. The chaos generates a state of fear that makes people welcome the worst kinds of repression from the most oppressive forms of government. Fear and paranoia are the essential ingredients of police states.

Nothing could be more appropriate for the warmongering Orwellian Empire than to have as its current public-relations person a Nobel Peace Prize laureate. His latest act of war, on February 11, 2015, was to send an official request to the US Congress to pass an AUMF against America's latest elusive enemy: ISIS (or ISIL).[8] The request to Congress, which was a gem in Orwellian rhetoric and legalese, mentioned that Obama "has directed a comprehensive and sustained strategy to degrade and defeat ISIL."[8] The irony and absurdity of it all is tragic. In the time of the Orwellian Empire, most people not only accept the notion that they must be protected against themselves, but also embrace it happily, as if they are singing cheerfully on their way to the slaughterhouse.

Facts are awfully stubborn, even in this era. Seventy years after the end of World War II, the US military still occupies the main losers of the conflict and current supposed allies. About 40,000 US troops occupy Germany, while 60,000 occupy Japan. Fifty-four years since the end of the Korean War, almost 30,000 troops occupy South Korea. Fourteen years after the invasion of Afghanistan, a Praetorian guard of 11,000 is still in that country, and 12 years after the invasion of Iraq a force of about 5,000 troops and quickly growing, remains there. Some other significant footprints of the US military on so-called sovereign countries are as follows: about 12,000 in Kuwait; 3,500 in Bahrain; 1,500 in Turkey; 11,000 in Italy; 10,000 in the UK, and 2,000 in Spain.

The overall US military force overseas occupies more than 150 countries and amounts to the staggering number of 160,000 troops, with an additional 70,000 deployed with either the Navy, Air Force, or Special Forces in contingency operations, i.e. active wars. A priority of further military expansion, in this case through NATO, is Eastern Europe, using the pretext of necessary defense against Russia's supposed aggressions. In spring 2015, NATO established command centers in Poland, Romania, Bulgaria, Latvia, Lithuania, and Estonia to oversee 5,000 troops. For 2016, the proposed DOD budget included, in addition to the base budget and money for various wars in the Middle East, $789 million to support NATO in the EU.

From time to time, despite the thick fog of disinformation and propaganda, where basic truth becomes meaningless, the empire's ideologues slip up and become candid. Such a chilling moment of semi-truth happened in the White House National Security Strategy report of February 6, 2015.[9] Vague literary flourishes do not hide the fact that the leadership of War Inc. does not intend to respect national sovereignty and pull out its Praetorian guard.

> Now, at this pivotal moment, we continue to face serious challenges to our national security, even as we are working to shape the opportunities of tomorrow. Violent extremism and an evolving terrorist threat raise a persistent risk of attacks on America and our allies. Escalating challenges to cybersecurity, aggression by Russia, the accelerating impact of climate change, and the outbreak of infectious diseases all give rise to anxieties about global security. We must be clear-eyed about these and other chal-

lenges and recognize the United States has a unique capability to mobilize and lead the international community to meet them.

Any successful strategy to ensure the safety of the American people and advance our national security interests must begin with an undeniable truth — America must lead. Strong and sustained is essential to a rules-based international order that promotes global security and prosperity as well as the dignity and human rights of all peoples. The question is never whether America should lead, but how we lead.[9]

There we have it. The global citizenry must challenge the US' Orwellian leadership that has driven the world from one war to another for the past seven decades. This is a clear-and-present danger to all of us. Nations, worldwide, must reclaim their sovereignty by first recognizing that the Praetorian guards of the Orwellian Empire are not allies but occupiers. Contesting the leadership of the US is the only way out of a perverse global construct where war is peace, freedom is slavery, ignorance is strength, and reality is fiction.

10

From Mujahideen to Taliban

TEXAS CONGRESSMAN Charlie Wilson died on February 10, 2010 at the age of 76.10 He was known in Washington as good-time Charlie for his excessive appreciation of beautiful women, booze, cocaine and hot tubs. But who could blame him? This had been during the swinging 1970s. Congressman Wilson also had a deadly serious side and a relentless ability to get things done, for better or worse. In 1979, he embraced the cause of the mujahideen in their fight against the Soviet Union. Wilson worked in conjunction with the CIA and Pakistan's Inter-Services Intelligence (ISI) to provide assistance to the Afghan fighters. He took numerous trips to the region to show his complete dedication to the cause of what was known at the time as Afghanistan's freedom fighters. After Ronald Reagan's election in 1980, Wilson's cause became easier. Republicans and Democrats were still fully living in the Cold War, and Reagan became extremely receptive to Wilson's goal of defeating the Soviets in Afghanistan. Massive amounts of cash and weapons started to flow to Afghanistan via Pakistan. As Wilson was pleading in Washington on behalf of the mujahideen, Rambo was doing the same on the screen for America's public opinion.

The Afghan resistance's main military challenges were the deadly and indiscriminate attacks being conducted by Russian helicopters. From his numerous trips to Afghanistan, Wilson became convinced that if he could provide the so-called freedom fighters with a weapon system that could take down the Soviet choppers, the Afghan resistance would prevail. The perfect weapon for this task was the one-man shoulder-triggered Stinger missile. Wilson worked tirelessly to convince the Reagan administration and his colleagues in Congress that, without the Stinger missiles, the Afghan resistance would lose. Thanks to his support from the CIA, Wilson won that battle. The provision of Stingers was the turning point in the war and the beginning of the end for the Soviet invasion. In retrospect, helping the Afghan resistance might have been one of Charlie Wilson's and the Reagan administration's biggest geopolitical miscalculations. Good-time Charlie's intentions were probably genuine, but those of Reagan-Bush Sr. were not.

Bush Sr.'s goal was to bleed the Soviet Union and bring the so-called evil empire to its end. This objective was accomplished: the war in Afghanistan was the final blow to make the Soviet Union, which was already crumbling for economic reasons, completely collapse. The part of the Afghan-Russian equation that was not considered by Wilson or the Reagan administration was the fact that soon thereafter, the very same freedom fighters, cherished by Wilson and financed and armed by Washington, would turn against the West. In the aftermath of their victory against the Soviets in 1989, the mujahideen became the Taliban.

The autobiography of Abdul Salam Zaeef, *My Life With the Taliban,* translated from the Pashtun and published in English in 2011, offered a unique and privileged look at the communities that formed the bedrock of the Taliban and the forces that motivated the Afghans to continue to fight.[11] Abdul Salam Zaeef was a principal actor in Afghanistan's domestic and foreign policies under the Taliban in the 1990s. His words supplied not only a personal history of an unusual life but also a counter-narrative to standard accounts of Afghanistan since 1979. Zaeef was born in Southern Afghanistan in 1968, in a rural area near Kandahar. His family was poor, and both of his parents died when he was young. Russia's invasion in 1979 forced him to flee to Pakistan. In 1983, he joined the jihad against the Soviets. During the war, he fought alongside several major figures of the anti-Soviet resistance, including Taliban top leader Mullah Mohammad Omar. After the war, Zaeef returned to a quiet life in Helmand Province, but factional conflicts soon broke out and, "disgusted by the ensuing lawlessness," he joined with other former Mujaheddin to form the Taliban. He recalled the movement's humble beginnings as follows:

> The first few days of the Taliban movement were a time of great needs. We had a few weapons, but no cars and no money. Mullah Abdul Sattar and I each had a motorbike. My bike broke down with an engine problem

on the very first day, though, which left Mullah Sattar's Russian motorbike as the Taliban's only means of transportation. It had no exhaust pipe and could be heard coming from miles away, roaring down the dirt tracks and back roads. We called it 'the tank of Islam.' After Mullah Masoom visited the villages, scores of people came to our checkpoints to see the Taliban for themselves. There was hope in their hearts for the first time in years.[11]

In the book, Zaeef recounted his times with Ahmed Shah Massoud, the leader of the Afghan resistance during the Soviet era, and as a civil servant and a minister who negotiated with foreign oil companies for the Taliban after they assumed power in 1994. Abdul Salam Zaeef was Afghanistan's ambassador to Pakistan on 9/11. In 2002, he was delivered to the American forces operating in Pakistan. He spent the subsequent four and half years in prison, including three years in Guantanamo, before being released without trial or charge. His book shone a light on what he called the phony war that had preceded the US-led invasion of Afghanistan. He lives in Kabul, where he has become a public critic of the US-backed corrupt Karzai government. Contrary to assumptions by the US media, the Taliban enjoy wide support, especially in the Pashtun areas of Afghanistan and Pakistan.

A reality that is often overlooked in the Western press is that the ISI has supported the Taliban for decades. The ISI, created in 1948, is often described as being a state within a state. In fact, it is the part of the Pakistani military that is involved in civilian politics, Islamic militancy and foreign affairs. The ISI has a long history of links to insurgents, not only in Afghanistan but also in Kashmir. In the 1980s the ISI became the key conduit for weapons and at least $6 billion in US and Saudi covert funds to the mujahideen. Since the CIA had heavily supported the mujahideen via the ISI, the two intelligence agencies have strong historical ties with the Taliban. Indeed the ISI helped to propel the Taliban to power in Afghanistan.

In 2001, the ISI officially renounced its support of Islamic militants, with the exception of those in Kashmir. In fact the ISI had helped the Afghan Taliban in the past and might still be doing so. In June 2010, British researcher Matt Waldman wrote a report, published by the London School of Economics, in which he accused the ISI of "playing a double game of astonishing magnitude."[12] According to Waldman's report, while fighting their own Taliban in Pakistan, the ISI was supporting the Afghan Taliban and had even compensated families of suicide bombers with 200,000 Pakistani rupees each. For his report, Waldman personally interviewed nine Taliban field commanders, and he said that former Taliban ministers and a UN official based in Kabul substantiated his claims.[12] Afghan President Karzai had in the past also accused the ISI of supporting the Afghan Taliban. Pakistani military spokesman Major General Athar Abbas, on the other hand, said that Waldman's claims were ridiculous and the allegations baseless.[13]

"Without a change in Pakistani behaviour, it will be difficult, if not impossible, for international forces and the Afghan government to make progress against the insurgency," wrote Waldman in the report.[12] The ISI strategy made more sense in the context of the ongoing regional conflict between Pakistan and India over their respective influence in Afghanistan. "This report is consistent with Pakistan's political history in which civilian leaders actively backed jihadi groups that operate in Afghanistan and Kashmir," Waldman told UK's *Sunday Times* on June 13, 2010.[14] It was unclear whether the ISI had acted with the full support and knowledge of the Pakistani government, or if the apparent support for the Taliban had come from rogue elements within the ISI.

Afghanistan, Burial Ground of Empires

The killing of Taliban Commander Baitullah Mehsud by a US drone strike on August 7, 2009, two weeks before the August 20 elections in Afghanistan, was a major early incident in the endless conflict.[15] The attack had been conducted by the CIA and had taken place in South Waziristan, a Taliban stronghold in Pakistan. Mehsud had commanded more than 20,000 fighters; most of them belonged to his own tribe: the Mehsud tribe. Since 2005, he had ruled South Waziristan as his personal fiefdom. The Pakistani government had accused him of ordering the 2007 assassination of Benazir Bhutto, and there was a $5 million reward on his head from the US. In a rare interview with the *BBC* in 2007, Mehsud said every Muslim had a duty to wage jihad "against the infidel forces of America and Britain."[16] His fighters were determined to reach this goal.

By putting the accent on military operations, both in Afghanistan and Pakistan, in advance of the Afghan elections, the Obama administration had brought into question the legitimacy of the elections. Predictably, Mehsud's assassination was followed by a series of violent incidents. On August 6, in one part of Helmand Province a bomb blast left five policemen dead, and in another part of the same province, a roadside bomb killed a group of people on their way to a wedding. Elsewhere in Afghanistan, three British soldiers were killed on August 7. Because of the violence, some Afghan officials said that as many as 700 polling stations might not open. International voices, including some from the British and French military, said that the only solution for Afghanistan was a political one and that, for this to work, elements of the Taliban would have to be included in the political process. The Taliban, for its part, called for a boycott of the elections and promised to disrupt them.

Two weeks before the second-round elections on November 7, 2009, the Obama administration seemed undecided on war strategy. Secretary of State Hillary Clinton, Secretary of Defense Robert Gates and General Stanley McChrystal favored sending more US troops. McChrystal requested an additional 40,000 troops, and he was a proponent of the so-called hold-and-stay strategy; in other words, he wanted to engage in nation building. By contrast, Vice President Joe Biden and Senator John Kerry appeared to want to put a brake on additional troops and focus instead on counter-terrorism operations.

Around the same time, former Marine Captain Matthew Hoh, became the first foreign-service official to resign in protest against the war. After making public, via the *Washington Post,* his letter of resignation from the State Department, he made the press rounds and publicly declared that he did not think anyone could justify the US and NATO presence in Afghanistan. In an interview on October 29, 2010 with *NPR's* Melissa Block, Matthew Hoh said:

> The losses of our soldiers do not merit anything that comes in line with our strategic interests or values. I have lost understanding of and confidence in the strategic purpose of the United States' presence in Afghanistan. I prefer to keep talking about: Is it even worth winning? Is it worth losing more lives? And is it worth spending billions of dollars that, frankly, this country does not have? The idea that we should continue fighting there just because we have been fighting there for the last eight years I think is completely irrational.[17]

Hoh pointed out that the US had been doing counterinsurgency since 2004, and that the Obama administration's strategy was just more of what had failed in previous years. He explained:

> I have a list of quotes from every commanding generals since 2004 in Afghanistan, assuring success, assuring that victory is one year away. They just need more troops and some more time. As every year we add more troops or spend more money, the Taliban grow in size, and support for the Karzai government decreases. The conflict is getting worse along any measures you want to measure: whether it is IEDs, civilian casualties and coalition casualties.[17]

Meanwhile a new radio station for British and US soldiers was launched in Afghanistan, in which the host kicked off the shows with a cheerful: Gooood Morning Afghanistan! This was exactly how a famous radio show had kicked off decades before in Vietnam. Irony or Freudian slip? Afghanistan was looking more and more like Vietnam, and Matthew Hoh, like a new version of a young John Kerry in his opposition to the war.

Taliban insurgents launched a wave of coordinated attacks on January 18, 2010 on the highly fortified capital city of Kabul, to show that Karzai's regime was fragile and that they could strike anywhere they wanted. Eyewitnesses reported that there had been a series of large explosions and gunfire near the presidential palace. Taliban spokesman Zabihulla Mujahid told *Agence France Presse (AFP)* from an undisclosed location: "It is our work, the targets are the presidential palace, the finance, justice and mines ministries and the central bank. Twenty of our suicide bombers have entered the area and fighting is ongoing. One militant has detonated a suicide vest at the entrance of the presidential palace complex."[18] The *BBC*'s Mark Dummett reported that Kabul was under lock-down, and at the same time the *BBC* interviewed a NATO spokesman who minimized the brazen attacks by painting them as being a few bad guys who got in an open window in an otherwise secure building.[19] Later it was discovered that indeed government buildings had been targeted and 12 people had been killed. The attacks had come one day after the government had said that Karzai would announce a plan to set up a peace process with the Taliban. Karzai, a Pashtun, had called for a political deal and gone as far as offering the Taliban some cabinet positions; however, the Taliban militia had refused any dialogue with the Karzai administration, whom they considered to be pawns of the US and NATO, until after a complete withdrawal of all international troops. Many Afghans viewed Karzai as a corrupt and illegitimately elected President, and they relied on the shadow government provided by the Taliban.

A major NATO offensive in Marjah, called Operation Moshtarak and involving numerous airstrikes, began less than a month later, on February 13, 2010.[20] This military operation killed 21 civilians and displaced thousands. It was the first deployment after a surge of 30,000 additional US troops had been decided by the Obama administration, supposedly to win hearts and minds in Afghanistan. On February 21, Karzai's government strongly condemned a series of subsequent botched NATO air strikes by saying that they were unjustifiable. One such bombing of a convoy of vehicles on its way to Kandahar had killed more than 27 civilians, including women and children.[21] "People still complain about how the house searches are being conducted. The joint force should not view every person here with suspicion of being a Taliban. When the government and its foreign allies want the people on their side, they should respect every resident here. People should not feel any sense of insecurity from Afghan and foreign troops," said Abdur Rahman Saber, head of a local council established right before the Marjah offensive.[21] General MacChrystal, the commander in Afghanistan, apologized to Karzai and the Afghan people a second time in a week. "We are extremely saddened by the tragic loss of innocent lives. I have made it clear to our forces that we are here to protect the Afghan people, and inadvertently killing or injuring civilians undermines their trust and confidence in our mission," said McChrystal.[22]

Shortly thereafter, on February 22, 2010, a suicide bomber blew himself up at a tribal leaders and Afghan government officials meeting and killed 15 people, including former mujahideen commander and a local tribal leader Haji Zaman Ghamsharik. According to *Al Jazeera*'s James Bays, reporting in the Helmand Province, it appeared that Haji Zaman had been the target of the attack. He had been a local commander in the Tora Bora Mountains when US forces had launched the botched operation to capture or kill Osama bin-Laden in 2001. "It is certain, I think, that the Taliban wanted Haji Zaman dead," said James Bays.[23] The bold attack proved that the Taliban were far from being on the run, despite the Marjah offensive and the loss, 12 days before, of Mullah Abdul Ghani Baradar, a key Taliban military commander who had been captured by the CIA and the ISI in Karachi, Pakistan.

If McChrystal's objective had been to break the back of the insurgency, he had failed. The capture of a Taliban commander appeared to have had little impact on the insurgency. On February 26, suicide bombers attacked the center of Kabul once again, this time at the Safi hotel and the country's biggest shopping complex, killing 17 people, including a Frenchman, an Italian, and 10 Indians. The coordinated attack was only the second on the heavily fortified capital city after the shock of the January 18 attack. The Indian victims appeared to have been the main targets because a Taliban spokesman said that the bomb had been "detonated in front of the Indians' hotel."[24] India's presence and influence in Kabul had considerably increased since the 2001 invasion. The attack had come while Afghans were marking the holiday Milad-Ul Nabi, the birthday of the prophet Mohammed. Zabiullah Mujahid, a Taliban spokesman, boasted to *Reuters* that the "holy warriors [had] managed to attack in the heart of Kabul once again."[25] Mujahid said that at least five Taliban fighters had launched the attack, including two suicide bombers who had detonated explosives-packed vests near the hotel. Witnesses reported explosions and the sounds of intense gunfire, followed by sporadic gunfire.

There grew concern that the suicide attacks would intensify as NATO's push against the Taliban continued. "The Taliban is showing that they too are very strong-willed and that they will attack anywhere and anytime they want," said Hoda Abdel-Hamid, *Al Jazeera's* correspondent in Kabul.[25] The US and its allies were fighting an asymmetrical insurgency warfare, in which the Taliban were picking when and where they would fight. They could hit whatever targets they deemed to be valuable. Unlike a traditional army, the Taliban had a bottom-up structure, as opposed to a top-down organization, which made the loss of a commander not that crippling for the insurgency, because someone else could quickly replace him.

A report by the International Council on Security and Development (ICOS), released in May 2010, confirmed that the Marjah offensive had not met its supposed objectives of emphasizing the needs of the Afghan people and winning hearts and minds, and that the attack could turn out to be a recruiting tool for the Taliban.[26] The ICOS reviewed the local perception of the Marjah offensive by interviewing more than 400 Afghan men from Marjah, Lashkar Gah and Kandahar in March 2010.[26] The report revealed that the operation had contributed to "high levels of anger among local Afghans," with 61 percent of those interviewed feeling "more negative about NATO forces than before the military offensive." Sixty-seven percent did not support a strong NATO-International Security Assistance Force (ISAF) presence in their province, and 71 percent stated that they wanted the NATO forces to leave; 45 percent said they were "angry at the NATO occupation, civilian casualties and night raids," and 78 percent of the respondents were "often or always angry." The report concluded that the mistakes of the operation could translate the legitimate grievances of the people of Marjah into more recruits for the Taliban.[26] Among those interviewed, 95 percent believed that more young Afghans had joined the Taliban in the last year, and 59 percent expected the Taliban to return to Marjah. Local Afghans were highly skeptical about NATO's chances to win against the Taliban: 67 percent stated that they did not believe that "NATO and the Afghan government would win against the Taliban," and 14 percent flatly said, "NATO would never win."[26]

A key issue was the refugee situation that had been created by the offensive. Thousands of displaced Afghans were forced to move to nonexistent or overcrowded camps with insufficient food, medical supplies and shelters. Of the Afghans interviewed by ICOS, 97 percent said that the operation had led to a new flow of internally displaced people. The Director of Policy Research at ICOS, Jorrit Kamminga, said: "The lack of humanitarian planning has been a propaganda victory for the Taliban, who will try to use the grievances of local Afghans to radicalize and recruit young men."[26] The report cautioned against similar operations in the future and recommended the adoption of a new "counter insurgency impact equation to balance any negative impact, and ensure that the positive impact is greater than the negative impact."[26]

The year 2010 turned out to be one of the deadliest ones in Afghanistan for US and NATO allied troops. By September, despite a 30,000-troop surge by the Obama administration, 530 troops had died, including more than 300 Americans. Corruption was rampant, violence had soared and, however one wanted to look at it, the momentum was still with the Taliban. History is not a US forte. If people had done their research in Washington before impulsively invading Afghanistan in 2001, they would have reconsidered their actions after learning that nobody had ever defeated recent history's best guerrilla force: the Pashtuns. The Taliban are mostly Pashtuns, and this fearless tribe has won the well-deserved reputation of providing a burial ground for empires. They did this with the British Empire and, in the 1980s, with the Soviet Union. The Reagan administration played a pivotal role in arming and funding what he called Afghanistan's freedom fighters when they were taking on the Soviet Union. A few decades later, Reagan's freedom fighters became the Taliban. Washington never made an effort to understand the Taliban and the reasons why they were such a tough and resilient enemy.

Drone Attacks a Recruiting Tool for Pakistan's Taliban

As NATO was bombing the Afghan Taliban, the US was launching drone strikes against the Pakistani Taliban. Since Obama's election in 2008, his administration's strategy had been to expand the war from Afghanistan to Pakistan. By doing so, he had turned an already unstable Pakistan into a ticking time bomb. His concept was well defined by the term AfPak, which had designated Afghanistan and Pakistan as being a single theater of operations. The Obama administration and the Pentagon viewed the conflict in Afghanistan and the engagement of Pakistan, either with drone attacks or Special Forces advising Pakistani forces on the ground, as a joined strategy to deal with the Taliban. The 2009 Nobel Peace Prize winner's weapon of choice was the drone, which Washington viewed as being critical in its global fight against Al-Qaeda. Despite claims to the contrary by the administration, human-rights organizations in Pakistan and abroad had condemned the drone strikes and reported heavy civilian casualties as a consequence of the drone attacks.

It was obvious why Obama had picked McChrystal to be the commander in Afghanistan: he had the perfect background for it. Under the Bush administration he had been the head of Black Ops. In 2010, he was running, not only the overt military operations in Afghanistan but also the covert ones in Pakistan. It was likely that he was coordinating, within Pakistani borders, the efforts of Delta Forces, Rangers and other Special Forces in conjunction with the CIA and ISI.

On February 2, 2010, according to Pakistani officials, US drones launched at least 18 missiles in the North Waziristan tribal area of Pakistan that targeted Taliban hideouts and killed around 35 people in one of the biggest drone attacks that had been carried out until then by the US in Pakistan. Pakistani authorities responded by saying that they had not given any tacit approval for the US to conduct such strikes. There had been tremendous opposition from a majority of Pakistanis to the US drone attacks, and it was growing. The government feared a backlash from the drone attacks, which had provoked anger among Pakistanis and boosted support for the Taliban.

The next day a bomb attack killed eight people including three US military personnel, a Pakistani security guard, and three children in North West Pakistan's Koto village. According to a local hospital, around 65 people were also injured. The attack coincided with the re-opening of a girls' school that had been rebuilt, with financing from a foreign NGO after a similar attack had destroyed it in 2009. According to *AP,* the US soldiers had been wearing civilian clothes and had been introduced as journalists by

Pakistan military handlers. The US embassy in Islamabad said that the Americans had been in the area to attend the re-opening of the girls' school when the bomb exploded; however an embassy statement said: "Three Americans were killed and two were injured in a terrorist bomb explosion at 11:20 a.m. today in the Lower Dir district.... The Americans were US military personnel in Pakistan to conduct training at the invitation of the Pakistan Frontier Corps."[27] Pakistan's Taliban claimed that the Americans were members of Blackwater. "We claim responsibility for the blast," said Taliban spokesman Azam Tariq.[28]

After the Pakistani government had routed the Taliban from their bases in places like South Waziristan, the Taliban spread to other areas. On April 5, 2010, a series of deadly blasts rocked Pakistan's North West Frontier Province (NWFP) killing at least 52 people and wounding more than 100 others, according to Pakistani authorities. In the first attack, a suicide bomber killed 46 people at a celebration in Timargarah organized by the Awami National Party, a leading secular party that had dominated the government of the NWFP.[29] Zahid Khan, a spokesman for the party said that they had been celebrating the recent decision to change the name of the NWFP officially to Khyber-Pakhtunkhwa, to honor its Pashtun-majority population, when the suicide bomber detonated.

The second attack followed a few hours later; it targeted the US consulate in Peshawar and killed six people.[29] Ariel Howard, the spokesman for the US embassy in Islamabad said: "We can confirm there has been an attack at the US consulate Peshawar facilities." In the attack, four Taliban came in two vehicles. According to Pakistani authorities, "the militants were well equipped and well organized." The Taliban had tried to enter the consulate but not succeeded. Two security guards were killed in the attack along with the four Taliban. Taliban spokesman Azam Tariq told *AFP*: "We accept the attack on the American consulate. This is revenge for the drone attacks. We have already between 2,800 to 3,000 Fedayeens ready. We will carry out more such attacks, we will target any place where there are Americans."[29]

In February 2010, another action within Pakistan by American operatives, either black ops or CIA, which created a backlash in the country, was the capture on Pakistani soil of Mullah Abdul Ghani Baradar, a Taliban military commander who was rumored to have favored peace talks with the Karzai administration. Hostility toward the US had grown even stronger than a year before when a Pew Research Center survey had found that fully 64 percent of Pakistanis regarded the US as an enemy, only 22 percent thought the US took their interests into account when making foreign-policy decision, and only 9 percent described the US as being a partner. In 2009, around 70 percent of Pakistanis believed that the 9/11 attack in New York had been an inside job conducted by the US government to justify the invasions of Afghanistan and Iraq. The increased presence of military personnel and CIA operatives in Pakistan had reinforced this viewpoint. By June 2012, about 75 percent of Pakistanis viewed the US as an enemy.[30]

In a book titled *Obama's Wars* and published in September 2010, Bob Woodward wrote that the CIA had created a 3,000-strong elite strike force composed of US Special Forces and Afghan paramilitary, which had conducted covert operations against the Taliban on both sides of the Afghanistan-Pakistan border.[31] NPR confirmed the existence of the secret Afghan unit with two sources. One US official said that the Afghan paramilitary force operated in small units called Counter-terrorism Pursuit Team. This is one of the best Afghan fighting forces, the official said, and it "has made major contributions to stability and security."[32]

Past news accounts had described the CIA's work with militias and other groups to go after al-Qaeda, as well as the close collaboration between highly-trained Afghan special forces soldiers and American Green Berets to go after Taliban fighters. What was new was the supposed work of the secret Afghan teams inside Pakistan, which NPR confirmed with an advisor to the US military in Afghanistan. The revelation would complicate diplomacy with Pakistan. Top US military leaders, principally Joint Chiefs Chairman Admiral Mullen, had worked hard to improve relationships with Pakistani security officials. "It was uncertain what, if any, major contributions these covert Afghan teams had achieved against the Taliban, in either Afghanistan or Pakistan. Even with such teams, the US had to send 30,000 extra troops to Afghanistan because the Taliban had grown so much in strength. The challenge of fighting the Taliban across the border in Pakistan remained. The American military command in Afghanistan was pressing for more US drone attacks against Taliban safe havens in Pakistan," said Tom Bowman reporting for NPR.[32]

The confirmation of the murkiness of the AfPak conundrum fueled some much-needed debates in Washington over whether the effort was worthwhile. Woodward's book also revealed the division of the Obama administration on AfPak strategy. Paul Pillar, a former CIA counter-terrorist operative, said that the US ought to look at the current commitment to Afghanistan in rigorous cost-benefit terms. Pillar said that Afghanistan was no longer a war of necessity, and the US did not need to defeat the Afghan Taliban because the group was not a national-security threat. "We are spending $100 billion a year, as well as an expenditure of blood that is now over 1,200 killed and countless others wounded. And we have lost sight of what this is or what this is not doing to keep Americans safe from terrorism," said Pillar.[33]

Feeding Red Meat to America's Imperialist Fervor
There is nothing like a good killing to shut down criticisms of military spending, make Americans proud and a president climb up in the polls. After the hit on Osama bin-Laden, on May 2, 2011, executed by US Navy Seals, Obama's approval rating jumped from 46 percent to 52 percent.[34] The US President was getting praise from such luminaries as former Vice President Dick Cheney. Most Americans were cheering without a second thought. After all, they finally got their bogeymen. The face of evil that had been used to justify the wars in Afghanistan and Iraq was gone. And because in the US, the perception of reality is a simplistic black or white without shades of grey, most people felt that the assassination of someone in a sovereign country was cause for celebration.

Despite the fog of war surrounding the mission ordered and observed live by the president, the American people asked very few questions. They were just happy that the bin-Laden chapter was closed, as if the death of a man in murky circumstances would bring the US back to the supposed innocent golden years before 9/11. On that day, the US feeling of invulnerability was lost. The country is still trying to recover from this deep open wound. On the day of bin-Laden's death, Americans felt proud, invincible, as if the killing of a symbolic figurehead could make everything all right again. Americans at large did not care about the geopolitical consequences of bin-Laden's assassination: they just wanted the ultimate bad guy to be dead. Besides the question of the photographic evidence of bin-Laden's death, few Americans asked themselves the real questions: Why now? Does it matter? Should the US declare its mission accomplished and get out of Afghanistan? Or would this mean an escalation of the conflict to Pakistan?

At first, US citizens were told that bin-Laden had been killed in a firefight. But they soon found out that, in the Navy Seal's fog-of-war theory, bin-Laden was killed cleanly, with a bullet in the chest and another in the head to finish him off. So it appeared that Osama bin-Laden had not fought and was killed unarmed, execution style. Actually, Americans could care less about the details, the repercussions, or even about the legality of the operation with regard to international law. What truly mattered was that the empire had successfully struck back and again appeared to be in the driver's seat. If some Americans were expecting that the closed chapter on bin-Laden would mean an end to the war on terror, however, they were grossly mistaken. It was the beginning of "war on terror: the sequel," but this time around, forget Afghanistan, forget Iraq, the target would be Pakistan.

The attack on bin-Laden's compound made the US' covert war in Pakistan fully overt. US Special Forces, but not CIA operatives, had conducted the assassination, in breach of Pakistani sovereignty; the Special Forces had obviously benefited from the complicity of part of the ISI and some Paki-

stani officials. The war on terror was still on. Bin-Laden's assassination en-
sured that Guantanamo would stay open a lot longer and that tools such as
the Patriot Act and other neofascist legal maneuvers would stay fully implemented. The endless war on terror was not only good business for the
military-industrial complex, but also good politics, judging by Obama's
boost in the US public opinion polls. Osama bin-Laden was dead, and
Americans would never see any credible photographic evidence, but they
had cheered the news as if it was about justice, although it was about revenge and the assertion of the empire's global reach.

If the Obama administration thought it had generated momentum in
favor of the US and against Pakistan's Taliban with bin-Laden's killing, then
this notion was short-lived. On June 9, 2011, more than 150 Pakistani Taliban attacked a military checkpoint in northwestern Pakistan and killed at
least 10 Pakistani soldiers. This bold attack, with rocket-propelled grenades
and heavy weapons, was the biggest one by the Taliban in several months
and was presumed to be retaliation. It occurred near the town of Makeen,
close to the Afghan border, in South Waziristan, where there had been a
surge in US drone strikes since bin-Laden's assassination. Washington had
put a great deal of pressure on the Pakistani government to take military
action in South Waziristan, which was described in US military and intelligence circles as being the most dangerous place on earth.

In an opinion piece in *Le Monde Diplomatique,* Chris Sands argued that
the assassination had not been a game changer, as described by US policy
makers and the US media.[35]

> Sympathy for the insurgents is particularly easy to find in the Pashtun
> community, Afghanistan's largest ethnic group. For many of them, bin-
> Laden's role in the anti-Soviet struggle still marked him out for
> admiration. Speaking in Kabul, a resident of the eastern province of
> Khost said: 'He left his house in the name of Islam, and now he is a
> martyr. If one Osama dies, hundreds will rise up, and hundreds of their
> friends will rise up'.
> NATO cannot win in Afghanistan. Even if al-Qaida and the Taliban
> were to be defeated in the short term, acts of retribution are inevitable. All
> it needs is for a young man who has lost a relative in a drone attack or an
> air strike to seek vengeance on the streets of Washington, Paris or Lon-
> don. Bin Laden's dream is very much alive.[35]

The drone attacks and retaliations continued relentlessly in a war that
sometimes seemed to be directly against the Pakistani government. In 2011
alone, there were around 65 US drone strikes in Pakistan. The final air strike
that year, on November 26, killed 24 Pakistani troops along the Afghan
border. Pakistan retaliated by shutting down US supply routes to Afghanistan and expelling from the Shansi Air Base US personnel who had used it
as a stronghold from which to operate drones remotely to target the Paki-

stani Taliban near the border with Afghanistan. The next air strike, on January 10, 2012 in North Waziristan, brought the already tense relationship between Pakistan and the US closer to a breaking point. According to the ISI, the drone attack killed four militants, three of them Arabs. One day later, a video surfaced, which showed US troops urinating on the corpses of Taliban fighters in Afghanistan. US Secretary of Defense, Leon Panetta, condemned the actions. "I have seen the footage, and I find the behavior depicted in it utterly deplorable. Those found to have engaged in such conduct will be held accountable to the fullest extent," said Panetta.[36] The damage had been done, however, and that video would increase anti-American sentiment, not only in Afghanistan but also in Pakistan and the Muslim world at large.

Under the direction of the CIA and with its help, the ISI had created bin-Laden and what would eventually become the Taliban in the 1980s. Part of the ISI still had an allegiance to Afghanistan's Taliban, although the ISI was fighting the Pakistani Taliban who threatened Pakistan's territorial integrity. The average American did not appreciate the complexity of this tricky geopolitical context where India, the archenemy of Pakistan, was playing a central role. If Americans thought that bin-Laden's assassination would end the US involvement in Afghanistan, they were deluding themselves.

NATO Is Winning in Afghanistan Like the US Was in Vietnam
Near the peak of the war in Afghanistan, around February 2010, the US-led NATO force was 133,000-strong, and half of it was composed of US troops. The remaining 61,000 troops were from 42 countries, including 26 NATO members. They had come from the ISAF, which had been established in December 2001. Washington had sent 30,000 additional troops in early 2010 and had counted on its European allies to muster 10,000 troops, but Obama's hope would be dashed, and he would get only 10 percent of that number. Overall, the war in Afghanistan was so unpopular in Europe that it became a dangerous political gamble for those governments that supported it. Opinion polls in the NATO countries indicated that the majority of people did not support their soldiers' presence in Afghanistan. In Britain, just like in Germany, France, The Netherlands, Italy and Spain, voters thought that additional troops would do no good and might even do harm by fanning the flames of the Taliban insurgency.

The government of Prime Minister Jan Peter Balkenende collapsed on February 20, 2010 over The Netherland's involvement with the NATO operations in Afghanistan. Earlier that month, Anders Rasmussen had asked The Netherlands to extend the military mission in Afghanistan until August 2011, which was a year later than the originally planned pull out. The deployment of the troops had been unpopular with Dutch voters. The

Netherlands already had around 2,000 troops in Afghanistan under NATO command, and 21 Dutch soldiers had been killed in the conflict. Some analysts warned that a Dutch decision to cut short the Afghan mission could have a domino effect among other NATO countries with troops in Afghanistan, like Italy and Spain, which had, respectively, 850 and 780 troops. "The withdrawal of Dutch troops would be a serious blow to both Afghan and NATO forces. The Netherlands is an important European and NATO country, and if it withdraws from Afghanistan, other European countries too — one after another — will consider leaving Afghanistan," said Ahmad Saidi, a political analyst in Kabul on February 20, 2010.[37]

On January 26, 2010, Chancellor Merkel had to do a difficult balancing act between NATO's request for more troops and the fact that the majority of Germans thought the mission was worthless and had become staunchly opposed to the war. The German troops already in Afghanistan numbered 4,330. In the end, the German government decided to send only an additional 500 troops. "This will be a new approach in the future, namely protecting the population and training Afghan soldiers in one go. This is a much more defensive approach, for which the German army's offensive capacities will be rearranged," said Merkel at a press conference.[38]

Britain, which had committed over 9,500 troops, by far Europe's largest contingent in Afghanistan, said it would send only an additional 500. Despite Washington's pressure to do so, Prime Minister Gordon Brown did not want to commit more troops because an election was coming up in Britain in 2010, and there was growing opposition to the war. In France, President Nicolas Sarkozy reaffirmed his country's commitment to maintain its 3,300 troops already in Afghanistan, but he said bluntly: "France will not send one more soldier."[39]

For the US, a major blow to the campaign in Afghanistan was the release of nearly 92,000 secret military documents about the conflict, on July 25, 2010, by the whistleblower website, *Wikileaks* (under Chapter 17). The military files covered the period from 2004 to 2010 and included details of covert operations against top Taliban, unreported civilian killings and NATO concerns that Pakistani officials, notably ISI agents, had helped to the Taliban. The White House condemned the release as being irresponsible and argued that the massive disclosure could endanger US lives in Afghanistan, although the Obama administration's failed policies and its refusal to recognize that the war in Afghanistan could not be won had been the real dangers to US lives in Afghanistan and the lives of thousands of Afghan civilians. The revelations confirmed that the war in Afghanistan was unwinnable, as many independent international analysts had argued for years.

Richard N. Haass, President of the CFR, in a July 18, 2010 article for *Newsweek* originally titled "We are not winning: it is not worth it," wrote:

"After nearly nine years of war, continued or increased US involvement in Afghanistan isn't likely to yield lasting improvements that would be commensurate in any way with the investment of American blood and treasure."[40] He advised the Obama administration to revamp US-Afghan policy towards decentralization and even negotiations to bring the Taliban into the Afghan political fold. "The war the United States is now fighting in Afghanistan is not succeeding and is not worth waging this way. The time has come to scale back US objectives and sharply reduce US involvement on the ground. Afghanistan is claiming too many American lives, requiring too much attention, and absorbing too many resources," concluded Haass.[40]

The *WikiLeaks* documents revealed, among other things, that a covert unit had been formed to kill or capture Taliban leaders, and that coalition forces had killed thousands of civilians in unreported incidents. The leaks prompted Amnesty International to call on NATO to provide "a clear and unified system of accounting for civilian casualties in Afghanistan," since the leaked war logs painted a bleak picture of an "incoherent process in dealing with civilian casualties."[41] Amnesty International's Sam Zarifi said: "The picture that emerges from the leaked data on civilian casualties is that NATO's leadership did not know exactly what was happening on the ground."[41]

On December 10, 2012, the Pentagon released a sobering 172-page report on the war in Afghanistan that had been ready before the US presidential election in early November but withheld, supposedly to respect the election cycle.[42] The delay from the Pentagon was viewed as an attempt by the Obama administration to hide the bleak findings from the American public before they went to the polls. During the election charade, both candidates had conveniently ignored the 11-year war in Afghanistan and all other meaningful US foreign-policy topics. The war was unpopular, and it had become a forgotten war for US politicians, although 68,000 US troops were still involved in Afghanistan's quagmire.

The raw numbers were grim, and the prospect of a real US withdrawal in 2014 seemed increasingly unlikely, unless the Obama administration declared victory and shortly thereafter let the Taliban take control. According to the Pentagon, only one of the 23 brigades of the Afghan National Army could operate without NATO support.[42] According to official data from the DOD, since 2001 the conflict had cost US taxpayers 2,146 American and more than $500 billion. In this war of attrition, thousands of NATO troops had already died and would keep on dying in vain.

"During the reporting period, enemy-initiated attacks (EIAs) were up one percent compared to the same period last year. The campaign continued to face challenges including a rise of insider attacks. The insurgency's safe havens in Pakistan, the limited institutional capacity of the Afghan government, and endemic corruption remain the greatest risks to long-term stability and sustainable security in Afghanistan. The Taliban-led insurgency and its al-Qaeda affiliates operate from sanctuaries in Pakistan. Although the insurgency's kinetic capabilities have declined from their peak in 2010, the insurgents remain resilient and determined, and will likely attempt to regain lost ground and influence through continued assassinations, intimidation, high-profile attacks, and the emplacement of IEDs (improvised explosive devices). Widespread corruption continues to limit the effectiveness and legitimacy of the Afghan government," revealed the Pentagon report, which spanned from April 1 to September 30, 2012.[42] US taxpayers should know that, according to the Pentagon, the estimated cost of the study and report for the DOD was around $161,000 for the 2012 fiscal year. This included $23,000 in expenses and $138,000 in DOD labor.[42]

The US never learned its lessons from Vietnam. In Vietnam, three million Vietnamese were killed and more than 50,000 US troops died in vain to maintain an illegitimate and corrupt government, all in the name of countering the spread of communism. The same Cold-War rationale was at play when Reagan became allied to Osama bin-Laden and his friends. This absurdly shortsighted US foreign policy was applied to Afghanistan with the NATO raids and strikes, and Pakistan with the drone attacks.

In Orwellian times, wars do not really end, instead they mutate periodically into other missions. On January 1, 2015, NATO's occupation of Afghanistan was renamed. It was goodbye ISAF, hello RSM! The rebranding of the International Security Assistance Force into the Resolute Support Mission did not trick anyone. While NATO's forces were reduced, they were in Afghanistan for an indefinite stay. The RSM was 13,195-strong and, of course, under the command of an American: US General John F. Campbell. Forty-two nations had contributed the RSM troops. In February 2015, the top contributors were: the US with 6,839 troops, Georgia with 885, Germany with 850, Romania with 650, Turkey with 503, Italy with 500, the UK with 470, and Australia with 400. Notably, France was gone from the NATO occupation's motley crew, which included countries as eclectic as Mongolia, Ukraine and Greece.

In its life span of 14 years and counting, the war in Afghanistan has followed the global empire's model of a permanent war that moved from being an acute war, launched in 2001 and employing at its peak more than 130,000 Western troops, to a chronic low-intensity conflict that required 13,000 troops in 2015. On October 15, 2015, Obama broke yet another of his cornerstone promises to Americans: the one where he said that he would end the war in Afghanistan. US troops will not be completely out of the country by the end of his second term; instead, the Obama administration has indefinitely committed 5,500 US troops to the country.[43] The Afghan poisoned gift will be passed on like a baton soaked in blood to the next tenant of the White House. Overall, Afghanistan remains an extremely attractive business proposition for the global military-industrial complex, especially considering that the conflict is no longer on the radar of news outlets. Nothing beats endless low-intensity wars running on the quiet.

11

Syria

SINCE SYRIA'S CIVIL WAR started in 2011, it has wrecked an 11,000-year-old country that has been called the cradle of civilization. The war has so far killed 250,000 people. Four million Syrians have left their country, and 6.5 million are internal refugees. Turkey, Jordan, and to a lesser extent, Lebanon, have so far absorbed most of the refugees. As of October 2015, Turkey alone was sheltering 2 million Syrians in its camps.

The drums of war were beating loudly from the US and its NATO vassals in December 2012. In Washington, the talk from the Obama administration and mainstream media regarded a red line that was not to be crossed by Bashar al-Assad; the red line was about the potential use of chemical weapons, mainly sarin gas, against his own population.[44] This was an all too-familiar song and dance to justify a foreign intervention. During the prelude to the invasion of Iraq by the US in 2003, the Bush administration had used a similar subterfuge to convince the public that the invasion would be a war of necessity. The supposed evidence that Saddam Hussein had possessed and planned to use weapons of mass destruction (WMD) was cooked up by the administrations of Bush in the US and Blair in the

UK. In both cases, they had the complicity of the mainstream media, including US news source of reference, *The New York Times.*

In the fog of civil war that enveloped Syria, all its communities have suffered, as regional powers like Saudi Arabia and Iran fought a proxy war, on Syrian soil, that revived a thousand-year-old conflict between Sunnis and Alawites. The US and Western Europe not only failed to take this sectarian war in the making into consideration but also were cynically fueling sectarian conflicts in the Muslim world, as they had done between Iraq and Iran in the 1980s, to fulfill their geopolitical agenda.

In the aftermath of the defeat of the Ottoman Empire, an ally of Germany during World War I, the two main colonial powers of the time, Britain and France, seized the opportunity to redraw the map of the Middle East and play kingmakers. In doing so, they largely ignored to take sectarian issues into consideration. In Iraq, the UK put a Sunni minority in charge instead of the Shiite majority. Consequently, the UK reignited and fueled a 600-year-old fire. Ever since the US invasion of Iraq in 2003, sectarian killings have gone on without any end in sight.

Sectarianism is widespread in Syrian society. An Alawite minority rules over a Sunni majority. The Assad family is Alawite, and this sect represents about 12 percent of Syria's overall population. It has been Syria's ruling class, entrenched in the country's power apparatus both in the public and private sectors, since Bashar al-Assad's father, Hafez al-Assad, rose to power in the early 1960s through Syria's Baath party. Alawites hold the key positions, not only in the government but also at the top level in business. In the army and security services, they make the critical decisions. It is difficult for a Sunni to rise to the rank of general, and if he does, the second in command in the division is always an Alawite. The Syrian army is made up of seven divisions, each one led by a commander. The one most important and best equipped is the fourth division, with around 45,000 men, all of them Alawites, commanded by Bashar al-Assad's mercurial brother, Maher al-Assad.

The future of Syria's 1.2 million Alawites is therefore tied to Assad's regime. Bashar al-Assad has always made a point of protecting Syria's sectarian and religious minorities, such as Christians, Druse and Kurd. By contrast, if the Sunni opposition to the regime had got the upper hand in the civil war, the retaliation against Alawites would have been indiscriminate and extreme.

By supporting the Sunnis in the Syrian civil war, the Obama administration and, more surprisingly, the governments of Western Europe, had failed to consider a potential for genocide or, at the least, an exodus scenario involving more than a million Syrian Alawites, who would have been unwelcomed almost anywhere in the Middle East, with perhaps the exception of Lebanon. If Assad had been toppled, with blessings and help from Saudi

Arabia, Qatar, and NATO, Syria's Alawites would have immediately become the targets of vengeful Sunni militias. The outcome would have been worse than when Iraqi cleric al-Sadr's militia went on killing rampages in Baghdad's Sunni areas.[45] A thousand-year-old conflict between Sunnis and Alawites remains at a boiling point in Syria.

Alawite dominance is recent in Syria's history. For centuries, the Alawites were Syria's poorest and most rural people, and they were oppressed and despised by the Sunni majority. Today the Alawites number about 1.5 million, of which 1.2 million live in Syria. For centuries, mainstream Muslims, i.e. Sunnis and Shiites alike, have viewed Alawites as heretics. Ahmad Ibn Taymiyya (1268-1328), a highly influential Syrian Sunni, wrote in a fatwa (religious decision or edict) that Alawites should not even be considered Muslims.[46] About 700 years ago, Ibn Taymiyya wrote:

> The Nusayris (older term for Alawites) are more infidel than Jews and Christians, even more infidel than many polytheists. They have done greater harm to real Muslims than have the warring infidels such as the Franks, the Turks and others. To ignorant Muslims they pretend to be Shi'a, though in reality they do not believe in God, his prophet and his book. Nusayris are always the worst enemies of Muslims.[46]

From the 14th century on, to express their contempt, Syrian Sunnis called the Alawites by the name Nusayri, a synonym for pariah. The full support that the Obama administration, Western Europe and, implicitly, Israel were giving to Sunnis in Syria and the Middle East at large was a gross miscalculation at best; at worst, it fell into the realm of Machiavellian geopolitics. This was indeed seeding crisis and potential sectarian wars in the Muslim world by inspiring an even greater Sunni anger towards Shiites and Alawites.

Washington seemed to be following the old adage, divide and conquer, in the Middle East. Some of this manipulation of Arab public opinion was apparently working. Jordanian Salafi leader Abou Mohamad Tahawi has said: "The Alawite and Shiite coalition is currently the biggest threat to Sunnis, even more than Israel."[47] Sunnis should be aware that, as happened to America's former good friend Saddam Hussein, the US and Western Europe could switch alliances on a dime, especially when the oil supplies run out. Sunnis are only the West's best friends in the region because of Saudi Arabia's oil and money. US diplomacy was also following the old adage: the enemy of my enemy is my friend.

Former UN Secretary General Kofi Annan sternly warned the international community, on June 30, 2012: "No one should be in any doubt as to the extreme dangers posed by the conflict — to Syrians, to the region, and to the world."[48] The main question for Syria remains whether Sunnis and Alawites would cohabit again with each other.

Henry Kissinger once tried to capture the forces at play in Syrian politics and history with the statement: "Damascus is at one and the same time the fount of modern Arab nationalism and the exhibit of its frustrations. Syrian history alternates achievement with catastrophe."[49] This mix of pride and injury is again at play in Syria: the oscillation between being controlled by outside players such as the Ottoman Empire or France, and being a player of consequence in the region.

Bashar al-Assad will probably prevail, but with such an incredible amount of bad blood between the two sectarian communities, it is unlikely that there could be lasting peace unless Syria undergoes a sort of Balkanization. Such a partition of Syria was not put on the table in 2012. This could and still can, in 2015, follow the model of Yugoslavia in the 1990s. Before Syria's demolition by four years of civil war, the country's religious and ethnic groups had a strong geographic concentration. Three quarters of the Alawites lived in the northwestern province of Latakia, where they constituted two thirds of the population. In the context of a potential Balkanization, Latakia could become strictly Alawite and Christian, two sects that have always gotten along well with each other, and gain autonomy from the rest of the Sunni-majority part of the country. In that scenario of federation, the Sunnis would control most of the center and south of Syria. The Kurds, who populate the North, would also become autonomous. The most difficult decisions would concern the fates of Damascus and Aleppo, where all sectarian groups are represented in large numbers. A partition of Syria would be challenging and have to provide protection and self-determination for all the communities in question.

US Policy on Syria Remains Incoherent

United Nations peace talks concerning the Syrian crisis took place in Geneva on December 8, 2012. The US did not want the two sides of the Syrian civil war to be represented in the talks; nor did it want the two proxy regional powers, Iran and Saudi Arabia, to be present. Instead, the five permanent members of the Security Council discussed Kofi Annan's plan to set up a transitional unity government that would exclude elements which would undermine it. This entailed excluding Bashar al-Assad from any unity government. Russia and China, for their part, wanted the crisis to be solved by Syrians, and for Assad and Alawites to be represented in any unity government.

Some vague diplomatic efforts also took place in Ireland, on December 6, 2012, between then US Secretary of State Hillary Clinton and Russian Foreign Minister Sergey Lavrov. Despite these supposed 11th-hour talks in Dublin, in Washington the reality and tone were quite different. Defense Secretary Leon Panetta said that "intelligence reports raise fears that a desperate president Bashar al-Assad is considering using his chemical weapons arsenal. I think there is no question that we remain very concerned…

that as the opposition advances, in particular in Damascus, Assad regime might very well consider the use of chemical weapons."[50]

Within four weeks of the supposed peace efforts, six Patriot missile systems were deployed in Turkey, along the border with Syria, by the US, Germany and the Netherlands, ostensibly to reinforce the NATO member air defenses. The surface-to-air missiles, which can intercept missiles, were transported to Turkey by sea. Two missile batteries were supplied by each, Germany and the Netherlands, with blessings from their parliaments. Each of the six Patriot missile systems could launch more than 500 missiles, and each system required around 100 soldiers to operate it, which meant that 600 troops from the US, Germany and the Netherlands were deployed to Turkey simultaneously with the Patriot missile systems.

The two world powers that opposed NATO's looming attack on Syria were Russia and China. If they had not done anything concrete — besides some rhetorical opposition at the UN — to block NATO's military attack and armed support of the so-called Libyan revolution to topple Gaddafi, why would they do anything to stop NATO from toppling Bashar al-Assad? Compared to the fate of Gaddafi, however the case of Assad was very different, especially for Russia, which after all had historical ties with Syria and the Assad dynasty since 1962. For decades, Syrians had attended Russian universities and, more often than not, returned with Russian wives. At the start of the civil war in 2011, the number of ethnic Russians or people with dual nationalities living in Syria was an astounding 100,000. The prospect that Russia might lose Syria as its strongest ally in the region would have been a crippling loss of influence. Like post-Gaddafi Libya, Islamist factions would have controlled a post-Assad Syria, if Russia had not militarily intervened in September 2015.

Possibly some geopolitical grand bargain was in the works between the US, Saudi Arabia, Qatar, and Western Europe — which were all actively supporting and arming the pseudo-Syrian revolution — and Russia and Iran. If so, what could this cryptic Western plan have been? For any of the players involved, what could have been gained by allowing the entire region to become Sunni dominated and come under the sphere of influence of Saudi Arabia, Qatar and the Gulf States?

People who run non-rational scenarios, and especially those who are obsessed by conspiracy theories about the so-called Illuminati and so on, like to talk about an end game: some mysterious twisted plan concocted by Henry Kissinger and his friends that is ultimately about absolute world domination and enslavement of the entire human race. This gives too much credit to a group of mainly elderly men whose core issues are more likely to be incontinence and memory loss than the establishment of a new world order with themselves at the helm. A more rational, albeit scarier, notion is that there is no master plan at all. If one thinks cynically about this, using the cold capitalist notions of bottom-line and quarterly profit, the business of war — any war, fought for any reason — is always a win-win proposition. Therefore a clear win in the Syrian proxy conflict that they fueled was never on the agenda of the Orwellian Empire.

Consider, for example, the fact that, in mid-December 2012, al-Nusra was declared by Washington DC to be a terrorist organization with ties to al-Qaeda in Iraq, although William Burns, from the Obama administration picked Sheik Ahmad Moaz Al-Khatib as the representative of the Syrian opposition, and the Sheik himself said that al-Nusra should not be considered a terrorist organization. So even in dealing with one person, there was no unity. Neither Washington nor Paris knew exactly whom they were backing and what was going on. Meanwhile, more than 100 Alawites were executed on December 16, 2012, strongly suggesting that US policy in Syria could trigger a massive genocide. Repercussions in Iraq and Lebanon were unavoidable once the Sunnis started persecuting Syria's Alawites and Shiites.

One month later, the window was completely shut for a political solution between the Assad regime and the opposition, which was never seriously pushed by the international community. This diplomatic failure belonged to all the parties involved in the proxy war, which for many was sold as a revolution. On one hand, the West had failed to recognize that the removal of Bashar al-Assad from Syria would likely put into power Islamists who were aligned with Saudi Arabia; on the other hand, Russia had failed to pressure Bashar al-Assad to diminish the power of his hardliner brother Maher al-Assad.

In the midst of the Western fumbling and a cabinet reshuffle by Obama, with John Kerry at the State Department, Hagel at the Pentagon and Brennan at the CIA, Israel conducted an airstrike deep into Syria's territory, on the outskirts of Damascus. The attack, on January 30, 2013, was clearly in violation of Syria's sovereignty. There were conflicting reports about the strike and its target, but an anonymous US source confirmed the strike and said that the target had been a military convoy on its way to Lebanon with anti-aircraft weapons. According to the Syrian army, the target was a weapons research center. Syria's ambassador to Lebanon responded to the attack by saying that "Damascus has the option and the capacity to surprise in retaliation."[51] The military in Lebanon, which shares borders with both Syria and Israel, reported that the presence of Israeli fighter jets in Lebanese airspace had sharply increased and that Israel's violation of Lebanon's airspace was occurring on an almost daily basis. Such actions by Israel, if they would have continued, would have expanded Syria's civil war into a regional conflict involving not only NATO and, at first, Lebanon, but also Iraq. One wondered if this was a way for the Jewish state to provoke Assad, and Iran's ally Hezbollah, into a retaliation that would justify a new invasion of Lebanon. Indeed, the Lebanon-based Hezbollah said in a statement the next day that the attack revealed the Jewish state's "motives towards [unrest in] Syria over the past two years, and the criminal thinking aimed at destroying Syria and its army.... and eliminating Syria's pivotal resistance."[52] They called the air strike a barbaric aggression and pledged full solidarity with Syria's army. Russia issued an emphatic statement the same day, arguing that any Israeli air strike on Syria would be unacceptable, according to the UN Charter. "If this information is confirmed, then we are dealing with unprovoked strikes against targets located on the territory of a sovereign state, which brazenly infringes on the UN Charter and is unacceptable, no matter the motive used for its justification," said the statement from Russia's foreign ministry.[53]

Israel remained silent on the attack, neither denying nor confirming it; however, as the news made the headlines in the Israeli press the next day, gas masks where distributed in the Golan Heights to feed popular paranoia. The news commentators indicated that Israel would never allow the transfer of sophisticated weapons systems to Hezbollah, which is an ally of Syria and Iran that is considered by both Israel and the US to be a terrorist organization. At the instigation of the all-powerful Jewish lobbying group, the American Israel Public Affairs Committee (AIPAC), the US Congress had passed a resolution on January 1, 2013 that urged the EU to designate Hezbollah as a terrorist organization. Likud party Member of Parliament Tzani Hanegbi, known to be close to reelected Prime Minister Netanyahu used another red-line metaphor to justify Israel's illegal action in Syria. "The best thing that Israel has been hoping for during a long time is that the West will take control of these weapons. But the world is not ready to take such a decision as it did in Libya or Iraq, so Israel finds itself facing a dilemma that we alone can resolve. Israel has always said that if sophisticated weapons coming from Iran, North Korea and Russia fell into the hands of Hezbollah, it would cross a red line," said Hanegbi to Israel's army radio station.[54] This statement echoed another one made a couple of months before by Netanyahu at the UN concerning Iran's nuclear program, as if Israel could put all its neighbors on notice by defining red lines that could not be crossed.

Some of the very same countries that had helped to create the atrocious situation in Syria by arming and financing Assad's opposition began to step in with so-called humanitarian help. First, help wreck Syria, then give candy bars and bottled water to starving kids. Leading wrecker-humanitarians who had been the anti-Assad Islamists' main backers included the United Arab Emirates, Saudi Arabia and Kuwait, each of which pledged $300 million in aid to Syria. Exactly one day before Israel's attack on Syria, US president Obama pledged $150 million of aid on behalf of the US in a playbook humanitarian imperialism move. One had to wonder if the White House had approved the strike or if Israel had just informed the Obama administration about it after it took place. The second option seemed to be the most likely one. Netanyahu's Likud party had been recently reelected, and the Obama administration was going through some important changes. This might have been Netanyahu's way to say nobody can stop us and try to bait Hezbollah and Iran into retaliation.

The regional escalation of Syria's civil war was well on its way in spring 2013. On February 28, 2013, Iraqi Prime Minister Nouri al-Maliki, a Shiite, warned that a victory of the Syrian opposition would spread chaos through the region. "If the opposition is victorious, there will be a civil war in Lebanon, divisions in Jordan, and a sectarian war in Iraq," said al-Maliki in an interview with *AP*.[55] On March 1, 2013 Iraq attacked the so-called Free Syrian Army (FSA), composed almost exclusively of Sunnis, which had been backed by Saudi Arabia, Turkey, Qatar and the West. Iraqi forces shelled FSA positions across the border of Iraq with Syria, and Iraq deployed a substantial amount of military assets near that border. This turn of events highlighted even more the incoherence of the Obama administration's evaluation and handling of Syria's civil war. Al-Maliki's forecast was similar to one I had made on February 19, 2012, more than a year before him.

Nobody was contesting that Syria had entered a civil war. Despite the efforts of Russia and China, the time for negotiating and defusing the crisis by a political solution was over. In the power struggle within the Assad regime, which had been unfolding ever since the start of the uprising, the hardliners, with Maher al-Assad in the lead, had taken control of the brutal repression, over the more conciliatory side of Bashar al-Assad. In retrospect, the situation might have been prevented at an earlier stage if Syria's three key allies, Russia, Iran and Hezbolla had put enough pressure on Bashar al-Assad to dismiss his own brother, Maher.

This being said, the situation had festered long enough to reach a point of no return without a coherent foreign intervention. While the big regional and international powers were interfering in Syria's affairs by siding with the Assad regime or the so-called opposition, they were not addressing what should have been a much bigger regional and global concern: would the war in Syria spread to surrounding countries and ignite a full-blown sectarian war between Sunnis and Shiites, and would it be a breeding ground for rogues jihadists? While the already precarious stability of the entire region was at stake, two countries were in the direct line of fire of the Syrian turmoil: Iraq and Lebanon.

In Lebanon, the balance between the Shiite, Sunni and Christian communities has been extremely fragile for decades. Hezbollah, which is Shiite, was mainly backed by the Assad administration and Iran. A regime change in Syria would have made Hezbollah much weaker, and they would have been inclined to show their strength, both internally and towards Israel, while they still could. In response, Sunnis and Christians could have wrongly assessed that the Syrian crisis was a perfect opportunity to diminish the power of Hezbollah. In Syria, the small Christian minority — always tolerated by Assad — had already left, seeking refuge in Lebanon or preferably in Europe, Canada or the US; but in Lebanon, the much larger Christian population would have been caught in the middle of a civil war between Hezbollah and the Sunnis.

If in Lebanon a civil war is always five minutes away, in Iraq the sectarian conflict between the Shiite majority and Sunni minority was ever present and hardly needed a spark to reignite it. Since the official withdrawal of the US military, the increased sectarian tensions could, at any moment, reach a boiling point. Even if Prime Minister al-Maliki's government was officially an ally of the US, al-Maliki had to perform an increasingly tricky balancing act with Iran. Al-Maliki also had to deal with the increasing power of the charismatic cleric al-Sadr, who was closely aligned with Tehran. In any case, sectarian issues for al-Maliki, who is a Shiite, would quickly supersede any other consideration, including the alliance with the US. Any other choice would have been suicide. Under pressure from al-Sadr and Iraq's Shiite community, al-Maliki might ultimately drop his alliance with the US and side with Iran.

Western powers assume that the Middle East operates according to national borders and interests but tend to forget that the main divide is between Sunnis and Shiites. The West, and especially the US, has fueled this tension for decades by implementing a rudimentary geopolitical strategy through the clumsy instigation of conflicts between Sunnis and Shiites. Syrians — Sunnis, Alawites, Kurd and Christians alike — were paying the ultimate price. The US and its allies had sided with the Sunnis and their key Saudis backers. This had been an ill-conceived plan against Iran and its ally Hezbollah. After the rise of ISIS, the collateral damage became all the communities in the region, including non-fundamentalist Syrians and Iraqi Sunnis. This disastrous geopolitical strategy might not have had as its motive the instigation of a war within Islam, but such a conflict became the outcome once the Syrian civil war had spread to Iraq though the jihadists. Neither Sunnis nor Shiites, and certainly not Islam, had anything to gain from such a fratricidal war.

Israel bombed Syria once again, ostensibly to destroy weapons destined for Hezbollah, on May 4, 2013. The air strike killed 15 troops from Bashar al-Assad's elite Republican Guard, together with more than 100 other Syrian soldiers. Israel was playing with fire. According to Washington sources, the White House was not even consulted. Israel might have been testing the waters to see how the international community would react if it attacked Iran. With this bombing, Syria won the sympathy of Turkey, which is mainly a Sunni country and not a friend of the Assads. Turkish Prime Minister Erdogan said the attack by Israel was absolutely unacceptable, and the Syrian opposition echoed the same outrage. With this attack, Israel tried to provoke Hezbollah into retaliation, but Israel appeared not to have considered that it could not simultaneously handle a front against Lebanon and another against Syria.

Russian Foreign Minister Sergei Lavrov met with US Secretary of State John Kerry three days later, but they probably did not look into a potential balkanization of Syria. Instead, the Obama administration focused on the chemical weapons issues and said it wanted to make sure it was right about this, but claims of chemical weapons in Syria brought a sense of déjà vu of Iraq to the international community. Obama's comparison of previous actions against bin-Laden and Gaddafi to possible plans for Syria was also a strongly implied personal threat against Bashar al-Assad.

As fighting raged in late-May 2013 for control of Qusair, a Syrian border town of critical strategic importance, the dense and toxic fog of that country's proxy war was spreading to Lebanon and Iraq. With Hezbollah becoming directly involved in the conflict to back Assad, the patchwork coalition of Syrian rebel groups and jihadist foreign fighters, with al-Nusra in the lead, was loosing ground and running on the defensive. Bashar al-Assad had three main objectives, which could be obtained with a full commitment from Hezbollah: first, taking back Qusair to reopen a critical channel between Damascus and pro-Assad Alawite militias on the Mediterranean coast; second, this would cut off the rebel-held areas between the north and south; third, and perhaps most importantly, this could have given Assad a stronger hand before a peace conference organized by Russia and the US, and scheduled to take place in June. Meanwhile, Arabs and Muslims in general were killing each other and doing the bidding of Israel and the West in what was quickly becoming a full-blown regional sectarian war between Sunnis on one side, and Shiites and Alawites on the other.

A meeting of the Syrian opposition in Turkey in mid-May 2013 had been a complete fiasco. The coalition's Western supporters, with the US, the UK and France in the lead, wanted more seats for liberals, but a Muslim-Brotherhood influenced bloc, supported by Qatar, defeated this attempt. In this regard, reflecting a change of course, the Western-backed part of the coalition was supported by the Saudis, as the Kingdom became concerned about Qatar's rising influence on Syrian opposition groups.

Alawites had also begun fighting against Sunnis in Tripoli, Lebanon. According to Qatari as well as Israeli sources, 5,000 Hezbollah troops had joined Assad's forces in Syria, and another 5,000 had been called to be deployed. On May 27, 2013, rockets fired by Sunnis targeted and hit Hezbollah-held areas of Beirut. Meanwhile, in a speech on May 26, Hezbollah leader Hasan Nasrallah said that his organization would stand firmly with Assad. "We will continue to the end of the road. We accept this responsibility and will accept all sacrifices and expected consequences for this position," said Nasrallah.[56]

By August 2013, it seemed almost inevitable that a NATO attack on Syria would inexorably take us all to witness another criminal madness. Officials in the US, France and the UK were working themselves up into an almost credible humanitarian warrior hysteria. Meanwhile their respective military were bringing more assets to the region and completing the preparations they had started about eight months before. One could not help but remember the same sense of riding a runaway train that we had collectively experienced in March 2003, before the so-called coalition of the willing attacked Iraq. In Iraq, the pretext for war had been WMD. This time around it was the use of a chemical weapon, presumably sarin gas, for which the West, without any proof, blamed Bashar al-Assad's government. Once again, a senseless war was about to engulf the region, and it would have been fought under humanitarian pretenses.

A short speech, delivered on August 27, 2013, by John Kerry was a gem either in pure hypocrisy or delusion.[57] "What we saw in Syria last week should shock the conscience of the world. It defies any code of morality. Let me be clear. The killing of women and children and innocent bystanders by chemical weapons is a moral obscenity. By any standard, it is inexcusable. And despite the excuses and equivocations that some have manufactured, it is undeniable," said Kerry.[57] "Conscience... code of morality.... moral obscenity." It takes a lot of nerve for a US Secretary of State to drape himself with such lofty notions. It is immoral to provide the Egyptian military junta $1.3 billion worth of weapons a year so they can kill their own people. The world's conscience should be shocked by the climbing death toll in Iraq in a war that is supposed to be over. It is morally obscene to have helped Saddam Hussein use a massive amount of chemical weapons on Iranians three decades ago or to have extensively used agent orange and napalm during your own morally obscene war in Vietnam, Mr. Kerry.

In an August 25, 2013 article in *Foreign Policy,* Shane Harris and Matthew M. Aid revealed that, in 1988 during the Reagan administration, the US had helped Saddam Hussein use chemical weapons, including sarin gas, against Iran.[58] Files from the CIA proved that the US not only knew that Saddam Hussein was launching extensive chemical attacks, but also assisted Hussein with the strikes by giving him intelligence on the Iranian army's positions. The CIA documents revealed how actively the Reagan administration had helped Saddam. "In contrast to today's wrenching debate over whether the US should intervene to stop alleged chemical weapon attacks by the Syrian government, the United States applied a cold calculus three decades ago to Hussein's widespread use of chemical weapons against his enemies and his own people," wrote Harris and Aid.[58]

Of all the top officials from the Obama administration, Kerry was making the strongest push for a strike on Syria. If the attack had come, the weapon of choice would have been the Tomahawk missile. The sabre rattling made the price of oil spike and sent the global financial market into a dive. One of the few exceptions was Raytheon, a weapons manufacturer based in Kerry's home state of Massachusetts that makes the Tomahawk missile. On the day of Kerry's speech, Raytheon stock rocketed to an all-time high of $75.50 per share, up 44 percent since February 2013. Besides drones, Tomahawk missiles were the Obama administration's weapons of choice. One such missile cost $1 million; Raytheon delivered 252 of them during the 2013 fiscal year and 362 in 2012. The attack on Syria, pushed by Kerry, would have meant great business for Raytheon.

The Obama administration defined the supposed red line for a US military intervention in Syria as being the use of chemical weapons, around summer 2012. As early as December of the same year, NATO was installing Patriot-missile batteries in Turkey. Despite paying lip service to Russia in its push for a political solution to the Syrian crisis, Washington had pursued a policy of regime change. From the start of the proxy war in Syria, the US had backed the FSA with extensive logistic assistance provided by the CIA to Saudi Arabia, Qatar and Jordan, to bring hundreds of military cargo planes full of weapons to the rebels. After it became public that the most effective fighting forces against Assad, such as al-Nusra, were linked to al-Qaeda and appeared on the US terrorist list, the help provided by the CIA became a source of embarrassment for Washington and was phased out. Qatar, Saudi Arabia, Israel and the West were certainly strange bedfellows, and this was reflected by the state of the supposed Syrian opposition coalition.

Despite the chest beating in Washington, Paris and London to push ahead with the so-called humanitarian war in Syria, some voices of caution did come from the US Congress. Congresswoman Loretta Sanchez of California, who sits on the House of Representatives' Armed Services Committee said: "Just shooting in some missiles isn't really going to take care of the situation, and might aggravate the situation. You have Syria tied to Iran, and also Hezbollah. The whole area is already a difficult area as it is. For Americans to believe that just by shooting a few cruise missiles we have made our statement and away we go, it is just not the way that it will play out if it happens."[59] A few voices in the international community also pushed for a peaceful solution. Nobel Peace Prize laureate Mairead Maguire said: "Contrary to some foreign governments' current policy of arming the rebels and pushing for military intervention, the people of Syria are calling out for peace and reconciliation and a political solution to the crisis, which continues to be inflamed by outside forces with thousands of foreign fighters funded and supported by countries for their own political gains."[60]

One hundred thousand people had already died in Syria by summer 2013, and the killing would have become more widespread if the Tomahawk missiles had started to fall in a less than precise fashion. Western powers were trying to convince their public that Assad in Syria needed to be taught a lesson. It was Russia and China that dissuaded NATO from a military attack. Considering that the UK and France had become respectively the 51st and 52nd states of the global Orwellian Empire, if NATO's hasty military strike on Syria had not been prevented by a tough stance of Russia and China, it would have had wide regional spillover and caused extreme international tensions. It would have further destabilized Lebanon and Iraq, which were both on the brink of civil and sectarian war. There would have been many more casualties than from any gas attack, and the images on TV screens would have been, once again, those of American bombs spreading mayhem in another Muslim country. How could anyone learn a lesson about conscience and moral obscenity by being bombed into oblivion? Such was the perversion of the humanitarian imperialism that had threatened to enter its phase of Syrian folly and had to be thwarted at all costs.

The Assad government had agreed to decommission its entire chemical arsenal; the deadline for this was approaching, but the political negotiations between Assad and the Syrian opposition, organized by Russia and the US, had failed. As the time ran out for drawing the red line that could not be crossed by NATO and Israel, and fear began to rise about Iran being next, Syria's deadly proxy war almost disappeared from the news, although the killings, displacements and destruction of the country continued.

On April 12, 2014, new accusations about the use of poison gas, presumably sarin gas, began to float back and forth between Bashar al-Assad's government and the rebel forces. The attack, which was believed to have killed two people and injured many, was reported in the village of Kfar Zeita. The Assad administration immediately blamed the al-Qaeda affiliated al-Nusra front while, predictably, the Western-backed Syrian National Coalition pointed the fingers towards the Syrian government.

New tension between Russia and the West over Ukraine made the already difficult task of a political solution for Syria almost impossible. In Ukraine too, a Balkanization seemed to be the only political way out of a deadly crisis, but this was not being discussed. Wrecking nations and engineering permanent crisis was good for business. In the Orwellian construct, it is common to pretend that gangrene is a trivial infection. In honest geopolitics, it is better to act quickly, inform the patient and amputate the gangrenous arm or leg.

V. The New World Order Is Chaos

12

To Wreck and Exploit

GERMAN PHILOSOPHER Friedrich Nietzsche announced, more than 125 years ago that God is dead. In light of the global events of the 21st century, Nietzsche's assessment was mere wishful thinking. His widely quoted statement was first expressed in *Die Frohliche Wissenschaft*, or *The Gay Science*, and again in his most famous book, *Thus Spoke Zarathustra*.[1][2] Nietzsche's philosophy would have never materialized without the French thinkers of the Enlightenment in the 18th century, whose principles were practically applied by the French Revolution. In *The Gay Science*, Nietzsche wrote:

> God is dead. God remains dead. And we have killed him. How shall we comfort ourselves, the murderers of all murderers? What was holiest and mightiest of all that the world has yet owned has bled to death under our knives: Who will wipe this blood off us? What water is there to clean ourselves? What festivals of atonement, what sacred games shall we have to invent? Is not the greatness of this deed too great for us? Must we ourselves not become gods simply to appear worthy of it? God is dead, but given the way of men, there might still be caves for thousands of years in which his shadow will be shown.[1]

In *Thus Spoke Zarathustra*, Nietzsche was setting up the cornerstone of his philosophy with the question: "Dead are all gods: now do we desire the uber man to live?"[2] Besides the last part of the above quote from *The Gay Science,* the one referring to men living in caves and still worshiping the shadows of dead gods, Nietzsche was wrong in his forecast. For about three decades, we have experienced a setback from becoming free of the shackles of religious beliefs and becoming the uber man Nietzsche wrote about.

Nietzsche, just like composer Richard Wagner, was wrongly accused of being a precursor of the Nazis, but in reality only a small part of his philosophy was used by the Nazi propaganda. Let us not forget that German soldiers wore belt buckles inscribed with Got Mit Uns, meaning God is with us, during World War II. This is yet another example that, at least in the context of their mass psychosis, many Germans wanted to believe they had God's blessings to perpetrate their hideous crimes.

Nietzsche was wrong. God is not dead. As matter of fact conflicting monotheist gods are more alive than ever since the Dark Ages. Today, globally, with some exceptions in secular Europe, more people are finding their way back to monotheist religious beliefs. This global rebirth of religious pursuit too often ends up, not in a place where it gives individuals comfort and peace, but in a move toward fundamentalism in the three Abrahamic religions, or so-called people of the book. Even though Christian, Jewish and Muslim fundamentalists are literally at war with each other, they share a common hatred of modernity, science, women's rights, and basic human rights. Their views against personal freedom, sexuality and free speech are cut from the same cloth. What they all want to do is set back the clock, without regard for the centuries of painful progress, to a time before the supposed perversion of modern days.

In Afghanistan, the Taliban are the lightning rod of this global historic regression, but they are very close in their principles to America's Christian fundamentalists and Israel's Jewish fundamentalists. If the Taliban in Afghanistan and Pakistan want to go back a few centuries, America's Christian fundamentalists, or so-called values voters, would be happy to return us to the 1950s in their Jesus time machine. In 2010, the annual Values Voter Summit in Washington DC, which began on September 16, had Christine O'Donnell as its star speaker.[3] The goals and political platform of the Values Voter Summit have been the same for decades: protect marriage, meaning oppose gay rights; champion life, meaning ban abortion but support the death penalty; limit government, meaning cut taxes for everyone, especially the rich; control spending, meaning cut social programs; and strengthen the military and defend our freedom, meaning fatten the military-industrial complex. O' Donnell was a great fit into this program as an everything-you-need-to-know-is-in-the-Bible type of gal. She didn't think evolution, climate change and global warming were real, and she not only opposed sex before marriage but also condemned masturbation. Propelled by the US Tea Party, O'Donnell had brought a populist hodgepodge anti-Washington ruling class elite message and, incredibly, promised a "revolution of reason." The 2,000-strong audience cheered as O'Donnell proclaimed: "They call us wacky, they call us wingnuts. We call us 'We the People'. They call us Reagan staffers and home schoolers. They are trying to marginalize us and put us in a box. We are not trying to take back our country, we are our country!"³

In Israel, Jewish fundamentalism is on the rise. Women are forced to ride in the backs of buses. Young girls and young boys are compelled to study in separate classrooms. In the Modern Orthodox youth movement, B'Nai Akiba, young men are ordered to leave a concert when men and women are together on the stage. This is obviously a great concern for Jews who are eager to enjoy the reality of our modern world. An even more disturbing example, and this time it is not against women or sex, but against science: to avoid conflict with the Orthodox fundamentalists' growing political clout, the guides in the Stalactite Cave Nature Reserve refrain from saying that the natural formations are hundreds of thousands of years old.

The three monotheist fundamentalists have an obvious common thread: they are anti-women, anti-gay, anti-sex, anti-science, and they want to curtail the most basic individual freedoms. All want to return to a time they view as being pure and untainted by our perverse modernity.

It is hard to contest that 9/11 was the opening salvo of the notion of clash of civilizations: a simple yet effective concept to justify a state of permanent war. Permanent wars against elusive enemies generate a constant state of fear, which, in return, allows governments to curtail some of the most basic liberties. What is better than a concept such as an endless war on terror to justify any action against any country? If the narrative of clash of civilizations started 14 years ago in the immediate aftermath of 9/11, more recent events in the Middle East show that we still live in this nightmarish engineered reality. The notion of conflict of civilizations has much more in common with crusades or clashes between religions than clashes between actual cultures or people. It is concocted and fueled by the rulers of the global system to create conflicts between people who are intrinsically on the same side. It is the ultimate tool of repression invented by the global 1 percent to keep the 99 percent divided.

The irrational emotional components that come with the three main monotheist religions are great tools to manipulate people who strictly follow this type of belief system. If 9/11 was a perfect excuse to attack and invade Afghanistan and Iraq, more recent events in the Middle East provide the perfect rationale for the US to deploy combat troops in Libya, Yemen and wherever else it will deem necessary, to protect US interests, personnel, and facilities. The troops are unlikely to leave anytime soon. Once again, the notion that we are in a state of permanent war can justify any and all imperialist actions. The current Muslim rage is creating fear in the West, which will conveniently prepare public opinion in the US and Western Europe with the notion that new invasions and wars are needed.

Anger directed towards the US, Israel and Western Europe has exploded all over the Middle East, starting with Libya, Egypt, Tunisia, Lebanon, Iraq and Yemen. It is now spreading as far as Bangladesh and Indonesia, and also to Europe and any country with a substantial Muslim community, such as Australia. Demonstrations, sometimes violent, have spread like wildfires across the world in the fronts of embassies or consulates and also businesses that symbolize the US. A spark on September 11, 2012 was an obscure and poorly made film, apparently directed by an Israeli citizen living in the US, which depicted the Prophet Muhammad as a womanizer and child molester.[4]

The rage engulfing the Arab world and far beyond all of Islam goes much deeper than a film. The wave of optimism that spread in 2011 in the Middle East has been replaced by deep frustration and a sense of alienation. The Arab people are realizing that they have been robbed of what they perceived to be the unstoppable 2011 Arab revolution called the Arab Spring (under Chapter 20). Autocrats have been kicked out of power from Egypt, Libya and Yemen, but they have been replaced by Islamist fundamentalists: all financed and acting on behalf of Saudi Arabia and Qatar, and directly controlled by the US and NATO. Overall, the US, Israel and Western Europe are meddling even more in the affairs of the Middle East than before the Arab Spring. The empire and its allies actively promote the Talibanization of the entire region with the enthusiastic support and complicity of the autocrats who rule Saudi Arabia and Qatar.

The Arab people, either Sunni or Shiites, and further, all Muslims, have come to realize that, despite all the claims to the contrary, they are the pawns in a tragic geopolitical imbroglio where fostering conflicts, to justify invasions and resource grabbing, is always on the agenda. Syria is a perfect case study in this sort of exercise, as was Iraq in 2003. The current alliance of Israel and Saudi Arabia is quite telling in this regard. The Saudis want a Sunni dominance in the Middle East under their control, and they are as eager as Israel to attack Iran to diminish the role of Shiites within Islam. The Saudis, the Islamist fundamentalists on their payroll, and the Israelis are only friends if friendship is defined by being the enemy of my enemy.

From Victims to Abusers
Groups of people, either nations or cultures, just like individuals, have a consciousness. Like individuals, a civilization's collective consciousness records and reacts to historical traumas. History leaves scars on people's collective consciousness. If some individuals tend to bury personal traumatic experiences under the false assumption that ignoring the pain will heal it, some cultures tend to do the same. The recall of the collective crimes of

Germans and Japanese during World War II is a taboo subject in both Germany and Japan, as if both cultures suffer from a collective amnesia. If you bring up in a conversation the atrocities committed by Japanese troops in Manchuria, Korea, the Philippines or Vietnam between 1936 and 1945, the standard answer from amnesic contemporary Japanese will likely be either "we didn't know," or "it was a long time ago." This applies to Germans as well, even though it is a crime in that country to deny the existence of the holocaust. Regardless, both cultures, as a defense mechanism, suffer from historical amnesia.

If Sigmund Freud were alive today and could put on his couch Israel or, more practically, Benjamin Netanyahu or his sidekick Igor Lieberman for a few psychoanalytical sessions, one wonders what he would find out. Most psychological studies of abusive personalities point in the same direction. This seems to be a paradox, but as individuals, most people who display abusive behaviors in relationships were abused as children.

At first thought, one would think that people who have been abused would be more sensitive, not less, to the pain inflicted on others, that they would, as individuals or a collective, show greater empathy. But more often than not, in the case of children who were abused, they grow up to become abusers. It is as if the psychological damage and trauma from early childhood turns our natural sense of compassion towards each other into a vicious cycle of borderline sociopathic behaviors, where inflicting pain becomes a source of pleasure. For individuals, this cycle of pain get passed on endlessly from one generation to the next. What applies to individuals is a good analysis model for a culture collective's psyche.

For thousands of years, between the Middle East and Europe, the Jewish people have been persecuted, abused and forced to move constantly around. In Europe, Jews were not allowed to own land and could not set roots as they were fleeing bigotry such as the Spanish Inquisition, slavery, pogroms and the despotic powers of the kingdoms of Europe and the czars in Russia. When tolerated, they had to live in ghettos such as the one in Warsaw. This precarious existence for Jewish communities in Europe, with the constant threat of having to leave, brought crafts, knowledge and money at a premium for Jewish survival. Books and money are portable, and the relentless persecutions against Jews very likely made them develop special skills in the areas of knowledge and finance. Jews became the people of the book, and to them knowledge, not material things, was the most precious possession.

"He who struggles with God" is the Hebrew meaning of the word Israel. But the Jewish state, as defined by Zionist principles, is not only fighting against the recognition of Palestine as a nation, but also against Judaism's humanist traditions. Many Jewish scholars view Judaism as a civilization: not just a religion. Part of this rich Judaic cultural heritage was passed on to more recent monotheist religions such as Christianity and Islam. This definition of Judaism more as a civilization than a religion is one of the main points made by Amos Oz and his daughter Fania Oz-Salzberger in their book, *Jews and Words*.[5] For Oz, a professor of literature at Ben-Gurion University and Oz-Salzberger, a writer and historian at the University of Haifa, "Judaism is not a bloodline but a text line." In an interview with *NPR*'s Scott Simon, Amos Oz said:

> For thousands of years, we Jews had nothing but books. We had no land, we had no holy sites, we had no magnificent architecture, we had no heroes: we had books. We had texts, and those texts were always discussed around the family table. I would add that you can never get two Jews to agree with each other on anything. It's difficult to find one Jew who agrees with himself or herself on something, because everyone has a divided mind and soul, everyone is ambivalent. So our civilization is a civilization of dispute, of disagreement and of argument.[5]

After the horrendous crimes committed against Jews during World War II by Nazi Germany, they decided that it would never happen to them again. They would not be the sacrificial lamb of human history, and they would no longer be victimized. But 67 years after the creation of the Jewish state in 1948, it is the one doing the victimizing, the one that is evolving from oppressed to oppressor. If Jews were treated like second-class citizens and were denied land ownership for centuries, they have now turned the table, and Palestinians are on the receiving end of the wrath of the abused turned abuser. Palestinians are denied land while Israeli settlers keep expanding into East Jerusalem and the West Bank. Just like the Jews of Eastern Europe, Palestinians are treated by the Jewish settlers and state as second-class citizens who live in an open-sky jail surrounded by thick concrete walls. Palestinians, just like Jews during World War II in the Warsaw ghetto, have become the victims, the collateral damage of history.

Saudi Arabia, Qatar, Israel and the West's Unholy Alliance

In the past few decades, Qatar and Saudi Arabia have seen their regional and global influence rapidly grow. The extraordinary wealth of both oil-rich nations gives them a lot of say and sway far beyond the Gulf area. As early as in the 1980s, the Saudis, together with the CIA, were financing and arming jihadists: the so-called freedom fighters of the Reagan era who fought the Soviets in Afghanistan. Nowadays both kingdoms have their hands in the political affairs of the Middle East and entire Muslim word. Their money allows them to proselytize a conservative and repressive brand of Sunni Islam, with a strict enforcement of Sharia law, through channels and vectors that include the Salafis, Muslim Brotherhood, and even al-Qaeda and ISIS.

Saudi and Qatari money builds mosques all over Europe and is also heavily invested in sectors of economic activity, from banking to the ownership of some of the biggest football teams, such as Paris Saint-Germain in France. Saudis and Qataris were at the forefront of the Syrian proxy war against the government of Bashar al-Assad, where they armed and financed the FSA and its more than 50,000-strong foreign jihadist mercenaries. Qatar and Saudi Arabia were instrumental in the toppling of Gaddafi in Libya, as well as the Islamist hijack of the Arab Spring.

In Qatar and Saudi Arabia, very few people control the wealth, while immigrants do more than 90 percent of the work under deplorable conditions. So few people are in charge of Qatar that it has been ironically called the nation of 300 people and a TV network. Qatar, with the help of its state-owned cable-TV station *Al Jazeera*, has cultivated the image of a modern moderate state, even a somewhat progressive society, at least compared to ultra-conservative Saudi Arabia next door, but this is deceptive both domestically and abroad. Qatar invests astronomical sums and spares no effort in spreading the fundamentalist teachings of Wahhabi Islam across the world. Lately, Qatar's money has been recruiting the faithful in Europe. From Greece to France and Belgium, and from Germany to Spain, the construction of mega-mosques is proceeding at record pace. In Munich, Qataris have financed a mosque of 65,000 square feet, which cost an estimated $50 million. This mosque is meant to be a key strategic point from which to spread fundamentalist Islam through Europe.

Domestically, Qatar imports almost all its workforce from poorer Arab countries like Algeria for white-collar jobs, while it exploits, often in dire conditions, 1.2 million migrant workers who are recruited from Pakistan, Bangladesh and Nepal for low-skilled labor. According to the UN International Labor Organization (ILO), Qatar is failing to implement the international convention that bans the use of forced labor.[6] The country only signed the ILO convention on slave labor in 2007. An exclusive report in *The Guardian* by Pete Pattisson has shined an international spotlight on Qatar's practices.[6] In this report, he revealed how Qatar was using slave labor for its 2022 World Cup mega-construction projects. The report included evidence of forced labor: workers whose passports were confiscated, whose pay was withheld for months so they didn't run away, and whose access to free drinking water was denied. "The investigation found evidence to suggest that thousands of Nepalese, who make up the single largest group of laborers in Qatar, face exploitation and abuses that amount to modern-day slavery," wrote Pattison.[6] Qatar was expected to ship in at least an additional 500,000 construction laborers — mainly from Nepal, Bangladesh and India — in preparation for its World Cup. Nepal's embassy in Doha, Qatar, reported that at least 44 Nepalese workers died in Qatar between

June 4 and August 18, 2013. According to the ILO, more than 4,000 migrant workers could have died in Qatar between now and 2022.

Unlike Qatar, Saudi Arabia makes no pretense of being a modern and socially liberal society. Saudi Arabia's record on human rights, from the death penalty to basic women's rights is appalling.[7] If oil gives the Saudi elite unlimited resources, Wahhabism and Salafism religious doctrines allow them to rule their people with the iron fist of strict Sharia law. Salafism is a branch of Islam fundamentalism that is based in Saudi Arabia but extends far beyond the Middle East. The goal of Salafists is to establish a Caliphate, i.e. an Islamic empire, across the Middle East, North Africa and, some say, Europe. Sharia law would exclusively govern the Caliphate, which would come under the geopolitical influence of the Saudis.

The Saudi Arabian oil-rich kingdom is not only a paradise for theocracy but also the world's most repressive patriarchal social system. Women are not allowed to drive a car. Worse, a strict Sharia law of sex segregation requires that a woman be accompanied by a male guardian, typically a relative, at all times in public. An egregious example of the application of such a law was the handling of the 2006 rape of a young Shiite, an oppressed minority in Saudi Arabia. The rape victim said she had boarded a car with a male student friend: a violation of Sharia law. Two men got into the car and drove them to a secluded area where seven men, three of whom also beat up her male friend, raped her. A Saudi court convicted the 19-year old woman for violating the strict Sharia law of sex segregation and sentenced her to 90 lashes. Later her sentence was increased to 200 lashes and she also received a six-month jail term because her lawyer, Abdul Rahman al-Lahem, a known human rights activist, had publicized his client's predicament outside of the country.[8]

Migrant workers appear to suffer the harshest punishments prescribed by Sharia law, such as: flogging for drinking alcohol, flogging for illegal sexual intercourse including 100 lashes for adultery, the amputation of hands for theft, and capital punishment by beheading in public with a sword. As recently as December 2011, a woman was decapitated for witchcraft.[9] People are routinely convicted based on confessions obtained under torture. Drug trafficking is a capital offense. Even theft can be a capital offense, especially in cases where the perpetrators are foreign workers and the victims are Saudis. Since the Arab Spring, the Saudis have executed over 80 people a year. By the middle of 2015, more than 100 people had already been executed for the year, some of them beheaded and then crucified.[7]

Saudi Arabia and Qatar are colluding to establish a Sunni-dominated Muslim word. They use their oil resources and considerable wealth to promote a repressive agenda well outside their borders. Qatar postures as a proponent of modernity and progressive Islam even as it finances and arms the jihadist foot soldiers of Islam from Algeria and Mali, to Libya and Syria.

In both Saudi Arabia and Qatar, millions of migrants from Pakistan, India, Bangladesh and Nepal build the wealth of emirs and sheiks with their blood, sweat and tears and quite often their lives.

Qatar, Saudi Arabia and Israel had formed a strange alliance, built on the principle: the enemy of my enemy is my friend. When one considers this, it is hard not to recall the pact of non-aggression signed in 1939 between Adolf Hitler and Joseph Stalin. On one hand, not having a front with the Soviet Union made wrecking Poland, Belgium and France easier for Nazi Germany. On the other hand, this gave Stalin the time he needed to build up the Red Army, knowing perfectly well that the pact with the Nazis would be short-lived. If Assad had been toppled, and Qatar, Saudi Arabia, Israel and the West had taken care of Hezbollah and Iran, the aftermath in the region and beyond would have been extremely messy.

During late spring 2013, more than 700 people were killed every month in Iraq, in sectarian violence between Sunnis and Shiites, according to the UN.[10] Sunni Iraqi jihadists were also reported to be fighting against Assad in Syria. An expansion of the Syrian civil war to Lebanon and Iraq had demonstrated, once again, that inflaming sectarian conflicts in the Arab world was a deadly strategy concocted by the West and Israel to divide and rule the Middle East. This geopolitics of chaos had already wrecked Iraq, Libya, and Afghanistan. The West and Israel wanted an encore in Syria by toppling Bashar al-Assad. Qatar and Saudi Arabia were working to establish an Islamist state in Syria. Using their money, they had exploited the Syrian opposition against Assad, and they had recruited and armed tens of thousands of jihadist foreign fighters. This was not the first time Qatar and Saudi Arabia had done this. Qatar was among the few Arab states that had offered active military assistance to NATO during the toppling of Gaddafi. Qataris were key suppliers of money and weapons to the so-called Libyan rebels. Qatar and Saudi Arabia's vision was that of a Middle East that would become Sunni dominated, under their influence, using the Muslim Brotherhood and the Salafis as their political instruments. Qatar wanted a Muslim-Brotherhood controlled Syria, but what would Israel have done if it had become surrounded by Muslim-Brotherhood or Salafi-controlled states sponsored by Qatar and Saudi Arabia? In that case, what would have happened to Israel's vision of territorial expansion to a Greater Israel?

To avoid an escalation that would have put us on course to World War III, Russia and China made a stand on Syria, as opposed to their inaction on both Iraq and Libya. In other words, Russia and China defined Syria as being a red line not to be crossed by the West, Israel, and their temporary allies from the Gulf. If Russia had dumped Assad's government, Hezbollah and Iran would have been next down the line, and Putin would have lost all geopolitical credibility.

Mairead Maguire, who headed a peace delegation to Syria and Lebanon in May 2013 that pushed for a Syrian national reconciliation, wrote in a report: "The Syrian state and its population are under a proxy war led by foreign countries and directly financed and backed by Qatar."[11] According to Maguire, 50,000 foreign jihadist fighters have come to Syria through Turkey, Jordan and Lebanon. These jihadists originated from many countries: they are Libyans, Saudis, Tunisians, Chechens, Afghans, Pakistanis, Emiratis, Lebanese, Jordanians, Europeans, and even Australians. Maguire urged the international community to "support a process of dialogue and reconciliation in Syria between its people and the Syrian government and reject outside intervention and war."[11]

Rise of ISIS: Geopolitics of Chaos Backfire
Some call it the Islamic State in Iraq and Syria, or ISIS; others call it the Islamic State In Iraq and the Levant, or ISIL, or simply IS. Whatever it is, a jihadist army with territorial ambition had grown and taken on a new dimension. jihadist fighters are nothing new. They have been around under names like mujahideen, or freedom fighters, in Afghanistan for more than 30 years. Just like al-Qaeda, ISIS is the secret love child of US imperialism and the kings and sheiks of the Gulf States. In other words, in the Middle East, the engineering of failed states has been on the US foreign policy agenda for decades. This was already at play in the early 1980s, when the Reagan administration, effectively run by Vice President George Bush Sr., had backed Saddam Hussein in Iraq's war against Iran.

An all-out regional sectarian war between Sunnis and Shiites might not have been the goal, but it was becoming the result. Anyone with even a rudimentary knowledge of the region should have known that Iraq, Libya and Syria, without strongmen like Hussein, Gaddafi, and al-Assad respectively at their helm, were likely to implode into chaos. Who might ultimately profit from fueling a fratricidal war within Islam? Could this be a strategy of ash and ruins, preliminary to the expansion of the Jewish state into the so-called Greater Israel project?

In 2003, under the pretext of the war on terror, the US invaded Iraq. Twelve years later, it was the jihadists of ISIS who could say: mission accomplished. Iraq and Syria are in ruins, soaked with the blood of several hundred thousand people, and without millions of their nationals, who are scattered to the winds as refugees. As this tragedy continues for Iraqis and Syrians, their former government officials are enjoying their retirements, without facing international tribunals for war crimes such as the use of depleted uranium weapons in civilian areas. They are more eager than ever to rewrite history and pass along the blame.

Policymakers in the US and the EU, as well as their mainstream-media echo chambers, acted as if they had been caught off guard by the rise of

ISIS. Were they sleeping at the wheel when their Machiavellian policy of playing Sunnis against Shiites, using Islamist fundamentalist soldiers of fortune, smashed into their faces? A 70,000-strong jihadist army had taken over large swaths of Iraq and Syria. They were on the move, combat hardened and with their own funds. ISIS was estimated to possess more than $2.3 billion in assets. When ISIS took Mosul in a three-day offensive, which also gave it control of Tikrit, it robbed all the assets of Mosul Central Bank: around $425 million plus a large amount of gold.[12] Consequently, the jihadists of ISIS no longer had to rely on the rule and deep pockets of Qatar and Saudi Arabia. They had the numbers, plenty of money to recruit new people and buy weapons, and they had their own agenda. ISIS was stronger than al-Qaeda ever was, and more ambitious: ISIS wanted to redraw the map of the Middle East.

Iraqi Prime Minister Nouri al-Maliki has accused Saudi Arabia and Qatar of having sponsored the jihadists of ISIS for about three years, ever since the start of the Syrian civil war. Al-Maliki should also have blamed the US and its European allies. By invading Iraq in 2003, toppling Saddam Hussein, and then fostering and sponsoring the jihadists in Syria since 2011, Qatar, Saudi Arabia and the US had opened a geopolitical Pandora's box. Out of it came ISIS. American foreign policy had been schizophrenic for decades, but it had reached the apex of contradiction. To please the Saudis and Qataris, Washington had supported the jihadist fighters against Assad in Syria; simultaneously Washington had lukewarmly supported al-Maliki's government against those same jihadists in Iraq.

The outcome was predictable, and one could wish that top policymakers could be held accountable for crimes of astonishing stupidity. As early as February 2012, I raised concerns that Syria's civil/proxy war could easily become a full-blown regional sectarian war between Sunnis and Shiites. Again, on June 26, 2012, I commented in a *Russia Today (RT)* interview that the US was backing a de facto Talibanization of the Middle East, just like the Reagan administration had done in Afghanistan during the 1980s.

The Islamist fighters had thrived, first in Iraq, where they had seized on the opportunities presented by the toppling of Saddam Hussein, the US withdrawal, and a Shiite-dominated Iraqi government that had largely failed to be inclusive of Sunnis. Then in 2011, ISIS and its many affiliates took advantage of a weakened Assad government in Syria. Flush with petrodollars from Qatar and Saudi Arabia, they quickly became Assad's leading military opposition. The jihadists of ISIS are an Islamist foreign legion. They come from, not only the entire Islamic world, but also Europe. Thousands joined their ranks in Syria. The leader of ISIS is al-Baghdadi, an Iraqi. ISIS controlled most of Iraq's Sunni-majority areas, and its goal was to impose a Caliphate: an Islamist state under strict Sharia law to encompass much of the Arab world.

The rise of ISIS was so worrying that it motivated some abrupt reversals of alliance. On June 18, 2014, the Obama administration announced that 300 military advisers would be sent to Iraq.[13] In the end, thousands of US Special Forces were sent to secure the Iraqi oil fields and the Green Zone in Baghdad. The crisis provoked a rapprochement between Washington and Teheran. Iran sent more than 2,000 of its revolutionary guards to protect Baghdad. During that time, American and Iranian special forces were allied against ISIS.

The ISIS crisis became an opportunity for Assad's troops, with the military help of Russia, Iran and Hezbollah, to reclaim Syria. Those who should have been most concerned about the jihadists' blitzkrieg in Iraq were ISIS' own biological fathers: the kings and sheiks of the Gulf States. If ISIS would have taken Baghdad, there would have been no way to stop the jihadist march on Doha in Qatar, Riyadh in Saudi Arabia, or even Amman in Jordan, in a most unwelcome return of the prodigal son.

Will ISIS Come Home to Roost?

RADIO SPUTNIK, FEBRUARY 6, 2015

Marina Dzhashi of *Agree or Disagree:* King Salman is the new ruler of Saudi Arabia who has acceded to the throne following the death of King Abdullah. The new ruler of the country asked the social media to help him "maintain security and stability, and protect the kingdom from all evils." What will determine the country's course and its relations with its neighbors and the rest of the world? Does a new ruler mean a new future for the country?[14]

Gilbert Mercier: One of the first moves of King Salman, very shortly after the death of King Abdulah, was to issue a decree to name one of his nephews, who is 55 years old and a grandson of the founder of Saudi Arabia, Prince Mohammed bin Nayef, as Deputy Crown Prince. So it gives some sign that the second generation, the founder's grandson, is actually going to start ruling the country.

MD: Who are the allies of Saudi Arabia in the region? Obviously, you cannot deal with a whole bunch of issues on your own these days.

GM: The Muslim Brotherhood has had the backing of Qatar in the region. Qatar sort of lost the Egypt affair. I have a feeling that Saudi Arabia has been actually weak for several years. There are two reasons. The main one is the fact that they have allowed, as the most powerful representatives of OPEC, something that is against their own interest, which is a drop of oil prices by more than 50 percent since August 2014. I am absolutely convinced, and it's just a logical argument, that the drop in question was manufactured from the US to suit their need of impacting the Russian economy.

MD: President Obama went to Saudi Arabia. Obama has said on a number of occasions that Saudi Arabia is one of the key allies of the US in the region. Ahead of his arrival, Obama suggested that he would not be raising US concerns about Saudi Arabia's flogging of blogger Raif Badawi, who was convicted of insulting Islam and sentenced to 10 years in prison. It's interesting that the human rights card is used sometimes by the West against some countries and conveniently forgotten when it comes to the protection of US interests. Why do you think the issue of human rights is overlooked?

GM: The West, and especially the US, has an interesting double standard in terms of human rights. They are critical of countries that don't serve their geopolitical interests. As an example: Michelle Obama came to the funeral with her husband, not wearing any kind of covering on her hair, which in terms of protocol is a grave insult to the royal family. It shows that there is definitely in the relationship between the US and Saudi Arabia a shift that makes me think that Saudi Arabia is getting a lot weaker in its relationship with the US. They're going to have to change. There is also a demographic issue, which nobody talks about. Out of 27 million in Saudi Arabia, I believe half of them are actually younger than 25 years old. So, there is a huge demographic push. Saudi Arabia has a generational problem: elderly men have ruled it for a very long time. So, there is a lot of push, both internal and of course external, with the instability in the region, and they will not be able to shelter themselves from it. I do think that the jihadists that the Saudis partially sponsor, and train and finance, will eventually come back to Saudi Arabia.

MD: Speaking about the shifts in the relationship between the US and Saudi Arabia. What are the things that both countries have in common, and what are the issues that they might in the future disagree on?

GM: In terms of the regional situation, Saudi Arabia and Israel have a common enemy, which is Iran. That doesn't necessarily make them best friends on any other issue. It is sort of the same vis-à-vis the relationship of Saudi Arabia and the US. Saudi Arabia will realize that down the line. I really want to bring back the issue of oil, which is a critical issue. The ultimate sign of weakness for Saudi Arabia right now is the fact that they didn't shut down the production to prevent a dive of the oil prices by more than 50 percent.

MD: What does Saudi Arabia gain from the global price collapsing? Let's talk about that.

GM: After taking out Iran, and also in the global context, going after Russia, they are siding with the US. I personally suspect, and I'm not the only one, that in late July, early August 2014, the US might have sold part of its 727 million barrels of oil reserves just to play with the market and get it to take a dive. The price of energy is something that is very important to geopolitical stability. And you don't play with that. There are repercussions.

MD: Are we likely to see some international changes in the country that will lead to the improvement of the situation with human rights, women's rights, and other things in the country that have been in the spotlight?

GM: The change, if any, can be of two kinds: it's either going to be a slow reform, or it's going to come from turmoil. I do not think that, considering the people who are the players now in Saudi Arabia, there will be much real change. Women in Saudi Arabia can still not drive cars. I don't think that's going to change very quickly at all. The change could happen through a reform, and there might be a desire for reforms from the second generation, from Prince Mohammed, but it's not going to be major, because it's an authoritarian system, and they need to keep a lid on protests, on liberty of expression. They need to keep a lid on things.

MD: As we see, there are problems in Saudi Arabia that are internally generated, and of course there are problems that are externally generated, and that is the issue of terrorism. What role does Saudi Arabia play in countering terrorism?

GM: In Saudi Arabia, the Wahhabis have been sponsoring jihadists and Islamic fundamentalists for decades. It's going on. It's been going on. They did it with al-Nusra in Syria. They did it with ISIS at the start, and that was actually the portfolio of Prince Bandar, who is now disgraced. His nickname is Prince Bandar Bush because of his close relationship with George Bush Sr. and Jr. They were playing with using the jihadists to topple Bashar al-Assad. Now they have lost control of ISIS. Nobody controls ISIS anymore: nobody at all.

MD: Do you agree that ISIS presents a threat to the Saudis themselves?

GM: Absolutely! I am convinced that the jihadists (a lot of them are actually from Saudi Arabia) will eventually come home to roost. There was an attack on the Saudi border with Iraq about three weeks ago. They will come back. What ISIS wants ultimately, what the Caliphate wants ultimately, is Mecca. That's what they're going to go after, down the line. That will be one of their goals. That is the jewel of the crown for them: for the Caliphate, it is to control Mecca.

MD: Are we dealing with a situation now, in which the genie is out of the bottle, and nobody knows how to get the genie back into the bottle?

GM: It's a little bit of a strange strategy from the US. It actually comes from the neoconservatives here, the theory of creating controlled chaos. It appears to be insane, but it is precisely applied to put a country in a favorable state to create chaos. I'll give you three examples: Iraq, of course, Syria, and Libya. Those countries are in a terrible state because of that. It is a strategy that is already backfiring because now the US and Saudi Arabia are fighting the same people that they have actually more or less created. ISIS has a lot of money. They have a lot of men. They control oil fields in Syria and in Iraq. In that region, it's going to be very difficult to deal with them. There should have been recognition from the US and the West — and of course that's never going to happen — that we screwed up. This wasn't supposed to happen. We need to forge an alliance with Russia and Iran. We need to say maybe Assad is not so bad after all and change policy.

The European Union's Predictable Refugee Crisis
RADIO SPUTNIK, SEPTEMBER 12, 2015

Andrew Korybko of *Red Line:* President Vladimir Putin recently laid the blame for the world's largest humanitarian crisis squarely on the shoulders of the West, saying that it wouldn't have been possible, had they not pursued their flawed foreign policies in the Mid-East. What are your thoughts on President Putin's assessment that this refugee crisis should have been expected and is due to the West's failing foreign policies in the Mid-East?[15]

Gilbert Mercier: I think that it's completely accurate, and it's actually not limited to the Middle East, but also includes Africa, Afghanistan, etc. It also includes Ukraine. It has been going on since the West hijacked the so-called Arab Spring to turn it into a regime-change policy. It worked well in Libya, but it didn't work so well against Bashar al-Assad in Syria. Today *Le Monde,* an old French newspaper and institution, sent 30 reporters world-wide to cover the immigration crisis; they should have thought about it four years ago and sent reporters to Libya and Syria when the French government was planning to join the US to bomb Bashar al-Assad in 2013. They are collecting on their misdeeds, and that is the consequence.

AK: How do you anticipate the West dealing with this massive influx of people, and what do you think the consequences will be in Europe?

GM: The thing is, Andrew, Germany, and you have to tip your hat to Angela Merkel, took the lead on the issue, and she wants, well — she has kind of a lead anyway because Germany is the biggest economy in Europe, and Francois Hollande is a poodle of Washington even more than she is — Merkel wants the EU, and it is going through in Brussels, to take on 160,000 refugees in the coming two years. France has already committed to welcome 24,000 refugees in the next two years. There will be a quota for each country. It is going to be mandatory. Angela Merkel insists on it. The other European countries will have to play along. It is only fair, considering that it is a situation that they largely helped create.

AK: What kinds of solutions do you think would satisfy both sides of this debate?

GM: The refugee crisis, Andrew, is absolutely huge! Just to give an idea to your listeners, there are two millions Syrians in Turkey, and I actually suspect that Turkey is negotiating some kind of deal with Germany, okay:

like, "We won't cut all the Syrians loose, but we need to get something out of it." The situation in Syria is even worse. The West and their various jihadist allies have destroyed the cradle of civilization. There are already four million refugees gone from Syria. Within Syria, there are 6.5 million internal refugees. This is the handy work of the West, with the support of Saudi and Qatari money. This is the stupidity of the West's geopolitics! What I hope is that this crisis in question in Europe — and again they are doing the right thing — will make them realize that being the poodle of Washington in terms of foreign policy is not a good idea.

PROGRESSIVE RADIO NETWORK (PRN), SEPTEMBER 9, 2015
Utrice Leid of *Leid Stories:* Our guest is looking today at Europe's refugee crisis as the predictable result, he says, of Western imperialism and its aggressive implementation of failed policies in the war-torn countries from which the vast majorities of these refugees are now fleeing.[16]

Gilbert Mercier: What is percolating in the Western media, especially European media, and from the politicians, is that they're talking about the effects of the crisis, which is this flow of refugees from war-torn countries. They are not talking, however, about the causes of that flow of refugees, and the causes are very simple. They go back, in the recent history of neocolonialism and imperialism in Africa and Northern Africa, to the invasion of Iraq in 2003 by the Bush and Blair administrations. That created a slew of refugees. They were absorbed in countries nearby including Syria, Jordan, Kurdistan, etc. People are not really informed. I don't think people understand the scope of the situation in Syria. Syria used to be a country of roughly 18 to 20 million people: among those, 250,000 have been killed since 2011, 4 million Syrians have already left Syria, and there are in Syria 6.5 million internal refugees. Syria is completely destroyed. We need to do a little bit of historical background here: Syria is actually a very old country; it was rightly called the cradle of civilization, and it has been around for 11,000 years. The miscalculations and misdeeds of the West, which is now collecting the fruits of its mistakes, have caused this country to become complete rubble. It is an incredible shame in terms of preserving humanity's heritage. And humanity's heritage, of course, it's mainly people, but it's also the past! Between Bush, Obama, Sarkozy and Merkel, tabula rasa was done with Iraq, then Libya. I really think that ultimately this is the policy. The policy is to implement regime change, in the case of both Gaddafi and Saddam, and in the case of Assad, through bogus revolutions.

I guarantee you, Utrice, that it is not only going to be used by the French far right and the Front National of Marine Le Pen, but it is also going to be used in Greece by the Golden Dawn party, which is neofascist. With this immigration flow, the far-right Front National will get more votes in France. I'll give you the example of a statement made to the French press; the mayor of Roanne stated, "the refugees are welcome if they are

Christians."[17] Mayor Yves Nicolin is only willing to accept refugees under the condition that they are Christians and persecuted by ISIS.[17] It is amazing that they are actually putting those requirements. Poland is doing that as a country! Poland is stating that it will only welcome Christian refugees. So, of course, it's going to shore up the far right; of course it's going to increase tensions between populations that are socio-economically oppressed, which are the Arabs in France, the Turks in Germany, and the Pakistanis in the UK.

UL: Do you feel that Europeans as a whole have a consciousness of the link between the actions of their governments and what is presented as a crisis today?

GM: Of course I do! I think that a lot of people are aware of this. And I actually think that the move to tackle those refugees is a good thing done under the lead of Angela Merkel, not of François Hollande and France. France has a long history of taking on refugees. France absorbed close to one million Armenians after the Turkish genocide in 1915. So, I think it's actually great that Germany is forcing everyone else, and there are going to be quotas; they are going to agree on what has to be done. There won't be internment camps. Now, setting up this news story as a new crisis? It's been a crisis for years! One of our colleagues, Ruben Rosenberg Colorni, wrote about it in *News Junkie Post*. He was one of the first ones to talk about refugee boats coming from Libya. Gaddafi had a deal with the Italian government to control the flux of refugees. Without Gaddafi, the flow of refugees became wide open. There you have it, the Italian problem of people coming from Africa. It is again a lack of understanding from the political class, and I'm talking specifically about the US political class, of course, because the EU have set themselves up as vassals of the US in all affairs. The question is: how come the US is not taking a million Syrians and Iraqis? After all, the US government was behind all this!

UL: The US so far has accepted 0.01 percent of the refugees. Is it widely recognized that the European Union is not dealing with this well, even under the leadership of Angela Merkel, who said that Germany will accept 100,000 refugees?

GM: I'm sorry Utrice, the complete EU will take 160,000 refugees; Germany will take about 30,000, and France will take about 24,000 in two years. There are already quotas.

UL: Since the refugees are heading towards Europe, one would have imagined that this is not something that just cropped up. They had to have anticipated that this was going to be a huge problem. What does it say about the state of the European Union now, under the leadership of Merkel?

GM: Well, there's no leadership. You cannot talk about the EU leadership. She's taking the leadership on this refugee issue, and Germany is the biggest economy of the EU. That's one of the reasons why she now has more say. When De Gaulle first conceived the EU, it was meant to be political. It was not meant to be just some kind of free market a la US for goods and services. They like the goods and services part, but the flow of population, they don't like. The problem is, and I've said it many times, it's a systemic failure of an empire that is based on wrong principles. Look at what is going on: the EU is cracking at the seams. Greece, well, they sort of want to get out. There are all kinds of problems cooking and, of course, this immigration flow. I suspect there might be some interesting dealings between Turkey and Germany to say well, we want this, or, if we don't get this we are going to make it very easy for the 2 million Syrians that we have in Turkey to leave. That could be one of the elements but, again, this could be very bad for the EU, because it is going to provoke a vote going to far-right parties that want to shut down borders.

UL: Do you get a sense of the us-against-them kind of attitude that prevailed prior to WWII? The kind of attitude that said: it's okay for us to invade other countries, but we don't want those people here! A reverse of the old system, where money used to stay put and the people moved around; now they want the people to stay put but the money to move around.

GM: Utrice, this is the poetic justice of it all. It's only fair. All those people — namely France and England — invaded half of the world for hundreds of years and now, those very same people they had invaded are coming back to the invaders a few centuries or decades later. Will they learn their lesson? Maybe some will, but the large majority will not. They will feel like they are invaded, which is pretty comical.

UL: The influx of refugees will change the demographics of many of these nations. Within those nations, they are not prepared for that. They don't want that. Even though the statistics are showing that, in many European nations, the populations are dwindling, and they are actually encouraging people to have babies. What do you expect will happen?

GM: Let's go back here to the fact that it is the Syrian middle class that is leaving. Once it is done, the middle class that could potentially help rebuild the country will be gone! Now, that being said, European countries are interested in Syrian or Iraqi engineers: people with qualifications. It also has a socio-economic impact. These are the people they want to welcome. France is welcoming Syrians, Iraqis and Eritreans. They will never welcome Afghans. I don't think Afghans would be welcome really anywhere, because they are Afghans.

UL: Are we likely to see a backlash that may even be more exaggerated, more violent, and more open against refugees and then the follow up of that being a deeper entrenchment of this notion of nationalism and nationalistic attitudes?

GM: It's, of course, going to be like that. In his speech, the mayor of Roanne mentioned the term Christian. It is a very specific term. Now what people forget in the US — they probably never knew that in the US, but they certainly knew that in France and the UK because they know a little bit more about history — is that the west should have supported Bashar al-Assad, because he is secular. He's not an Islamist. They wanted him out for geopolitical reasons. We need to put the blame where the blame belongs: what is going on in Syria and Libya is specifically the fault of the US and its European military allies in NATO, and also the fault of Saudi Arabia and Qatar. I will explain again: the people who did the fighting against Assad turn out to be jihadists. Those were the ones doing the fighting, with financial and logistic help from Saudi Arabia and the CIA. And this is official. They will never be able to say: well, we really screwed up on this one. They don't say that, but they did screw up! And they keep doing it. They did that in Ukraine again. There will be a flow of refugees coming from western Ukraine to Poland and Germany within a year or two.

UL: So, what are we to see right now as the EU scrambles to fashion something of a policy, and something of a way to manage this inflow of refugees, and at the same time maintain political balance within their respective countries, the indigenous peoples and the citizens of their respective countries.

GM: They're trying to do the right thing, and you have to give credit to Angela Merkel and François Hollande for following through. However, in the UK, David Cameron doesn't want to play along. What he wants to do is to welcome refugees, but he has to pick them himself directly from Syria. He doesn't like the other refugees. There's dissension, and of course Italy and Greece — because most of those people coming from Syria via Turkey, are ending up in Greece, which already has enormous problems as it is; so does Italy. There needs to be a coordinated policy, and apparently there is going to be one. Will this be a wake up call for people to dismiss the racist neofascist EU far right? I certainly hope so. But unfortunately it might, at least for a short time, reinforce local nationalism, which is not good. It is better to have some kind of coordinated policy.

UL: But in the meantime you see this as a form of poetic justice that the European Union and its member nations have to deal with.

GM: Yes, it's like we say in France: "l'arroseur arrosé." It's basically the person watering that gets water splashed all over his face. If it weren't tragic for millions of people, there would be some kind of comedic element to it. People have to keep in mind that this is the biggest refugee crisis worldwide since the end of World War II. That's a lot of people. People need to imagine those millions sitting in camps in Turkey with little food supply, with little water access, and living like people who were in the Warsaw ghetto, or who are currently in Gaza. That is not humanity. That is not humanity at all! If I may add something else, Utrice, and this is not a personal view; this is just a rational projection. Very soon, within about 10 to 20 years, the world will have to deal with the climate-change-event refugees, and we are not talking about a few millions. We are talking about 600 million people worldwide.

Russia's New Projection of Military Might

Vladimir Putin made his move on Syria in late September 2015 in a well-planned deliberate fashion, seizing the strange political vacuum in the White House. Washington was already in a full-blown election cycle and scrambling to keep the appearance of competency in foreign affairs. The Obama administration was fully leading from behind: reacting about events, and not anticipating much of anything. Foreign-policy decisions made for the past seven years have turned out to be a complete fiasco. Since the invasion of Afghanistan in 2001 and Iraq in 2003, the footprint of the West in the Middle East and South-East Asia had been enormous and overall a complete disaster. Some policymakers in Washington, Paris, London and Berlin were fully aware of this, even though they would never acknowledge it in a public statement.

There were so many conflicting narratives in Washington that it was hard to pinpoint who was in charge of the situation with ISIS in both Syria and Iraq. But it was clearly not the so-called leader of the free world. The key moment for Putin to green light his military operation in Syria was a visit of Israel's PM Netanyahu to Moscow on September 21, 2015.[18] Israel and Turkey, the two regional players, allies of the West with real armies, had to be consulted and be more or less on board before a full-blown Russian and Iranian military involvement could occur in Syria. Both Netanyahu and Erdogan probably gave Putin the explicit guarantee that they would not interfere with Russia's military operations. They indeed stayed on the sideline and, in the case of Turkey, stopped assisting ISIS or al-Nusra. The Americans, their European and regional Sunni allies would also probably stay on the sideline while Russia, Iraqi Shiite militias under command of Iran's Revolutionary Guard, and Hezbollah fought ISIS. The West was quite happy to stay out of the way. The narrative in Washington was full of contradictions. While Mr. Obama was more or less stuck in his 2013 talking point of Assad must go, Vice President Joe Biden admitted that it had always been a challenge to find some moderate Syrian able to fight Assad.[19] As matter of fact, moderates of the so-called Free Syrian Army have always been harder to find than a needle in a giant haystack.

Russia's plan in Syria was to degrade ISIS strongholds, command centers, ammunition depots and oil fields. After this, a ground operation would start. Russian troops and Assad's forces would come from the Allawite-controlled north, while Hezbollah would move more forces from Lebanon in the west. In a coordinated fashion, Iraqi Shiite militias and even Iraqi troops, under Iranian command, would come from the south to take back

ISIS-controlled areas of Iraq. The jihadist army would have nowhere to go, but they would likely be formidable opponents using their tanks and armored vehicles, all proudly made in the USA, and they would have snipers in position blending into the ruins of Syria. Regardless, if the coalition of Russia, Iran and Hezbollah committed enough troops on the ground, they would probably prevail.

A success of the Russian-led coalition against the jihadists would mean a substantial gain of regional geopolitical clout for Iran, in direct proportion to the likely diminished influence of Saudi Arabia — meddling in Yemen's affairs — and Qatar. The regain of influence of Russia in the Middle East could become a source of stability for the region. After all, Syria had been an ally of Russia since 1946 and, during that time, Syria had not been a source of major conflict in the Middle East. It was in the interest of Washington and even more Europe that this coalition of Russia, Iran, Iraq's Shiite militia and Hezbollah succeed in crushing ISIS and flushing it out. In the meantime, Putin had played a shrewd geopolitical chess game, while the West was playing checkers.

At the start of the so-called Syrian revolution against Assad, Russia's mistake in dealing with Bashar al-Assad was not to put pressure on him to sideline his brother Maher al-Assad. Syria is destroyed: it is literally tabula rasa. The best outcome, which might be the only option, would be to structure Syria as a federation with a map that follows sectarian divisions, which have become extreme. Syria would need something like a Marshall Plan, and it is reasonable that the leading culprits of the destruction, such as Saudi Arabia, Qatar, the US, the UK, France, Germany and Turkey should contribute the most. Perhaps then, millions of Syrian refugees could come back from Turkey, Jordan and elsewhere and start a slow process of rebuilding and relearning to cohabit despite the bloodshed, trauma, and misery that they have experienced. In Iraq, a similar process of restructuring and reconciliation should also take place.

Reset of Imperialist Borders

History is almost always written by the winners, and world maps are mostly drawn with the blood of the losers. Because certain groups of people want to expand their territories through wars and conquests, other ethnic groups have been oppressed or even exterminated. Five hundred years ago, the conquest of the Americas by Europeans meant the start of the genocide of native tribal populations, from current-day Canada all the way to Brazil. Large-scale European colonialism, and its hideous helper slavery, redrew the world map entirely on all continents. Empires come and go, but they leave deep scars on world maps that foment conflicts for long periods. Most of the conflicts at play today have their origins decades or even centuries ago, and they can usually be traced back to the criminal follies of European colonial empires.

Many of the current problems in the Middle East originated from decisions by Great Britain and France in the aftermath of World War I, after they defeated the Ottoman Empire. Instead of splitting the Kurds between Turkey, Iraq, Syria, and Iran, a state of Kurdistan should have been created. The treaty of Sevres, signed in 1920, provided for the recognition of a Kurdish state, but the agreement was never implemented. Kurdistan still does not have recognized boundaries on any maps. Another colossal geopolitical blunder, with dire consequences, was the 1948 rubberstamping of a Jewish state's creation in Palestine.

History stubbornly continues to challenge the arbitrary geography that imperialists have imposed, and the struggles are often violent. People all over the world, including the Scots, Catalans, Tuaregs, Crimeans, Kurds, Pashtuns, Basques and Palestinians are fighting for the right to have their own states. They want to control their lands and destinies and reclaim their national identities. Nations are usually defined by the common grounds of culture, language, and ethnicity within certain natural boundaries, such as rivers, seas and large mountains.

Despite the power and oppressive natures of Turkey and Israel, for example, neither the Kurds nor the Palestinians will ever relinquish their legitimate aspirations to have a state to call home. Besides Western instigation, the civil war unfolding in Ukraine has its roots in the ill-conceived and abrupt dismantlement of the Soviet Union in 1991. Paradoxically, a major challenge to globalization, which can be regarded as an extreme kind of imperialism, may take the form of a return to older cultural divides. This is happening even at the heart of former colonial powers like Spain, with the case of Catalonia, and the UK with Scotland. Soon to follow could be independence for the Basques that would involve France as well as Spain, and perhaps even a push for independence of Corsicans from France.

For Scotland and Catalonia, self-determination will probably come peacefully through an electoral process. In Ukraine, the east and the west have slid into a civil war; in Syria, after four years of civil war turned proxy war, hundreds of thousands are dead and millions are displaced; and in Iraq, a sporadic but long-term sectarian war between Shiites and Sunnis is killing thousands of people every year, compliments of the 2003 US invasion. In Turkey, Syria and Iraq, the Kurds are still denied the right to call their home Kurdistan; in Mali, Algeria, and Libya, the Tuaregs remain stateless; Palestinians have been denied a proper state by Israel since 1948; in Afghanistan and Pakistan, the Pashtuns of both countries are separated by an arbitrary border designed in London. Some identities will outlive any form of persecution. For example, although Kurdistan, Pashtunistan and

Tuaregistan do not yet exist, these national identities do. Whether a Kurd lives in Turkey, Iraq, Syria, or Iran, he will always define himself as being Kurdish. The same goes for a Tuareg in Mali, Algeria or Libya, and a Pashtun in Afghanistan or Pakistan.

Two decades ago, the prospect of globalization seemed inevitable and positive in many respects. After all, borders between countries may be viewed as artificial separations that divide humanity and fuel conflict. The EU was at the forefront of this dream of open borders to heal the deep historical wounds of centuries of warfare. In the aftermath of two world wars, what could have been a better place than Europe to realize this Utopia, with former archenemies like France and Germany co-existing harmoniously and trading with a single currency? Some imagined that nationalism and its primitive impulses would disappear. Twenty-eight European nations bought into this Utopia, which quickly became a scheme to gather a global capitalist empire under US tutelage. The idealistic EU of free circulation of people and ideas turned into an opportunity for banks and corporations to maximize profit by reducing labor costs.

In its present state, the EU is quite dysfunctional: not an EU for the people by the people, but rather, a monstrosity where a rarefied technocratic elite rules without popular consent. For Europe to continue as a political entity, it must become democratic and inclusive. The EU and globalization in general were promoted to citizens as being vectors of progress for the many; instead they have worked wonders for very few. Therefore it should not come as a surprise that, in this new historical cycle, more and more people are challenging the world order of corporate imperialism. This reaction is so strong that some ancient national entities, heirs of previous empires, are also cracking at the seam. Imperialism has arrogantly trampled ethnic groups and tried to destroy cultural entities. The new era is one of backlash against arbitrary geopolitical divides as a push to regain democratic governance and reset boundaries on authentic ethnic, cultural or sectarian differences. A flip side of this trend is the confusion of nationalism with religious fanaticism and xenophobia, as illustrated by increased sectarian warfare and the rise of European far-right parties. In a few years, new world maps might include Scotland, Catalonia, Basque, Kurdistan, Tuaregistan, Pashtunistan, Corsica and several others as fully independent countries. Local government of manageable size for democratic rule could be an antidote against various kinds of imperialism, including that imposed by globalists. A return to smaller government is a natural reaction against the disempowerment, loss of specificity, and vertigo caused by a global empire that thrives on destruction, consumption and greed.

13

Human Trafficking

MOST PEOPLE THINK that slavery is a crime of the past. This notion could not be any further from the tragic reality of a well-organized criminal activity that victimizes more than 30 millions women and children worldwide. As matter of fact, more people are enslaved today than at any other time in human history. There are two distinct facets of this modern slave trade: one concerns victims who are sold, bought and used as sex slaves, the other pertains to people who are exploited for their labor. Here, we will only examine the global sex trade aspect of human trafficking.

In areas of the world where people are made destitute and displaced by wars and natural disasters, sex trafficking is rampant. It is more profitable than drug and weapon trafficking for a very simple reason: once a 100-kilogram shipment of cocaine or heroin has been sold in the streets, it is gone. By contrast, the so-called investment made by human traffickers on the buying end, in women and children, keeps turning a profit over a fairly long time. Often, large criminal organizations work together to control the recruitment, transit and enslavement of the victims at the destination point. The Russian mafia and Albanian gangs have the upper hand in Europe, and they often work in association with pimps/traffickers in the Middle East, where the biggest distribution point is Beirut, Lebanon, to provide

Estonian, Ukrainian or Lithuanian women, who are in high demand from the rich buyers in the Gulf.

Although sex slavery is associated with the brothels of Thailand, Cambodia, the Philippines or the Dominican Republic, in countries where prostitution is legal, like Germany, traffickers, pimps and dangerous crime organizations such as the Russian mafia and ethnic-Albanian gangs control most sex workers, even those who claim to be independent. Around 200,000 children between the ages of 12 to 15 are sold for sex by pimps/traffickers every year in the US. The problem is epidemic. Until the communication revolution of the Internet, sex trafficking was mainly confined to brothels and street corners. The information super highway has given criminal organizations a great tool to turn sex trafficking into a multi-billion a year enterprise.

Starting in 2012, the Obama administration, under the impulse of Secretary of State Hillary Clinton, declared January to be the human trafficking prevention month. Although this marked a desire from the US government to focus on the issue, the problem is so vast that this action is unlikely to make a dent in it. The only positive impact has been to raise some public awareness. The US State Department has been active in tracking the traffic worldwide. Unlike previous reports, its "Trafficking in Person Report 2011" had the honesty to identify the US as one of the hubs for modern-day slavery.[20]

In Africa, the two biggest sources for human trafficking are Nigeria and Ghana. In a scheme that is more or less universal, women recruit other women locally, under the pretense of job opportunities abroad. Once they reach their destination, usually Italy, Greece, Belgium or Germany, pimps confiscate the women's passports, and they are deprived of legal immigration status. They are forced to prostitute themselves, usually after being severely beaten and raped, to pay off the debt of their transit to Western Europe. According to a report from the British police, Albanian gangs in the UK control 75 percent of the sex trade. In Germany, 75 percent of sex workers come from former Eastern-block countries.

In the West, the Internet has become the number-one platform for buying women and children for sex. Victims from various countries of origin are trafficked through pseudo-independent, but in reality pimp-controlled escort services, chat rooms, and even dating web sites that openly advertise on the Internet. In the US, countless brothels are disguised as massage parlors, and in the strip-club business industry, exotic dancers turn tricks in the VIP rooms. Coyotes, working with local pimps, Mexican gangs, and the Salvadorian-US gang MS13, lure migrant women from Central America, either from Guatemala or El Salvador, into crossing the US-Mexico border in Texas, Arizona and California. The women usually end up as sex slaves in cantinas or massage parlors.

Though the cynics say that prostitution is the world's oldest profession, few women willingly enter this line of work. They are forced into it by adverse socioeconomic circumstances, in virtually all cases. The fall of the Soviet Union in the early 1990s, and the rapid rise of Russian organized crime in its aftermath, flooded Western Europe and the Middle East with an unprecedented influx of former Eastern-block women seeking a better life and hoping to support their families back home. It is the same for poor women and children in rural areas of Thailand, Cambodia or the Philippines, who are bought by local recruiters, for sometimes as little as $150, and then shipped to Japan, where they become sex slaves in brothels that Yakuzas control.

Sophisticated criminal organizations are exploiting a situation of despair created by a global system where human beings are not much more than a commodity. Mega international corporations have outsourced countless jobs to seek a labor pool that can be paid slave wages, just like global organized crime has found a gold mine in human trafficking. Fundamentally, the Albanian gangs, Russian mafia, MS13 or the Mexican drug cartels apply the same brutal rule of free-market capitalism, which is to satisfy a demand by providing a product, in this case 30 million enslaved human beings.

Putting Human Trafficking in the Spotlight

NEWS JUNKIE POST, FEBRUARY 2, 2012

The Boston Initiative to Advance Human Rights (BITAHR) organized a three-day film forum from February 3 to 5, 2012, titled Fighting Trafficking Through Film, to raise awareness about the epidemic of human trafficking and promote the cause of the anti-trafficking movement. BITAHR is a nonprofit organization whose goal is to eliminate commercial sexual exploitation. BITAHR's Executive Director, Rebecca Merrill, gave *News Junkie Post* an exclusive interview.[21]

Gilbert Mercier: What triggered originally your interest in fighting human trafficking?

Rebecca Merrill: I was driven by the impact that *The Day My God Died,* a film featuring Anuradha Koirala and Maiti Nepal had on me both personally and professionally. After nearly a year of research, and the development of my own documentary during law school, I had the opportunity to sit with Anuradha and to discuss life's passion and how it often drives one's career. During that meeting, Anuradha admonished me to listen to my heart and to open my ears. Her voice was delicate but commanding as she asked me simply: "How can you not be passionate when you listen to the stories of these women and girls? How can you not do something about it?" Those words, the stories, had a lasting impact on my academic studies and now professional life. I think it is a wonderful complement to pair the human voice and images with the research and theory.

GM: Sex trafficking is a multi-billion-dollar global business that is getting more and more controlled by large organized-crime networks and no longer by small-time local pimps. Do you think we need a global strategy to fight such sophisticated criminal organizations and, if so, what would you recommend?

RM: Second only to drug trafficking, human trafficking is the largest criminal industry in the world, and it is the fastest growing. We need a holistic and multifaceted international strategy just to keep up with the growth of the industry, never mind to eradicate it. There are numbers of non-profits, agencies, and individuals doing great work around the world. That said, we really need national governments and law enforcement to work together against trafficking. We need governments to recognize that victims of human trafficking are victims in need of social services, not criminals subject to detention and deportation. There are circumstances where return to countries of origin is appropriate, but agencies have the responsibility to ensure return isn't directly into the hands of the victim's traffickers. All too often, victims are simply deported to the countries from which they were recruited, most often subjecting them to the same vulnerable circumstances and a mixture of societal shaming, family rejection and condemnation, and an inability to rejoin the workforce. Moreover, the circumstances giving rise to vulnerability are not typically eliminated but rather exponentially and detrimentally made worse. If governments worked together to provide victims with social services, after exploitation abroad and at home, re-exploitation would not be such a threat. In addition, while we are seeing an increase in transnational crimes of exploitation, the independent contractors, if you will, still operate and regularly increase in number. This can be linked in large part to economics. Where there is a profit, particularly of the margin available through commercial sex exploitation (CSE), entrepreneurial criminals will find a way.

GM: Some countries, such as Germany, have legalized prostitution. Do you think it is a valid approach to end sex trafficking?

RM: No. I cannot recognize the legalization of prostitution as a valid way to end the sex trade. Legalization would not end modern-day slavery; it would simply empower pimps to continue manipulation and exploitation with less likelihood of identification, because the line between legal and illegal would be so fuzzy. The rationale for legalizing prostitution is relatively easy to understand. Legislators, often pushed by well meaning advocates, may believe or accept that prostitution will happen regardless of legalization and, if legal, the laws will at least document the industry and license the workers, making it theoretically easier to provide healthcare and other services to prostituted women. There is also the feminist argument that a woman should be empowered to do what she wishes with her body, including selling sex. These arguments are flawed. Legalizing prostitution does not reduce the enormously harmful physical and psychological effects that being sexually exploited inherently caused. Women and girls who engage in prostitution do not choose to do so. The idea that prostitution is a choice does not take into account that, in order to choose something, one needs to have several options. The majority of those in the sex trade — admittedly not 100 percent — in countries where prostitution is legal and illegal alike, are vulnerable to commercial sexual exploitation due to a complex set of circumstances often including economic desperation, unrest or instability in homes or even communities or countries, psychological manipulation and more: not because it is a viable choice.

GM: Traffickers make an extensive use of the Internet and even of social media sites to lure, recruit and exploit victims. Should these types of activities be more closely monitored by law enforcement agencies, with perhaps the help of anti-trafficking organizations, such as yours, acting as a network of whistleblowers?

RM: It is true. Traffickers may use social media sites to recruit underage girls into commercial sexual exploitation. Once recruited, the sites are used to advertise sex with the exploited individuals: children and adults alike. The illegal age of children is disguised using language like youthful, fresh, barely legal, and tight body. The Internet provides anonymity for the exploiting pimps and endless choice and anonymous shopping and exploiting for the Johns who are purchasing sex. In some areas, ordering sex is easier and cheaper than ordering a pizza. Screen names and pseudonyms make it harder to identify and prosecute the pimps. In addition, the handles protect the Johns from the negative stigma that buying sex should carry. In reality, companies that facilitate this type of exploitation are just as guilty as the pimps that exploit minors, because they too are making hundreds of thousands of dollars off the sale of the bodies of very young girls and boys. Not only should law enforcement agencies monitor this type of behavior, they should shut down the websites. The problem is that, regardless of our pointing out that commercial sexual exploitation is happening online, the criminal facilitation must be prosecuted and punished. In addition, advertisers must take some responsibility by removing their ads and reducing the facilitators' bottom-line profitability.

GM: In a phone conversation we had sometime ago, you mentioned that we are living in a hyper-sexual world fueled by popular culture, online pornography, etc., and that it could be one of the reasons why a substantial number of men seek commercial sex or indulge in sex tourism. Would you elaborate on this?

RM: Of course. Over the past few decades we have seen a shift from the most risqué magazines, including one spread with a suggestively clad woman, to a society where pre-adolescent boys see literally hundreds of thousands of images of nudity before they even reach middle school. When sex education comes in the form of magazines, the Internet, song lyrics and popular culture, instead of from teachers and parents, it can be a very confusing topic for young men and women alike. By hyper-sexualizing children at a disturbing young age, we have diminished the gap between buying the idea of sex in the form of a magazine subscription, or a calendar, to buying the act of sex in a massage parlor, in a hotel or car, or even in one's own home. When we see so many images of women in circumstances that suggest that they are happy naked, exposed, in sexually dominated manners, we are normalizing the notion that girls and women should be dominated, subordinated and subjected to sexually violent and aggressive behavior. These progressive and persistent images make it harder to believe that the exploited are victims. Moreover, products like lingerie for four to six-year-old girls feed into this idea of children as sex objects and sexy as an ideal for children.

GM: A cynical view of commercial sex, and a stereotypical rationalization of it, would be to say that prostitution will never be eradicated because it is the world's oldest profession. Do you think, one day, men and women will be able to free themselves from the sick correlation between sex and money?

RM: It is true that commercial sex has existed in various forms over centuries throughout most, if not all countries. It is also true that women have historically been subjected to oppression, domination and silencing. I am not sure that as a society we will ever be able to eradicate the correlation between sex and money. It is my hope, however, that as this topic becomes a priority for the feminist movement and society at large, and as women everywhere continue to fight for equal opportunities, one day women and girls will have sufficient opportunities so as not to be vulnerable to coercion and forced into prostitution. Females need sufficient opportunity to utilize their skills and abilities in ways that positively contributes to society. It is also our organization's goal to spread awareness, in collaboration with a global coalition, such that it minimizes demand by educating purchasers about the harmful, long-term repercussions their exploitative conduct has on children, families, and the community.

GM: In countries of origins for victims of traffickers, socioeconomic factors play a huge role. Does your organization reach out to local organizations in human trafficking hubs such as Cambodia, Nepal, the Dominican Republic, Lithuania, Estonia, Nigeria and Ghana?

RM: We are cognizant of trafficking atrocities around the world and do our best to spread awareness about it in each and among all countries. We are mindful, however, that to utilize our resources effectively, we cannot work in every country or every issue in the complex effort to combat trafficking. We focus most intensely on domestic trafficking within the borders of the United States. We are also working in conjunction with the

Congolese-US NGO, Promote Congo, on a program that will focus on aid for girls and boys being trafficked for labor or sexual exploitation in the artisanal mines in the Democratic Republic of the Congo.

GM: Do you think, realistically, that human trafficking can be one day abolished and how?

RM: At present, human trafficking is extremely profitable for exploiters. If we apply a standard cost-benefit analysis, we can see that the economic benefits of human trafficking far outweigh the miniscule risk of being prosecuted and the repercussions that might follow. As long as human trafficking is extremely profitable, criminals will continue to take the calculated risks. To reduce the occurrence of sex trafficking, we must continue to raise the cost associated with prosecution, so that the risk of being caught and punished is no longer worth the economic benefits of trafficking, while simultaneously reducing the revenue. To achieve this, we must change the way society looks at trafficking. We must realize that the victims of this exploitation are just that: victims. Instead of thinking of labor trafficking as poor individuals deserving of unfair labor standards, or girls that wear too much make-up or parade around in provocative clothing as criminal prostitutes, we must identify these exploited people as victims and punish the traffickers. Without this identification, victims will continue to be plagued with negative stigmas, fear and vulnerability: some of the factors that very likely led to the exploitation at the onset.

14

A Runaway Train Hurtling Us into the Abyss

A S WE APPROACHED December 21, 2012, anxiety was building up for many. This was due to the predictions of the Mayan calendar, Nostradamus, and Christian fundamentalists that the fateful judgment-day phase had begun, with a few potential candidates to play the role of the anti-Christ. As a rationalist, I could not adhere to any of this and especially not the part about the return of Jesus. On the other hand, anyone able and willing to analyze our current predicament knew that we were on the threshold of a very challenging period for our own survival. The world did not end in 2012, but we might have entered the phase of the end of the world, as we know it, because most of us are unprepared to make any significant adjustment to our social behavior.

While the notion of a pending apocalypse is impossible to argue rationally, its emotional impact is nonetheless potent. The horsemen of the apocalypse, identified in this chapter as overpopulation, climate change, food crisis and war, are not symbols like their mythological counterparts. Instead, they are real, deep systemic problems that we have created or that we have collectively failed to tackle due to a global lack of vision and political will. The horsemen, working on the behalf of transnational disaster capitalism, are joyfully pushing the next generations into the abyss, and they should be identified as the main danger to our survival as a species. We are heading for a cliff, to be forever sent to oblivion, and we can only blame our own arrogance, selfishness, stupidity, and lack of foresight. Despite the evidence piling up, most people are still not connecting the dots, but unless some radical changes are implemented in terms of global governance, we are in for a very rough ride. We are too many; we consume too much; we gobble energy, food and resources like millions of leeches sucking the blood of a magnificent water buffalo. Planet earth has been a generous host, but we have become billions of parasites killing our own support system. If the Leviathan that is global imperial capitalism had a voice and conscience, it would scream: what have I done?

Our largely incompetent governments are content with their expanding tax bases and economic growth, and they are not tackling our plethora of problems that are related to overpopulation, climate change, and social inequality. With a world population already at seven billion, the failure to address this quickly ticking time bomb is the equivalent of global suicide. We live under a delusional concept of stability and permanence, as if our trivial mentality of business as usual will always prevail. The UN projects that the global population will climb to about 10 billion by the year 2050.[22] Some even more pessimistic academics argue that, unless birth rates are lowered sharply through voluntary family planning, which entails easy access to contraceptives, the tally of humans on the planet could reach the unsustainable level of 11 billion by 2050. Every week, the world population increases by one and a half million. Naturally, this is a recipe for accentuating the impact of the ecological disaster we have created with climate change.

The current rate of the human population explosion, in conjunction with climate change, is unsustainable even in the short term. One of the reasons why the overpopulation issue has been ignored for so long is that aggressive population control policies constitute a human-rights issue. The exponential increase in global population is quickly exhausting our limited resources, energy supplies, and it is also accelerating pollution, leading to global warming. Unless deep systemic changes are made, there is no doubt that rapid population growth will lead to hunger, failure in education, an increasing numbers of failed states, mass migration, and conflicts.

Man-made climate change through global warming is not seriously contested by anyone in the scientific community, unless they are on the payroll of oil companies. According to the National Oceanic and Atmospheric Administration (NOAA), climate change is now largely irreversible. NOAA has established that a significant portion of the carbon dioxide (CO_2) emitted by human activities stays in the atmosphere for thousands of years. If CO_2 is allowed to reach 450-600 parts per million, which is likely to be our course due to global inaction, the results will include dramatic increases in extreme weather, such as floods and hurricanes, and persistent decreases in dry-season rainfall. This latter phenomenon will be comparable to the 1930s North American dust bowl drought, widened to include southern Europe, northern Africa, southwestern North America and western Australia. The impacts would differ by regions, but they would include a decrease in water supplies, an increase in fire frequency, an expansion of deserts, and such other drastic ecosystem changes as the disappearance of the honeybees. Dry-season wheat and maize agriculture in regions of rain-fed farming, such as Africa, would also be dramatically affected. These factors, combined with overpopulation would compound the global food crisis.

Another outcome of climate change will be a global rise of sea level. Considering just the expansion of warming ocean waters, without even adding melting glaciers and polar ice sheets, the irreversible global sea level rise by the year 2100 would be at least 1.3 feet and up to 2.5 feet. Of course, if the melting of glaciers and polar ice were taken into consideration, this would increase the overall rise to between 2.5 feet to 4.0 feet. Such a rise of sea levels will submerge coastal areas and islands that provide habitat globally for more than 1.5 billion people. Fertile and highly populated areas worldwide will become flooded and uninhabitable for 600 million people within less than 20 years. The floods will displace vast numbers of people, and these large migrations will create conflicts between populations. Imagine a world where one out of 10 people are climate-change refugees. A world where Manhattan, Hong Kong, New Orleans and most of the Netherlands are under more than 6.5 feet of water. Imagine a world where killer hurricanes, typhoons, cyclones, severe droughts and giant fires are always on the menu. Imagine a world with depleted energy resources, drinking water and food, trying to feed around 14 billion people, which is the absurd projection given for 50 years from now.

A striking aspect of our world in disarray is the universal lack of political will. Our elected leaders, for better or worse, stopped leading a long time ago. It is as if all of them are hostages to a system that functions primarily to oil the gears of the capitalist machine from time to time. The machine is greased with money but also requires, like Cronus devouring his own children, human sacrifices. A prime example of this myopic political leadership is Mr. Obama, who has two teenage daughters yet causes one to wonder if he ever reflects on the type of world they will inherit from our generation. He might think, like other rich people, that his wealth will shelter his children and perhaps also his grandchildren from the realities of an overpopulated, flooded world, but his two girls might be in for a rude awakening. By ignoring the clear-and-present dangers of our times, Obama and his colleagues from Europe, China, India, Russia, Brazil and elsewhere are all modern-day Cronus, feeding on their own children: all precipitating by neglect the doom of future generations.

The human footprint on this planet has become so heavy since the industrial revolution of the mid-1800s, that we are starting to harvest the poisoned fruits that were seeded about 160 years ago. Since the industrial revolution, the focus has been on a constant growth of production and the labor force to accomplish it. To accommodate this exponential development drive, our insatiable appetite for natural energy and mineral resources has compromised the natural ecological balance necessary for our survival. This obsession for energy and resources is even more prevalent today. We have collectively raped the planet for one and a half century. Some of us are already paying the price: just ask the Japanese after their natural and man-made disasters in Fukushima. With extreme weather spreading destruction all over the world, and its impact on man-made technologies, such as nuclear-power plants poisoning our food supply, it seems that humans have created an unstoppable army of Frankensteins.

My own experience with a preview of such an apocalyptic scenario, in post-Katrina New Orleans, gave me a precise idea of what life can be when first-world amenities like electricity, gas, water coming out of the pipes and stores to buy food fall apart (under Chapter 5). In disaster situations like the New Orleans hurricane, Haitian earthquake or Japanese tsunami, governments usually fail to some degree, and the survivors have to fend for themselves. Then it is back to the basics, and this translates into the two most absolute human necessities: water and food. Los Angeles, California, is overdue for a major earthquake, yet, is the population prepared? As a former resident of the City of Angels, I can say that the community is absolutely not ready to handle the challenge. Globally, we should ask ourselves some critical questions. How would we survive if all our water and power were cut off for weeks to months? How and where would we get water and food for our families and ourselves?

Capitalism is a nightmare-producing dream machine, and just like in Hollywood movies, the global capitalist propaganda needs a happy ending. Like mainstream popcorn entertainment, capitalism has no need for intelligent audiences or critical thinkers who examine their lives or question the validity of the system: it only needs consumers. The disaster documentary of our own making is unlikely to end happily, and it is unfolding live. Leaders are not leading but serving the universal god machine that is global capitalism. In the early 1970s, there was still time to act on climate change and overpopulation, and to rethink seriously our modes of economic and social development without extreme hardship to all. Since then, we have entered a tunnel of imbecility and oblivion at blinding speed in an accelerating bullet train without pilot or brake. Jumping off the train is no longer an option. Sabotaging the train and derailing it by a world revolution could be our only hope before the train plunges into the abyss.

Today, humans are stupid enough to fight for the exploitation of resources such as oil, natural gas and charcoal. If we cannot curtail this madness, in the very near future, the wars will not be about energy, control of transport and access to cheap labor. Instead, they will be about food and water. To feed a growing world population, the global food output will have to climb by 70 percent by 2050. This is according to the UN's Food and Agriculture Organization (FAO).[23] Rising food prices were the trigger for the uprisings across North Africa and the Middle East that toppled Ben Ali in Tunisia and Mubarak in Egypt in 2011 (under Chapter 20). That February, the world food price index, tracked by the UN, rose to a record high. Rising oil prices due to the uncertainty in the Middle East, and the increased cost of global food production and transport, had contributed to the food-price hikes.

World financial markets also had a negative impact on food prices, as investors poured their money into the commodity market. For example, wheat prices jumped 65 percent between 2010 and 2011, after droughts and fires in Russia and Eastern Europe prompted these countries to restrict the volumes of their exports. In the US, a spate of dry weather curbed the corn output while the rising demands for corn for livestock and ethanol put an additional pressure on the crop's price. Floods in China, India and Pakistan also impacted and restricted rice supplies. The USDA predicted that the global inventories for all grains would drop by 13 percent before the next harvest.[24] This was the first decline since 2007, and surging food prices in 2008 had triggered more than 60 riots worldwide, from Haiti to Egypt.

The title of a book by Eric J. Weiner in 2010, *The Shadow Market: How a Group of Wealthy Nations and Powerful Investors Secretly Dominate the World*, sounds a lot like a line that new-world-order conspiracy theorists would use, but in this volume, Weiner, who is a serious writer and journalist, articulated his claims in a completely rational and well-documented way.[25] Weiner demonstrated that the strongest force in global commerce today is not the US Federal Reserve, the international banks, governments of the G7 countries, or the EU. Instead, it is a multi-trillion-dollar network of super-rich, secretive and largely unregulated investment entities: namely foreign sovereign-wealth funds, government-run corporations, private equity funds, and hedge funds that are quietly buying up the world, in large valuable chunks. Unlike Wall Street, or other world financial markets, the shadow market does not have a physical headquarter. It also does not have a formal leadership. Instead, it is composed of an ever-shifting global network, where large sums of money flow rapidly and mix with geopolitical power and long-term policy objectives. Needless to say, the big national players of the shadow market are cash-rich countries like China, Kuwait, Abu Dhabi, Saudi Arabia, Singapore and Norway.

The Great Recession of 2008 turned out to be an advantage for the shadow market, due to the lack of liquidity in the US and European banking systems. The shadow market's big players spent huge amounts of cash to control the capital market and secure, not only a massive amount of shares in multinational corporations, but also huge tracts of farmland and natural resources across the world.

In response to a request by Bob Moon, on the *NPR* show Market Place, to define the shadow market and what could be its geopolitical impact, Weiner explained:

> What you have is countries that have digested the lesson of the market, and that, is that you gain control over things and you have a much greater opportunity to create the returns. So, what you're seeing is massive land grabs going on in Africa and other developing nations, because many of these rich countries have concerns about their natural resources, about their food supply, so they're basically going in and cutting deals by offering them very low-interest loans or outright giving them grant money, whatever it is, and they are in effect, creating a new colonial system.[26]

Further in the interview, when asked about the role of China, one of the biggest players in the shadow market, Weiner described how the shadow market is likely to alter our geopolitical predicament:

> China builds allies with other countries that we would like have influence in. And it's not just China. For example, Saudi Arabia owns a farm the size of the state of Connecticut in Indonesia and they're going to grow crops that are in demand in Saudi Arabia. This creates a natural ally between Saudi Arabia and Indonesia in ways that we can't even comprehend, because we're not participating in this.[26]

Breeding Ourselves to Extinction[27]

The UN has held countless major meetings on climate change, at great consumption of fuel, which have amounted to nothing but reports and promises of more talk. After many of these alarming reports, the G20 leaders, in November 2014, decided to throw several billions of dollars at the problem.[28] Despite climate-change denial becoming politically incorrect, as long as a discussion of overpopulation, in the context of climate-change mitigation, remains a taboo, we may be sure that nothing will be achieved. If we are serious about reducing our carbon footprint, we must rethink the flawed capitalist concept of unending economic growth and consider reducing the number of human feet in the world. Overpopulation must be discussed in the context of climate change. A major impediment to this discussion has been the assumption that Africa and Asia would be the main targets for depopulation, with eugenics intent towards black and brown babies. In reality, there are too many human babies of all kinds: especially in industrialized countries with high rates of consumption.

Earth's current human population is 7.27 billion, and it is increasing at a rate of more than one per second. By the middle of any given day, for example, there are about 205,000 births, compared to 84,000 deaths. Superficially, Asia and Africa are the most populous continents in the world, with the 10 most populated countries being China, India, the US, Indonesia, Brazil, Pakistan, Nigeria, Bangladesh, Russia and Japan. On the other hand, if we consider the human impact on greenhouse-gas emissions, the most heavily industrialized countries contribute more per capita to the burden of overpopulation on climate change.[29] Specifically, in 2012, China, the US, and the EU alone contributed 56 percent of the world's carbon dioxide (CO_2) emissions from fuels: 29 percent from China, 16 percent from the US, and 11 percent from the EU. India and Russia were a distant fourth and fifth, at respectively, six and five percent. The rest of the entire world only contributed 33 percent of the total carbon emission! This includes all of Africa, South and Central America, Australia, and all the less industrialized countries of Asia.

According to Paul and Ann Ehrlich, who sounded the alarm about overpopulation several decades ago and have analyzed it for many years, "our species' negative impact on our own life-support systems can be approximated by the equation: $I = P \times A \times T$."[30] In this equation, I, the impact of a population is equal to its size (P), multiplied by the per-capita consumption (A), and finally also multiplied by the energy use (T) for the technologies to drive that consumption. By this analysis, the US is by far the most overpopulated country on the planet. The rapid growth in consumption by China and India, and the global aspiration to follow the US' footsteps are terrifying and should have dire consequences within 25 years or less.

The human population should have crashed from famine in the 1970s but was rescued by modern science. In particular, Norman Borlaug's green revolution allowed our consumption of food to rely more and more on fossil fuels than on solar energy. We have come to depend on industrial fertilizers that require vast amounts of oil for their production, plus a heavily mechanized agricultural industry that also consumes large quantities of hydrocarbons.[31] Indeed, for many years, the patterns of food, fertilizer, and oil prices over time have been superimposable. Today, we can say with confidence that it takes three quarters of a gallon of oil to produce a pound of beef. Consequently, the idea of cheap oil has become regarded as a guarantee of affordable food. There are three problems with this notion: for one, oil is a finite resource; secondly, in a vicious cycle, cheap and abundant oil will, at best, postpone the inevitable human population crash to a much higher population; and finally, all the oil will eventually wind up in the atmosphere as CO_2.

According to a November 2014 report from the International Energy Agency (IEA) that projects the state of the planet and its energy resources to 2040, humans will not have to face a shortage of energy.[32] The IEA projects, that by 2040, the world will consume greenhouse-contributing energy like oil, gas and coal, compared with so-called green energy like wind, solar, and nuclear, in a 1:1 ratio. A worldwide expansion of fracking is expected to keep carbon energy cheap and plentiful. This fact plus a projected two-billion-people increase on Earth mean that energy consumption would increase by 37 percent by 2040. This rate of growth and consumption implies a rapid increase of greenhouse-gas emissions, which in turn translates into a 3.6-degree Celsius global warming by the year 2100. This, according to the IEA report, is a catastrophic scenario.[32]

About 20 years ago, when the human population was 5.7 billion, our species was already consuming 40 percent of the Earth's primary productivity. In other words, 40 percent of the total solar energy converted to organic matter was being consumed by a single species.[31] We are quickly approaching a tipping point in the planet's sixth mass-extinction event, attributable to human folly. The planet simply cannot accommodate another human doubling. Whether or not there is sufficient hydrocarbon to permit such a doubling, it will be prevented by the ravages of climate-change events, such as floods, hurricanes and droughts due to global warming, by famines due to the disappearance of key members of our ecology like the bats and honeybees, and by infectious diseases, like Ebola, from human infringement on the habitats of other animals. Our runaway overpopulation, overconsumption, and our obsession with economic growth are carving a sure path to collective suicide.

Procreation is still viewed as being a blessing and accomplishment, although this is an obsolete notion from an era when many hands were needed on a farm, and life expectancy was short, especially for women (many of whom died in childbirth) and young children. In an overpopulated world, parenthood is an act of self-indulgence: the ultimate act of selfishness against the society at large and even toward the children themselves, who are being delivered to a world in crisis. So far, the only country that has seriously tried to control its population has been China. For 35 years, from 1979 to 2014, China's unpopular one-child policy helped to avert a population growth of more than 400 million. More recently, China's capitalist ambitions to grow a domestic market for its goods have led it to relax this policy to allow two children per couple if either parent is an only child.[33]

Population control policy is needed globally and can be achieved without coercion. In most industrialized countries, parenthood currently comes with substantial tax breaks and an assortment of benefits. This must end. Instead, parenthood should be heavily taxed in proportion to the number of children, and adults without children should be those to receive the tax

breaks. The notion that children are a burden to the community at large —
and not a blessing — must become part of the discourse. Ultimately, this
should become incorporated in the culture to such a degree that the sight of
a mother or father with three or four children will become obscene. To
have any future as a species, our population needs to drop, as does our consumption. We must challenge capitalism and adopt a degrowth model, and
if we are to make any progress on mitigation of climate change, we must
urgently address the problem of overpopulation.

VI. Fear and Paranoia

15

A Kafkaesque World

G EORGE ORWELL officially started on the journey to create his masterpiece, *1984*, as tuberculosis made his life a living hell.¹ It was a desperate race against time to write what Orwell called "a Utopia in the form of a novel."² *Nineteen Eighty Four* was published in June 1949, and Orwell died shortly afterwards in early 1950. The novel is said to have started to germinate in Orwell's mind during the Spanish Civil War, but according to Orwell, the book was also partly inspired by the 1944 Teheran meeting of Stalin, Roosevelt and Churchill where, Orwell claimed, the three allies "consciously plotted to divide the world."³ In any case, the bleakness of Orwell's book is deeply rooted in the dreadful emotional landscape of post World War II Britain.

Orwell's nightmarish Utopia became strangely real on 9/11. Earlier signs were present since the explosion of the Internet in the 1990s, but the information superhighway was regarded mainly as a great tool for data dissemination and free access to knowledge, not as an instrument to spread disinformation. The Internet symbolized the pre-9/11 world paradox: the potential for complete freedom and empowerment due to access to free knowledge by everyone, versus the unlimited power of corporate governance's Big Brother to oppress and spy on everyone. September 11, 2001 was not Big Brother's birthday but his coming of age. The events gave oppression and casus belli their raison d'être, and this became a permanent "raison d'état" to justify the invasions of Afghanistan and Iraq, and the never-ending global war on terror. September 11, 2001 further became a global primal-fear event: a moment so traumatic that its impact cannot be erased. Constant war had become the new norm. If soldiers return from today's killing fields, the fear that has kept burning into their guts for months becomes a post-traumatic stress disorder (PTSD). Our society at large suffers from PTSD, and the original trauma that feeds the fear and paranoia occurred on that fateful day in September.

Fourteen years later, the wounds that had been opened by the collapse of the Twin Towers still fester. A poll released by the *Washington Post* in 2010 revealed that 49 percent of Americans held a negative view of Islam.[4] In several press conferences Obama has reiterated that the US is "not at war with Islam," but against Al Qaeda or ISIS.[5] For a lot of people in the US and Europe, however, the distinction between Muslims in general and Islamists has become dangerously blurred. On both sides of the Atlantic, far-right parties are exploiting this irrational anger. On September 11, 2010, American right-wingers gathered at ground zero in New York to voice their opposition to the Park-51 Islamic Community Center. They were there to deliver a clear anti-Muslim overall message and say "no mosque."[6] Far-right Dutch politician Geert Wilders spoke at the rally to promote his message of violence to all Islam and paint Muslims as the enemy from within, who threatens both the US' and Europe's way of life. Across the US, right-wing radio hosts and preachers of many stripes cranked up their virulent rhetoric and spread hatred of Muslims. Anti-war leftist organizations organized a counter protest. The NYC Coalition to Stop Islamophobia said: "a toxic atmosphere of bigotry, fear and hatred stoked by right-wing demagogues like Pam Geller, Robert Spencer, Sarah Palin and Newt Gingritch has led to a rise of anti-Islam in the US."[7]

September 11, 2001 will leave a permanent mark on everyone. It is the historic turning point when irrationality won over pragmatism as the deciding factor in global geopolitics. In this sense, Osama bin-Laden and his associates were fully successful in their attack. The target was picked for its symbolic value as a key center of America's global empire. The overall cost of organizing the attack on the Twin Towers was estimated to have been $300,000. Because of an irrational reaction in the aftermath, in the form of the invasions of Afghanistan and Iraq, the US and Europe have spent many trillions of dollars on their response, and this ongoing expenditure has no end in sight. Bin-Laden accurately calculated that the US and its Western allies would impulsively embark on a spree of revenge and almost immediate retaliation. Of course, at the time, the neocons were running the show both at the Pentagon and the White House. They saw in the tragedy a unique opportunity for what could be a final consolidation and expansion of their American empire project. Bin-Laden and al-Qaeda outplayed and outsmarted the neocons as well as the West's financial elite. The goal of the attack was not to kill a few thousand people and take down a few tall buildings, it was to bankrupt the American and European economies. The so-called war on terror has turned out to be the empire's Achilles heel, and in this sense, that dreadful day was the start of the decline of the US global empire.

March 2003 marked the creation of the Department of Homeland Security (DHS). The name alone is Orwellian. The word homeland sounds warm and motherly, and the term security gives a sense of a father-state figure to the children-citizens that we are supposed to be. The Big Brothers of the DHS and their affiliates at the Transportation Security Administration (TSA) are supposed to keep us safe from all the real or imagined dangers that lurk everywhere. The DHS should be called the DFP. Fear and Paranoia are its psychological impacts on the collective consciousness.

Consider, for example, the nationwide campaign called, "If You See Something, Say Something," which was rolled out as a prelude to the Christmas season in 2010 by the DHS to Walmart shoppers, subway riders in New York or Washington DC, and sports fans at big sporting events.[8] The campaign was an open invitation for people to spy on each other and become unpaid informants for the federal government by reporting any suspicious activity. Big Sister Napolitano's voice replaced the Muzak, aisle cleanup announcements and familiar smiley faces as the entertainment in the Walmart megastores. Shoppers across the country were treated, free of charge, to her fear inducing video message as they stood in the checkout line. "We are expanding 'See Something, Say Something' in a number of venues. It is Walmart, it is Mall of America, it is different sports and sporting arena, it is transit systems. It is a catchy phrase, but it reminds people that our security is a shared responsibility," Napolitano told *NPR* in justification of the measure.[9] In subsequent months, the DHS, as promised, continued to expand its campaign nationally with what it called "public education" and "outreach tools designed to help America's businesses, communities and citizens remain vigilant and play an active role in keeping the country safe."[8] Between this campaign and the blatant invasion of privacy of the body scans and searches conducted by the TSA at US airports, it was debatable if US citizens should feel protected or threatened by a federal government that had become more intrusive by the day.

A hallmark of the fear and paranoia strategy is the assignment of generic names to the enemies of the repressive global order. Terrorist and other extremist can mean anything and its opposite for different people and in different contexts. An example of this was a 2012 post-US election report that the Occupy movement, or more accurately, the US Day of Rage movement, had been under FBI surveillance and treated potentially as a home-grown terrorist movement.[10] The effect of circulating this information through some of the big voices of the US media's left was to amplify the fear and paranoia by implicitly carrying the message that protest is barely tolerated. Further, media and social media combined convey mostly a sense of despair and alienation, as if some of these are being exploited for the purpose of psychological operations, i.e. PSYOP. The Big Brothers on top of the global order of corporate governance expect their workers-consumers to be predictable and above all compliant, even on their final trip to the slaughterhouse.

In our global Orwellian totalitarian state, life appears almost pleasant at times. Obey, stay in line, and rewards may be expected from conformity. Rebellious behavior, on the other hand, is no longer tolerated. The US is a prison nation, and incarceration has become the school system of the oppressed. During the McCarthy era, communists or people suspected of so-called anti-American activities were prosecuted, but now anywhere in the world a person suspected of being a terrorist or other extremist can be blown to smithereens by a drone. Never mind due process. Collateral damage: who cares? Vaguely defined enemies of convenience are killed anywhere, at any time. The anonymous Big Brother has become judge and executioner, and the killing is done remotely with machines. The cowardly war of the drones is not the war of the future; it is the war of today. What can we do to overcome this apparatus with which the powerful exercise control over the population through fear and paranoia? Although Orwell's warnings were not heard in time, throwing in the towel and giving up the fight is not an option.

"Writing a book is a horrible exhausting struggle, like a bout of some painful illness. One would never undertake such a thing if one were not driven by some demon whom one can neither resist or understand," wrote Orwell.[11] Perhaps Orwell's *1984* was an effort to understand the demons that overtook the world during the six long years, from 1939 to 1945, and make sure they would not rise again.[1] What is astounding is that the "Utopia in the form of a novel" written by a dying man almost 70 years ago has turned into our dystopian reality.[2] It is as if Orwell's closeness to death gave him this incredible foresight. Orwell's intention might have been to give us a warning. Instead, we have followed the premises of *1984* like a blueprint for what we are about to become: the little people under the thumb of a universal Big Brother. We have become enslaved by our own fears and paranoia for the benefit of corporate global capitalism. The ultimate form of capitalism is slavery, and our history is in the process of regressing to this. The turning point might be when a large majority of people has nothing to lose. Perhaps then, we can reverse the tide, return to a sense of ownership over our own destinies, and embrace the deep belief that the human spirit cannot be kept permanently shackled and will triumph against all odds.

Patriot Act and NDAA: Welcome to the Police State of America!

There is nothing patriotic about the USA Patriot Act, unless you define patriotism as being the passivity of citizens who give up their civil liberties for the illusion of security under the constant intrusive eyes of a Big Brother government. The Patriot Act was first passed by the US Congress by a wide margin and signed into law on October 26, 2001 by George W. Bush, in the aftermath of 9/11.[12] In February 2010 the US Congress passed, again with a wide majority, a one-year extension on the three controversial provisions of the Patriot Act without making some much needed amendments to the overreaching bill which had, de facto, transformed the US into a police state. Vague legal language, opacity and secrecy were the key ingredients of the sweeping powers given to the government's executive branch by the Patriot Act, which had created a surveillance superstructure.[12]

In May 2011, the Congress extended three provisions of the Patriot Act, which should have been scrapped altogether, and Obama signed another extension of the Act into law.[12] The three provisions were a blatant case of government overreach and a clear danger to the essence of democracy, because they gave the government unlimited power to spy inside the US on individuals who are not suspected of any wrongdoing. Section 215 of the Patriot Act authorized the government to obtain "any tangible thing" in connection with a terrorism investigation. The notion of a thing is of course vague and ill defined, and it doesn't have to pertain to suspected terrorist activities. This provision allowed the government to start investigations that infringe on a people's privacy without a requirement to show probable cause or even reasonable suspicion. Section 206, known as "roving John Doe wiretap," allowed the government to wiretap either a person or a facility without reasonable cause, or the need to identify the person or target, before obtaining an intelligence surveillance order. Section 6001, also known as the Lone-Wolf provision, permitted secret intelligence surveillance of non-US persons who are not affiliated with a foreign organization. This section was in breach of international law and a clear abuse of the US government's investigative power within its borders. Another disturbing part of the Patriot Act, which would continue, was the use of National Security Letters, which allowed the government to obtain the communications, financial information, and credit records of anyone "deemed relevant to a terrorism investigation," even if that person is not suspected of any unlawful action. Tens of thousands of these letters are issued every year, and they come with a gag order that prevents a court from determining whether the gag is necessary to protect national security.

Despite the window dressing amendments made to the Patriot Act since it was first enacted, and except in cases where regulations sought by the government were discovered and challenged, the public never received any real information about how the law was to be implemented to collect information on Americans. On September 27, 2010, *The New York Times'* Charlie Savage reported that the FBI and the NSA were seeking sweeping new regulations for the Internet.[13] "Essentially, officials want Congress to require all services that enable communications, including encrypted e-mail transmitters like BlackBerry, social networking web sites like Facebook, and software that allows direct peer-to-peer messaging like Skype, to be technically capable of complying if served with a wiretap order. The bill, which the Obama administration planned to submit to lawmakers in 2011, raised fresh questions about how to balance security needs with protecting privacy and fostering innovation. And because security services around the world face the same problems, it could set an example that is copied globally," wrote Charlie Savage in his article.[13] The Obama administration argued that it had simply hoped to keep up with the new technology and emulate the Communications Assistance to Law Enforcement Act (CALEA), which mandated that telephone companies rework their networks to be wiretap ready. The bill would have required companies like Facebook, Microsoft, Yahoo, and Google to build backdoors into their programs for government surveillance.

During the Bush era, in the sweeping intrusive context of the Patriot Act, US citizens found out that their international communications were being spied on with the complicity of their trusted telephone companies. These actions were, until 2008, clearly outside the norms of the defined wiretap authorizations given by the Foreign Intelligence Surveillance Act (FISA). Furthermore, the US Congress had already granted the executive branch virtually unchecked power to conduct dragnet collections of Americans' international e-mails and telephone calls without a warrant or suspicion of any kind under the FISA Amendment Act of 2008 (FAA). The later proposal would have provided the legal apparatus for the government to broaden yet again its already overbroad surveillance authority. ACLU's Christopher Calabrese explained: "Under the guise of a technical fix, the government looks to be taking one more step toward conducting easy dragnet collection of Americans' most private communications. Mandating that all communications software be accessible to the government is a huge privacy invasion. With concerns over cyber-security at an all-time high, this proposal will create even more security risks by mandating that our communications have a backdoor for government use, and it will make our online communications even more vulnerable. Congress must reject the Obama administration proposal to make the Internet wiretap ready."[14]

So far, the Internet companies have resisted the government initiatives, more for fear of losing business than over ethical issues. The Patriot Act was renewed again in 2015; in addition, a law called the USA Freedom Act restored until 2019 those parts of the Patriot Act that had been allowed to expire in 2015.[12] Consequently, for more than a decade, the Patriot Act has given the US government unlimited legal options to pry into all aspects of the lives of Americans and visiting foreign nationals, including world leaders. It is sold to the public as an indispensable tool to protect US national security, but in fact it is a dangerously intrusive instrument that guts civil liberties and assaults the core principles of democracy.

Yet another tool of legal repression, together with the Patriot Act and the omnipresent DHS to crack down on basic human rights and civil liberties, is the National Defense Authorization Act (NDAA or Levin/McCain bill). The NDAA takes the US yet further from the rule of law and towards a fascist system where order and repression are its top priorities. In one of his characteristic flip-flops, and despite earlier promises to veto the NDAA, Obama announced in December 2011 that he would sign the controversial bill into law.[15] According to the ACLU, the NDAA gives unlimited war authority to the US executive branch. The NDAA also authorizes all future US presidents to order the military to imprison people indefinitely without charging them of any wrongdoing or putting them on trial. The far-reaching provisions in the NDAA codify indefinite detention without trial into US law for the first time since the McCarthy era in 1950, when the US Congress overrode the veto of president Truman to pass the Internal Security Act.

Human rights and civil rights organizations worldwide condemned the bill in the strongest terms. The ACLU said that the provisions of the NDAA are inconsistent with fundamental American values embodied in the US Constitution, and that the bill is an "unacceptable attack on fundamental freedoms."[16] Kenneth Roth, executive director of Human Rights Watch said: "By signing this defense bill, President Obama will go down in history as the president who enshrined indefinite detention without trial into US law. It is a sad moment when a president who has prided himself on his knowledge of and belief in constitutional principles succumbs to the politics of the moment to sign a bill that poses so great of a threat to basic constitutional rights."[17] Roth added that Obama cannot "justify this serious threat to basic rights on the basis of security," and he argued that the signing of the NDAA would provoke a "global outrage that will delight recruiters of terrorists."[17] Amnesty International also vehemently criticized the law. "The NDAA enshrines the war paradigm that has eroded the United States human rights record and served it so poorly over the past decade as the country's primary counter-terrorism tool. In doing so, the NDAA provides a framework for 'normalizing' indefinite detention and making Guantanamo a permanent feature of American life. This legislation establishes a two-track system of justice by distinguishing between US persons — citizens and resident aliens — and foreign nationals. It is a betrayal of the most fundamental principles of justice and equality before the law," said Amnesty International's Tom Parker.[18]

Feeding the War on Terror Within the US[19]

We might never learn the motive behind the Boston Marathon bomb attack on April 15, 2013, which was reported to have killed three people and injured more than 170. It could be as simple as an unhinged individual going postal on tax day or a sinister message to Americans from a foreign national illustrating the proverb, "you can run, but you can't hide." In any case, the improvised explosive devices (IED) were amateurish and ineffective at causing maximum casualty. According to investigators, the crude IED were made from rigged pressure cookers loaded with gunpowder, nails plus ball bearings, and triggered by egg timers. The clumsy work suggested an unbalanced individual rather than an organization. Nevertheless, almost immediately and for many days after the bombing, the US media talked about a terrorist attack, and the story became the only story. What mattered more, however, was the way policy makers and their media sycophants worldwide exploited the incident.

Overall, the tragedy was a minor incident in the scope of world affairs. Around the same time: in Iraq for example, a wave of bomb attacks killed 50 people and injured 300; in Afghanistan, 30 people at a wedding party were killed and about 90 more were wounded because a US bomb missed its target. Nevertheless the Boston bombing had already raised the level of fear and paranoia. Just like 9/11 was used to justify the invasions of Afghanistan and Iraq, as well as the start of the global war on terror, repressive governments would exploit the Boston Marathon incident to justify an ever-growing war economy, to benefit the military-industrial complex. Private security and surveillance companies would grow, and US citizens could expect the DHS to become a bigger monstrosity. One could easily foresee that, at upcoming big crowd gatherings such as sporting events, drones of all functions, shapes and sizes — some presumably designed to look like hummingbirds — would fly overhead to protect us from ourselves. In the aftermath of 9/11, many young Americans joined the military with the fervor of naive patriotism. With unemployment being high, it was likely that the Boston Marathon incident would lure more young men and women into becoming cannon fodder for the war machine.

Before the marathon incident, the top news stories in the US suggested that Americans might be regaining their senses and worrying about the erosion of their civil liberties. A foremost concern was the free dissemination of information and protection of privacy. Earlier in 2013, the Cyber Intelligence Protection Act (CISPA) had been reset into motion by an executive order and a vow from Obama, during his State of the Union address, to "strengthen our cyber defenses by increasing information sharing."[20] CISPA was about to be put to a vote in the House of Representatives. If passed in its state, it would have allowed companies to collect the confidential e-mails and web-browsing histories of private individuals and share the information with the government, including its military and intelligence agencies, ostensibly to counter cyber threats.

To the US government, the epitome of a cyber threat was Private Bradley Manning. Manning had been detained for over a year without trial and more than 1,000 days without a conviction, for whistleblowing about US attacks on Iraqi and Afghan civilians. He was charged with espionage, not because he had knowingly shared classified information with a foreign agent but because some of his information had been published online and might have been used by a hostile foreign agent for some unspecified nefarious purpose. Manning enjoyed considerable sympathy, and it was not lost on the Internet community that some of the charges against him represented an attack on all online publishers, who obviously have no control over who uses their information.

For what seemed to be the first time since 9/11, Americans began again to express publicly their sympathy toward some Muslim foreign nationals. In a *New York Times* editorial of April 14, 2013, which was exceptional for allowing an incarcerated Muslim to present his plight directly to the US public, Samir Naji al Hasan Moqbel detailed some of the horrors he had suffered in Guantanamo during his 11 years of detention there without trial.[21] The story was damning. More than half of the 166 prisoners at Guantanamo were on a little-publicized hunger strike that had started over two months before, and 16 of them, including Moqbel, were being force-fed. One man weighed only 77 pounds. Moqbel, whose weight had dropped to 132 pounds, described that: "During one force-feeding the nurse pushed the tube about 18 inches into my stomach, hurting me more than usual.... It was so painful that I begged them to stop feeding me. The nurse refused.... When they come to force me into the chair, if I refuse to be tied up, they call the E.R.F. [Extreme Reaction Force] team. So I have a choice. Either I can exercise my right to protest my detention, and be beaten up, or I can submit to painful force-feeding."[21]

Comments about the editorial were overwhelmingly sympathetic; the readers recognized, not only that prisoners everywhere are entitled to decent treatment, but also that Moqbel, in particular, had never been charged with or found guilty of anything. This outpouring of sympathy stopped as suddenly as the Boston Marathon explosions, which were immediately presumed, without proof, to have been orchestrated by a Muslim.

Even a few days after the bombing, there were already some alarming signs of the ways the tragedy would be used in a broader geopolitical context. On April 17, the *Times of Israel* announced that police chief Yohanan Danino and "other senior police officers" had left the Jewish state to help the FBI with the Boston Marathon investigation.[22] This was the highest-ranking police delegation ever sent overseas by Israel. President Shimon Peres, during a foreign diplomatic gathering, expressed his condolences and jumped on the opportunity to crank up the terror narrative. "Today the real problem is terror, and terror is not an extension of policy: their policy is terror, their policy is to threaten. Terrorists divide people, they kill innocent people," said Peres.[22]

To keep the global war on terror in the limelight is to lull the public into docility despite the continuous assaults on its civil liberties and human rights. So long as terror can regain its place as the number one public-opinion priority, CISPA may be implemented with the blessings of a large majority of US citizens, Manning can stay in prison, and Guantanamo can remain open.

Data Mining by the NSA, Search Engines and Social Media
In the surreal world we live in, reality has become stranger than fiction. The information superhighway could have produced a completely transparent world, yet the elusive corporate and governmental nexus of Big Brothers has surrounded itself with layers of opacity, secrecy and deception. Meanwhile, ordinary citizens are probed, exposed and have become open books to organizations such as the US National Security Agency (NSA) and the corporations that run search engines and social media. In one case, it is done in the name of security and prevention of terrorist attacks, in the other it is done in the name of commerce. Factual and fictional have become so blurred that many dreams have a more logical structure than current events. It is as if reality is trapped, like a fly in a spider web, in the matrix of a nightmarish and grotesque virtual construct. Perhaps the best way to understand this layered reality — both hyper-connected and paradoxically disconnected — is to look into fiction.

The general context of the novels *The Trial* and *The Castle*, which were started by Kafka about a century ago, is an exploration of oppression by a mysterious power and of the alienation of individuals.[23] [24] In both instances the power structure is opaque and removed from its victims. The premise of the Guantanamo Bay Detention Camp echoes Kafka's *The Trial*: a remote and inaccessible authority arrests people and does not disclose the alleged crimes to the person detained, and the public or reader.[23] In *The Castle*, Kafka focuses on alienation as a by-product of bureaucracy. The main character, identified only as K, struggles as a land surveyor to get access to the mysterious power that resides in a castle and governs the village below. K acts like a reporter trying to crack the opacity of power and reveal its deceptive nature. "All the authorities did was to guard the distant and invisible interests of distant and invisible masters," wrote Kafka.[24] This diffuse power fog could easily apply to the NSA's overreaching or overzealous decision — authorized or not — to spy on more than 35 world leaders. Just like in *The Castle,* the elusive multi-layered authorities running our world, which does not mean the puppet figureheads used as window dressing, could say that "One of the operating principles of authorities is that the possibility of error is simply not taken into account.... There are control agencies, but they are not meant to find errors... since no errors occur, and even if an error does occur... who can finally say that it is an error," wrote Kafka.[24]

"One must lie low, no matter how much it went against the grain, and try to understand that this great organization remains in a state of delicate balance, and that if someone took it upon himself to alter the dispositions of things around him, he ran the risk of losing his footing and falling to destruction while the organization would simply right itself by some compensating reactions in another part of its machinery — since everything is interlocked — and remain unchanged, unless indeed — which was very probable — it became more rigid, more vigilant, severer, and more ruthless," wrote Kafka in *The Trial.*[23]

The rationale expressed above seems to be the governing principle of the rulers' media sycophants. By constantly milking and peddling the NSA-Snowden story and the like, media outlets promoted passivity and inertia. They conveyed a sense of helplessness and despair, not any indication that something could be done. Fear and paranoia are ultimately amplified to make people believe that it is absolutely pointless to fight a systemic anonymous monster.

While it is true that whistleblowers like Assange, Snowden, Manning and Swartz are not traitors, it is difficult to see them as being heroic. Assange is in a golden cage at the Ecuadorian embassy in London; Snowden fled his country to seek political asylum in Russia; Manning is psychologically crushed and imprisoned; and Swartz committed suicide. If nothing else, all four are poster children for: "Look what happens if you oppose us." Heroes, providing they are not cinematic clichés, overcome the system they fight rather than become victimized by it. For better or worse, Charles de Gaulle, who headed and led the French Resistance against the Nazis was the last heroic figure of France. Fidel Castro might well be the last one standing in the context of true heroes of our times.

Further, these times call for strategic collective fights. *WikiLeaks,* for example, was more powerful before Assange became a public figure. The Anonymous network draws it strength from operating below the radar. Individuals cannot effectively oppose an oppressive system that is widespread, diffuse and opaque, because individuals are too easily muscled into deals or targeted for destruction.

There is a great paradox and flagrant contradiction in all of this. The data mining or data surveillance enterprises, public and private, want to know everything about you, but they don't want you to know much about them. On one hand, they probe into the minutiae of people's lives — against their will in the case of the NSA, but with their active collaboration in the case of social media — and on the other hand, they want to maintain as much opacity as possible on why and how they do it. According to NSA staunch defender Paul Rosenzweig, a former Deputy Assistant Secretary for Policy at the DHS, "too much transparency defeats the purpose of democracy."[25]

"In the new domain of dataveillance, the form of oversight should vary depending upon the extent to which transparency and opacity are necessary to the new powers authorized. Allowing some form of surveillance is vital to assure the protection of American interests. Conversely, allowing full public disclosure of our sources and methods is dangerous and could be used by terrorists," writes Rosenzweig, who has fully embraced the booming business of private security and data surveillance, or dataveillance, as he calls it.[25] As head of Red Branch Consulting, a homeland-security consulting company, and a senior adviser of the Chertoff Group, Paul Rosenzweig represents the crème de la crème of the privatized security and data-mining business. Chertoff, Rosenzweig and company are, in all respects, a lot scarier than even the NSA, because they are not subject to public oversight.

If the private business of security and data surveillance has a definite Big Brother neofascist flavor to it, the apparently friendly and borderline warm and fuzzy social networks do some thorough spying of their own, and they collaborate with the authorities. In this case, the user is a willing victim. Though they should not be, some were surprised when it was revealed that social networks collaborate with the police or the Internal Revenue Service (IRS). It is naive to think that they would not. After all, social media are corporate entities, and as such they are invested in maintaining the status quo. On October 26, 2013, thousands marched in Washington DC against the NSA's widespread surveillance program in a Stop Watching Us rally.[26] Needless to say, it is wishful thinking to imagine that they — the Big Bothers consortium Leviathan of the NSA, Chertoff Group, DHS, search engines and social media networks — will stop watching us. They will not stop watching merely because they are asked to do so. What political activists can do is watch them, give them the middle finger from time to time and, as regards social media, and set up their own independent nonprofit network.

16

Xenophobia à Gogo

AFTER WORLD WAR II, and especially during the economic boom of the early 1960s, European countries needed migrant workers to do the type of work that the European middle class no longer wanted to do. Large migration phenomena during those periods were closely linked to the ends of the British and French empires. The turmoil between India and Pakistan, following India's independence in 1948, brought to the UK large numbers of Indians and Pakistanis who sought a safer and better life. In Germany, the economic boom triggered by the Marshall plan would have been impossible without the influx of a large migration coming from Turkey. The beginning of the end of the French Empire came with the loss of Indochina, i.e. Vietnam, Laos and Cambodia, in 1951. A large number of Vietnamese, Laotians and Cambodians later decided they would rather move to the former colonial power than stay in Indochina.

In the early 1960s, it was the turn of West Africa and North Africa to win or be granted their independence from France. Algeria earned its independence after a nasty war that spanned eight years and started in 1954. France had almost 500,000 troops in Algeria during the darkest days of the conflict. Some of the torture that the French forces committed on the insurgents of the Algerian Front National de la Liberation (FNL) were so brutal that they defy the imagination. An important turning point for

Algeria's war of independence was a massacre of civilians by the FNL insurgency near the town of Philippeville in August 1955. Until then, FNL's policy had been to attack only military and government targets. The killing of 123 people, including elderly women and babies, caused Jacques Soustelle, the French Governor General, to call for a massive retaliation. Soustelle claimed that 1,273 guerrilla fighters were killed, but according to the FNL, more than 12,000 Muslims were slaughtered by the armed forces, police and colon gangs. After the Philippeville incident, an all-out war broke out. With the loss of Algeria in 1962, it was over for the French empire.

After their independence, many formerly colonized populations wind up migrating, in search of a brighter future, to the same nations against which they had fought so hard. This seems paradoxical, but it is not. After all, Algerians, Tunisians, Moroccans and Senegalese spoke French. Indians, Pakistanis and Kenyans spoke English. For this reason, Europe became a logical destination for ambitious individuals who were willing to work hard and take a chance on displacement. Besides, from post-World War II to the 1960s, the rich European countries needed the influx of cheap labor.

The landscape has changed in the past decade. The EU has been struggling with a recession, and the need for new migrant workers has vanished. Some Europeans, especially those among the lower middle class, view the migrants as being invaders who are challenging Europe's lifestyle and cultural values. Far-right anti-immigration rhetoric has been on the rise everywhere in Europe, and some Europeans have been acting out violently against migrants. All over Europe, the political discourse and, in many instances, legislation have reinforced a twisted perception of a direct connection between migrants, petty crime, and even terrorism.

As early as November 29, 2009, in a sign of the rise of racist far-right European parties that focus their agenda on anti-Islam and anti-immigration issues, over 57 percent of Swiss voters approved a ban on the construction of Muslim minarets.[27] Minarets are turrets, attached to Mosques, from where Muslims are called to prayer. Switzerland had four minarets; the new legislation blocked further construction of these edifices. The country's biggest political party, the Swiss People's Party (SVP) forced the legislation on the government under Swiss electoral regulations that allow a referendum if 100,000 signatures or more are collected on a specific issue. The right-wing SVP claimed that minarets "symbolize a political-religious claim to power."[28]

Only four cantons in Switzerland rejected the proposal. The Swiss government also opposed the ban and warned that it would harm Switzerland's image. "Muslims should be able to practice their religion and have access to minarets in Switzerland too," said President Hans-Rudolf Merz before the referendum.[28] In Switzerland, a country of 7.5 million people, there were an estimated 400,000 Muslims in 2009, a large fraction of them originally from Bosnia.

The very next day, far-right parties in France and the Netherlands called for referendums over minaret construction and other issues. "What is possible in Switzerland should be able to happen here. We will call for our government to make this referendum possible in the Netherlands," said Dutch anti-Islamic politician Geert Wilders.[29] In France, the Front National's Marine Le Pen called for a vote to tackle the problem of immigration. "I would like a national referendum on immigration and community politics, because the problem is deeper and more serious than a simple question of minaret," Marine Le Pen told *AFP*.[29]

French Minister of Foreign Affairs, Bernard Kouchner, described the Swiss vote as an expression of intolerance. "If we can't build minarets, that means we are oppressing a religion," said Kouchner in an interview with the radio station RTL.[30] France's Muslim population is the largest in Europe; it is composed mainly of Arabs from France's former colonies in North Africa and represents about 10 percent of the country's population.

The Muslim world strongly condemned the Swiss referendum. In Indonesia, the vote was described as a manifestation of religious hatred. In Egypt, Mufti Alo Gomaa, the government's key official on Islamic law, referred to the minaret ban as "an insult to Muslims across the world, and an attack on freedom of beliefs."[31] In Pakistan, Vice President Khurshid Ahmad said it "reflects extreme Islamophobia among people in the West."[31]

During the French 2010 elections, in which the Front National targeted the so-called threat of Islam taking over Europe, the party's poster so closely resembled one that the Swiss far right had used in its anti-minaret campaign, that a Swiss advertising agency threatened to sue the Front National for plagiarism. The poster showed a woman in a Burka next to a map of France covered with an Algerian flag; minarets appeared as missiles over France's map, and a caption above the image read "Non à l'Islamisme."[32]

Algeria quickly filed an official protest. The North-African country argued that the campaign poster represented an abuse of the Algerian flag. "We need to respect the symbols of one another. This is the position of our country, and we will ensure that it will be respected," said Mourad Medelci, Algeria's Foreign Affairs Minister on March 8, 2010.[32] The next day, the French Foreign Ministry said that Algeria's official complaint was "legitimate."[32] Simultaneously several French rights groups, such as Licra, MRAP, and SOS Racisme launched legal actions to get the controversial poster banned. The Front National's reaction to the attacks was to declare, "Paris is on its knees before Algiers."[32] A few months later, in December 2010, Le Pen compared Muslims praying in the streets to the German occupation during World War II.[33]

In Rosarno, Italy, between January 7-9, 2010, 11 African seasonal migrant workers were badly wounded and required hospitalization after drive-by shootings and mob attacks with iron bars.[34] Racism and xenophobia towards migrants and any non-ethnic Italians had become a serious problem, especially after a 2009 law made undocumented entry and stay in Italy a criminal offense. Prime Minister Berlusconi even went so far as to say that his government "rejects the idea of a multi-ethnic Italy."[35]

A spike of undocumented migrants from North Africa in the aftermath of the Tunisian revolution exacerbated the situation with regard to racism and xenophobia. When the EU's interior ministers met in Luxembourg on April 11, 2011 to discuss the new migration, Italy alone was reporting that 26,000 migrants had entered the country since the North African unrest had started in January 2011. One of the numerous threats by Gaddafi, after the West had militarily intervened in Libya, was to flood Europe with African migrants. The European far right called the influx of new migrants a human tsunami, and the amplified crisis gave it an opportunity to make substantial political gains.

Most of the migrants who reached Italy in 2011 were Tunisians. Italy tried to transfer its migration problem to the other EU members, as if the Berlusconi administration had forgotten to take into account that a European law stipulates that the country where migrants first arrive is obligated to assess their status before allowing them to leave. Under this law, migrants who are authorized to apply for asylum are sent to detention centers, whereas economic migrants are returned to their respective countries. The so-called human tsunami, together with the aftermath of the 2008 financial crash had already put a major stress on the EU's unity.

At the Luxembourg meeting, Italy threatened to leave the union, after receiving extremely negative reactions over its migrant policy across the board. The Dutch minister for immigration and asylum, Gerd Leers, accused Italy of "passing its problems to others without prior notice."[36] Germany's interior minister, Hans-Peter Friedrich, denounced Italy's decision in even stronger terms: "We cannot accept numerous economic migrants arriving in Europe through Italy. This is why we expect Italy to respect the existing legal framework."[36] France, Austria and Germany were all tightening controls at their borders and threatening to send back migrants to Italy. The Berlusconi administration's view was that the sudden increase in migration should be handled by all the EU members and not only by Italy. Berlusconi correctly argued that 80 percent of the Tunisian migrants were hoping to join their relatives in France.

Many of the North African migrants were kept in detention on the southern island of Lampedusa in the squalor of cramped facilities, with little access to basic sanitation. Lampedusa has a population of 6,000 people, but since the Arab Spring, the island had received around 8,000 Tunisian migrants and had become the flashpoint of what the European racist far right called the immigration problem. In March 2011, Marine Le Pen traveled to the Italian island together with another EU far-right political leader, Mario Borghezio from the Northern League party. "I want to draw Europe's attention to what is happening. European officials are averting their gaze and are trying to play down the risk of immigration flows," said Le Pen.[37]

The racist anti-immigration platform of Le Pen's Front National had already gained considerable traction among the French electorate, despite the party's anti-EU agenda. In 2011, the French far right enjoyed historic gains in the local elections, with more than 15 percent of the votes. According to a poll by the daily newspaper *Liberation,* 21 percent of those who said they favored Le Pen had voted for Sarkozy in 2007.[38] A March 7, 2011 poll, by the daily newspaper *Le Parisien,* shocked France's political class and public opinion by showing Le Pen to be briefly in the lead for the 2012 presidential election, with 23 percent, against 21 percent for Sarkozy.[39]

François Duprat, François Brigneau and Jean-Marie Le Pen founded the Front National in 1972. Le Pen began to lead it later the same year. After 10 years on the margins of French politics, the Front National began a period of spectacular growth in 1981, campaigning on the slogan "France for the French," as French fascists had done in the 1930s, and linking high unemployment and crime to the presence of immigrants. By using such arguments against immigrants, the Front National and its founder Jean-Marie Le Pen had stirred up, once again, racism and xenophobia. The Front National needs to be called what it is: a neofascist movement. The core of its political appeal is its stand against immigration and in favor of expelling foreigners from France, its current focus being on Muslims and North-African immigrants. In the 1930s, the party in France that was aligned with the fascist ideology of the current Front National was Action Française, which then blamed France's problems on Jews, just like Adolf Hitler was doing in Germany. Indeed, put in an historical context, the current European wave of xenophobia should bring to mind the fact that, the last time far-right parties all across Europe built popular support on similar themes of racism and intolerance was in the 1930s, with the Nazis in Germany and the fascists in Italy and Spain.

Since Turkey released a massive number of its two million Syrian refugees to Europe, through Greece and the Balkans, in September 2015, the immigration problem in the EU has reached the stage of a substantial crisis compared to 2011 (under Chapter 12). Because of the situations in Iraq, Libya and Syria, which were largely created by the US and its Western allies, countries like Germany were talking, in October 2015, about welcoming as many as one million refugees from the Middle East. Germany's economy might be able to absorb this influx, as opposed to the EU's poorer countries, which are dealing with their own serious economic problems. In any case, the factor of xenophobia will play a much larger role in European politics. This, in turn, will shore up the far-right parties across Europe and, in the case of Germany, it will trigger a significant revival of its small but very active neo-Nazi groups.

The rise of Islamophobia in Europe has already become a recruiting tool for Islamic fundamentalists, just like the wars in Iraq, Afghanistan, Libya and Syria. The US and NATO troops in the Middle East increasingly have two targets on their backs: one that says invader and another that says Christian crusader. The climate of xenophobia manifests a fear of the other. This is a slippery slope and a departure from the European aspiration for a more diverse and tolerant society. Instead of rejecting the idea of a multicultural and multiethnic Europe, Europeans should embrace their diversity and learn to value the ethnic, cultural and racial global melting pot that is the future of humankind.

17

Free Speech Vs. Police State

IN OUR CURRENT ORWELLIAN construct, control is key. It has expressed itself by a constant effort to criminalize dissent and keep a vigilant eye on non-conforming human activities of any kind. Since the inception of the Internet, this monitoring has been done in both the real and virtual worlds. The expression of rebellious thoughts on social media, which some people wrongly view as their own private space in the web matrix, can be easily labeled by the legions of Big Brother's little helpers as criminal subversive actions. The ultimate and final frontier for the handlers of the Orwellian Empire is to intrude into people's minds and police their thought process. Through state or corporate owned mainstream media, the empire's ruling class largely controls the narrative and the flow of information, but notions such as free speech, still enshrined in the US Constitution, constitute a threat and must be, from their twisted perspective, curtailed. Voices of dissent can still climb on soapboxes, but the controllers of the empire make sure they do not have the bullhorns to amplify their messages and have a real impact. In this brainwashing operation of millions of people, conducted through most of the media apparatus, an organization such as *WikiLeaks,* which made its raison d'être in the disclosure of state secrets, remains a major threat: intelligence, as it is called in the world of spies, is not meant for common mortals but only for the elite. Therefore, *WikiLeaks'*

founder Julian Assange and whistleblowers such as Bradley Manning immediately became dangerous enemies of the state. Free speech only matters if one can make his or her voice heard, and so far they have not managed to silence *WikiLeaks*, which remains, with very few media outlets such as *Charlie Hebdo* in France, a small island of truth in a sea of lies.

Despite a cyber attack that took down its main website on November 28, 2010, the next day *WikiLeaks* started to publish 251,287 cables, including 15,652 that were classified secret, from 274 US embassies around the world.[40] Assange described the release of the documents as the exposure of a "diplomatic history of the United States" covering "every major issue."[41] *WikiLeaks* promised that the diplomatic communications, which dated from 1966 up until the end of February 2010, would appear in installments over the next few months. Governments worldwide scrambled to salvage the little dignity they had left, however they could, after being exposed. Government representatives voiced an overwhelming and almost universal condemnation of the release of the US State Department's secret communication files from France, Britain, Iran, Germany, Saudi Arabia, etc. A few weeks before, the cables had been delivered to five major international news organizations: *The Guardian, The New York Times, Le Monde, Der Spiegel* and *El Pais.* "The cables show the extent of US spying on its allies and the United Nations; turning a blind eye to corruption and human rights abuse in 'client states'; backroom deal with supposedly neutral countries; lobbying for US corporations; and the measures US diplomats take to advance those who have access to them. This document release reveals the contradiction between the US' public persona and what it says behind closed doors — and show that if citizens in a democracy want their governments to reflect their wishes, they should ask to see what is going on behind the scenes," said *WikiLeaks'* Cable Gate page. The Obama administration and many governments worldwide braced for the worst.

Apart from revealing the secret details of some of the world's most tense crises, the leaked diplomatic documents also painted most world leaders in an unflattering and undiplomatic light. More seriously, the documents exposed the State Department as being a giant intelligence gathering structure where the diplomatic mission had taken a back sit to the spying one. Highlights of the cables included a call by Saudi King Abdullah for the US to "cut off the head of the Iranian snake," and a Chinese government attempt to hack into Google.[42][43] Despite the unflattering US memos about Prime Minister David Cameron, the British government said it would continue to work closely with the US. The memos gave embarrassing views of Cameron and described former PM Gordon Brown as being weak.[44] Similarly, in France, despite the fact that President Sarkozy had been described as "touchy, authoritarian, and an unpredictable emperor with no clothes" in the US State Department cables, the Sarkozy administration called the revelations "irresponsible" and "a threat to democratic authority."[45] In an interview with *Europe 1* radio station, Francois Baroin, the French government spokesperson, said: "We stand united with the US administration on the desire to avoid that which not only damages states' authority, the quality of their services, but puts men and women who have worked in the service of the country in danger."[45]

The day the cables began to appear, *Forbes* magazine published an interview of Assange with Andy Greenberg that had been conducted in London earlier in the month. Assange told Greenberg that, after the release of the Pentagon and State Department documents, he would target a major US bank, and the files would be made public early in 2011. When asked by Greenberg what he would expect from the release of these documents, Assange said: "It will give a true and representative insight into how banks behave at the executive level in a way that will stimulate investigations and reforms, I presume. For this, there's only one example: it's like the Enron emails."[46]

Twenty-three-year old Private Bradley Manning, who had been assigned to an army unit in Iraq as an intelligence analyst in 2009, was accused of leaking the information to *WikiLeaks*.[47] This involved over 75,000 classified reports on the war in Afghanistan, including a video of a May 2009 airstrike in Garani village that had killed over 100 civilians. Manning was also accused of leaking the famous video titled "Collateral Murder" to *WikiLeaks*.[47] It showed an Apache helicopter attack in Baghdad in 2007 killing several civilians, including two *Reuters* employees. Manning was arrested in May 2010, transferred first to a camp in Kuwait and two months later to Quantico Brig, in Virginia. On his transfer to the US, the army issued the statement: "Preferral of charges represents an accusation only; Manning is presumed innocent until and unless proven guilty. The case will be processed in accordance with normal procedure under the Uniform Code of Military Justice."[48] Military-appointed attorneys initially represented Manning, and they refused to comment on any charge against him.

While some politicians and commentators were going as far as calling Manning a traitor, a large number of peace activists were speaking out and demonstrating against Manning's arrest, and they embraced his alleged role in the documents' disclosure as being patriotic. As early as Summer 2010, the anti-war groups World Can't Wait, Code Pink, Veterans for Peace, and Iraq Veterans Against the War had organized several huge demonstrations. They took place in New York, Oklahoma City and Virginia to protest Manning's arrest. Many viewed as a parody of justice the fact that Manning could not pick his own defense team. Among them was Mike Gogulski, the founder of The Bradley Manning Support Network. In Gogulski's opinion, Manning's arrest was unjustified. By August 2010, Gogulski's organization had already raised $50,000 to help hire a civilian attorney for Manning, and

WikiLeaks had pledged to match the fundraising effort. "I think the grand dream that I and many others share is that someone in the Obama administration will wake up and realize that what they are dealing with here is not a case of treason, but rather a heroic act to bring transparency to the prosecution of these wars," said Gogulski.[49]

Only two years before, the US and most of the world had been infatuated with the new President-elect, Barack Obama. He had vowed to increase government openness to citizens with a never before seen level of transparency and accountability. "The Bush administration has been one of the most secretive closed administration in America's history. An Obama presidency will use cutting-edge technologies to reverse this dynamic, creating a new level of transparency, accountability and participation for America's citizens," said the site set up by the President-elect.[50] An ambitious promise of the new administration, on ethics and government, was to conduct regulatory agency business in public. "Obama will require his appointees who lead the executive branch department and rule making agencies to conduct the significant business of the agency in public, so that any citizen can see these debates in person or watch them on the Internet," claimed the site.[51] Another declaration was even more damaging to the administration's truth-meter standard, when it is applied to Private Manning: back in November 2008, the president-elect had also pledged to protect whistleblowers. "Often the best source of information about waste, fraud, and abuse in government is an existing government employee committed to public integrity and willing to speak out. Such acts of courage and patriotism, which can sometimes save lives and often save taxpayer dollars, should be encouraged rather than stifled. We need to empower federal employees as watchdogs of wrongdoing and partners in performance. Barack Obama will strengthen whistleblower laws to protect federal workers who expose waste, fraud and abuse of power in government," said President-elect Obama on Change.gov.[51]

As president, however, Obama stopped talking about protecting whistleblowers. Instead his administration tried to prosecute Julian Assange under an obscure law, dating from 1917, called the Espionage Act. "We are deeply skeptical that prosecuting *WikiLeaks* would be constitutional. The courts have made clear that the First Amendment protects independent third parties who publish classified information. Prosecuting *WikiLeaks* would be no different from prosecuting the media outlets that also published classified documents. If newspapers could be held criminally liable for publishing leaked information about government practices, we might never have found out about the CIA's secret prisons or the government spying on innocent Americans," said Hina Shamsi from the ACLU.[52]

On January 24, 2011, Amnesty International accused the US of inhumane treatment over Manning's detention because, among other things, he was being held for 23 hours a day in a bare solitary cell. Manning had been deprived of a pillow, sheets and his personal possessions since his arrest. One week before making this public accusation, Amnesty International had written a letter to US Defense Secretary Robert Gates that called for the restrictions on Manning to be reviewed on the ground of basic human-rights violations. Manning had just been placed on suicide watch, which resulted in him being stripped of all his clothes except for his underwear. The confiscation of his prescription eyeglasses for most of the day, according to Manning, had left him "essentially blind." Furthermore, he had the status of a maximum-custody detainee, which meant that he was shackled at the hands and legs during all visits. He was also detained under a Prevention of Injury (POI) status, although his military psychiatrist had recommended that this would not be necessary, and Manning's lawyers had challenged this status. Prisoners with POI status are subject to extra restrictions such as checks by prison guards every five minutes, which results in constant sleep deprivation. The Department of Defense gave no reason for Manning's maximum-custody and POI detention status. "We are concerned that the conditions inflicted on Bradley Manning are unnecessarily severe and amount to inhumane treatment by US authorities. Manning has not been convicted of any offense, but military authorities appear to be using all available means to punish him while in detention. This undermines the US commitment to the principle of presumption of innocence. The repressive conditions imposed on Manning breach the US' obligations to treat detain-ees with humanity and dignity," said Susan Lee from Amnesty International.[53]

Manning was charged with 22 offenses after being held in custody for two and half years. The charges included aiding the enemy: a capital offense for which he could have been sentenced to death, or life in prison without the possibility of parole. During a hearing on November 27, 2012 his de-fense Attorney, David E. Coombs, argued that all the charges should be dismissed on account of "unlawful pretrial punishment."[54] Simultaneously, peace groups like Veterans for Peace in the US and the UK, and others in Canada and Australia protested in an international day of solidarity with Manning. The charges presented by Coombs were very damaging to the US military. Private Manning had been held for nine months in solitary confine-ment under conditions described, by UN chief rapporteur on torture Juan E. Mendez, as "cruel, inhuman and degrading."[55] The US military and, by extension, the US government had acted with complete disregard for their own legal framework. Manning had been denied a speedy trial, as stipulated in the military code, and the codified rule of a maximum of 120 days had become 635 days. He had also been subjected to well-documented illegal pretrial punishment. In summer 2013, Manning was convicted of violations of the Espionage Act and other offenses, but not of the most serious charge of aiding the enemy. He was sentenced to 35 years in prison, without the possibility of parole until after eight years.[56]

Under the Obama administration, the US had often lectured other countries on their human rights and justice-system records. But this was fundamentally hypocritical, considering the flagrant disrespect of basic principles of justice or even international law that had been practiced by the Obama administration and previous ones. Despite the promises from candidate Obama in 2008, the Guantanamo prison camp remained open for business, and an assassination program was run from the White House in complete breach of countries' sovereignty. In a real democracy that valued truth and justice, Manning's exposure of war crimes would have been praised as a public service.

Charlie Hebdo

PROGRESSIVE RADIO NETWORK, JANUARY 8, 2015

Utrice Leid of *Leid Stories:* We're going to be overseas today, taking a look at that development yesterday.[57] One suspect has surrendered, and the hunt is on for two others, two brothers allegedly, in a murderous attack on the Paris-based headquarters of the satirical magazine *Charlie Hebdo* that left 12 people dead and at least 12 others seriously wounded. President François Hollande has declared today a national day of mourning, and the attack, the second in three years since the magazine started, has drawn condemnation from heads of state all over the world. We are fortunate to have our guest discussing the attack in the context of France's foreign policy especially in the Middle East, the rise of the ultra-right in France and throughout Europe, and a virulent strain of racism and anti-immigrant and anti-Arab sentiment. Of course, these are rather horrible developments in Paris. The attack is being associated with a jihadist element within Paris. Things do not happen in a vacuum. It is helpful for people to understand what the context is. What is the environment of the story from your point of view as a French man, as a journalist, as a person who has been writing about these developments for so many years? How would you encourage us to understand the context of these awful events yesterday?

Gilbert Mercier: Unfortunately, it's being depicted by many people in France as France's 9/11. I certainly hope that the reaction to what happened after 9/11 in the US, which was the enactment of repressive legislation such as the Patriot Act, is not going to entice the current French government of François Hollande, or the coming one, to crack down even more on protest and turn themselves even more into a police state. Indeed, it is a national day of mourning in France. There are going to be three days: today is the big day; it is also a day of mourning for all of us journalists, for all of us who cherish free speech.

The jihadists, according to some French government sources, appear to be from al-Qaeda and are likely to be connected with al-Nusra, a Sunni faction fighting Bashar al-Assad in Syria that is connected to ISIS. There is definitely a connection there. The two main suspects are still at large, but the French police have already arrested seven people. One of the suspects was arrested in 2008 for being in a network that was recruiting foreign fighters to fight in Iraq. So this is the background. Now, what I personally fear, more than anything else, is confusion from the French or European public opinion. They might feel like it's a sort of war on their society, on their culture, from Islam. This notion of clash of civilizations really is something that fundamentalists want. They want this type of situation.

Attacking *Charlie Hebdo* is incredible, because *Charlie Hebdo* is a weekly magazine that has been around since 1971. It's really the magazine that carries on in France the spirit of May 1968. And that is what they tried to kill in this attack. However, a lot of people are reacting worldwide in a way that is, I think, the way to react against this kind of attack on free speech. I'll give you an example: in Quebec today, the 12 leading newspapers republished some of the most controversial cartoons published by *Charlie Hebdo* in 2006. They carried a drawing, a picture of Prophet Mohammad. The caption said: "It is hard to be loved by idiots." It has the kind of humor *Charlie Hebdo* was carrying: a humor marked by secularism and irreverence. *Charlie Hebdo* was a leftist version of *The Onion,* if you wish, for your American audience. It was irreverent: attacking all forms of religion, not really respecting anything, which is what cartoonists, what satirical journalists, should do. We cannot let those people succeed. The next edition is going to be next week. *Charlie Hebdo* will come up. They've decided to print one million copies next week. Just to give you an idea, the normal weekly circulation of *Charlie Hebdo* is 45,000. In a gesture that is really incredible, everybody is stepping in. Newspapers like *Le Monde, Radio France, Liberation,* they're all stepping in, and they have donated working space and money to the people of *Charlie Hebdo* to continue their work. It is quite remarkable.

UL: This is a very serious question that pertains to media and other outlets. *Charlie Hebdo,* as you said correctly, is a satirical magazine. In the United States, we hear the arguments, and you raised them as well, about free speech. People operate sometimes with the idea that free speech, or any so-called right is absolute. And it isn't. With every right comes a corresponding duty to exercise that right responsibly. There was an attack on *Charlie Hebdo,* I believe in 2005, by presumably the same elements over presumably the same issues. Is there a line to be drawn? Or should it be assumed that, under the cover of free speech, you don't necessarily need to respect anybody's deepest sentiments? This is not to say that I'm rationalizing the attack. I think it's a horrible thing to do: an awful, awful act. The question does raise the issue here that in France, there is incipient and now raging anti-Muslim sentiment, and it is evident both on the left and on the right. The left says we don't have to respect anything, the right says we don't respect anything. What are your thoughts about this as a journalist?

GM: The question is, Utrice, where do you draw the line? The issue that Muslims have is that there should not be any image representation of the prophet. It's an absolute. What your listeners have to understand vis-à-vis France is that we have a very long tradition, established since the French Revolution, of secularism. The main trigger for this thing, the icing on the cake if you wish, was the fact that France, in September 2010, banned face covering. France has been in the crosshairs of fundamentalists ever since. This is not just about cartoons. It is a stand that says: look, you come to our country, you come to live with us, and there are certain things that you have to do. That is the way I feel about it. This is something that is very personal to me. I don't think that the practice of the burka, those kinds of coverings imposed on women by men, is something that should be really tolerated. So in that sense, I completely agree with that French vote in 2010. Only one person opposed the vote in France's Parliament, it was almost unanimous.

UL: On the other hand, France never has adjusted to the mandates of other countries when French people go to other countries. When the French go as tourists to Lebanon, or they go to Tunisia, Morocco, or anywhere in Africa in any of the francophone former colonies, they don't adjust. They don't change their culture, and they don't change their ways. They still have their baguettes, and they still walk around in shorts in places where people are frowned upon for exposing their legs, etc. The point I'm making here: France has had a history of targeting the people of its former colonies. The tenor of the times in France right now seems to be harkening back to the days when we started hearing arguments about immigrants causing impurities to the language, intermarriage causing impurities to the genetic line, and that France needed to purify itself. Thus began this heavy anti-immigrant sentiment. Because a large number of the people in France, especially in Paris, were people of color coming from francophone nations in Africa, the Caribbean, the Middle East live, it was all bundled together. And so we have a virulent strain of racism taking hold in France.

GM: It's not only in France, but also in Germany. There's an organization in Germany called the Pekita. They are on a fast rise, and their acronym stands for Patriotic Europeans Against the Islamization of the Western World, which gives their agenda. They said today that the attack is a proof that they are right and that there is a threat from Islam. I'll give you another example of that discourse, which is absolutely unbelievable: the editorial of *Le Figaro,* which is a right-wing conservative newspaper, which would be like *The Wall Street Journal* here, said that France is at war, maybe tomorrow in a civil war, and France's new enemy is radical Islam. This is a very dangerous situation. You mentioned the far right, which is in France mainly the Front National. They will make political gains. There were already today three attacks on mosques in different parts of France. The backlash is going to come. A lot of the people from the former French colonies in North Africa who came to France are secular Arabs and secular Africans who don't care about Christianity or Islam. A lot of the Arabs in France, the friends I had, Algerians came there to get away from fundamentalists. Some people, for political reasons, will create that confusion and make that simplistic equation, Arab equals Muslim equals terrorist, and that is very dangerous.

UL: Arabs make up about 10 percent, but they are not the only distinct cultural or religious group that has experienced targeted actions against them in the last two decades, maybe even longer, in France. We do have the Front National in France, the right-wing party, growing by leaps and bounds, but it is the same throughout the European Union. All throughout the EU, we're seeing the rise or rabid racism, anti-Semitism, and anti-Islam.

GM: Anti-immigrants in general. Some parties have on their platform that immigrants should be completely kicked out of France, Germany, the UK, etc. There is definitely that discourse. You were talking about the tradition of colonialism in France. It is an irony of history that the people who were invaded by France went back to France after their own independence. It's something that should normally work out in a very nice manner, because France has been a racial melting pot for generations now. It could come to a situation where it's not the case anymore, and that's also reinforced by very short-term views of foreign policy that Sarkozy and Hollande have carried. This is mainly a blind support for Washington, which implies a blind support for Israel in the region. There's a lot of resentment in the Middle East and the Muslim world in general against that type of position.

UL: I've been reading that the largest group leaving France right now is Jews, because of the anti-Semitism against them.

GM: They are indeed. They are leaving France because they are afraid it's going to be a situation where they are going to get attacked by Islamists, that they will get caught in the crossfire. That's one of the reasons why they're leaving; however, it's been drummed up by the US media, this large exodus of Jewish people from France. The number of Jewish people in France, which is one of the largest in Western Europe, is a little bit more than half a million. What people need to understand is that the Front National came from a group called Action Française, from the French pro-Nazi government of Petain. That's really the core heritage of the Front National, meaning: well, it's France, we don't like foreigners, and we don't need foreigners. It's right-wing Nazi nonsense.

UL: I would like you to really address this. Even in the left, they operate as if there are no rules that need to be observed, no respect that needs to be paid to the very serious vital, cultural religious values of the people living there. In a sense it's a twisted expression of supremacy that, if it is not important to us, it is not important. The representations of the Prophet Muhammad, peace be upon him, have always been negative. They've never been anything uplifting, and they know that this is a huge problem for many in the Muslim world. They don't need to be jihadists or terrorists to have that feeling. But they are, many of them Muslims. Many of them, even if they are secular, identify with and respect the religion of their ancestors. This is not something that should be toyed with. The fact that the left takes the position that, we are well within our rights to disrespect everybody, and everybody should live with it because that's a freedom. This idea that we have absolute rights is crazy. We have no absolute rights. All rights are conditional and predicated on the corresponding duty that we will take advantage of these rights in a responsible way. I have the right of free speech, but under the so-called coverage of free speech, I don't have the right to impune your character or defame you.

GM: You do have a point that free speech shouldn't give you the right to insult other people. It's a very interesting consideration here. For example, if people wearing KKK outfits were starting to burn crosses in the backyards of French houses, could that be considered free speech? I don't think so. You're right. There is a limit. The problem, Utrice, is that since 9/11, we have entered a time of collective madness. Unfortunately, actions trigger other actions, like the invasions of Afghanistan and Iraq. Well, there are still consequences to pay for that. *Charlie Hebdo* in many ways paid those consequences. The complete editorial staff paid for the consequences of the policies of François Hollande, who wanted Bashar al-Assad, a mainly secular person, out of Syria and implicitly supported the flow of weapons and money coming from Saudi Arabia and Qatar. Things have repercussions. You do have a point when you say that maybe they went a little bit too far. The question for me is, what is really the point in drawing pictures of the Prophet Mohammad in a provocative and vaguely insulting way?

UL: Again, there is the expression of white supremacy even in the left, in *Charlie Hebdo* and other leftist organizations, the attitude being: the way we see the world is the way the world ought to be or the way the world is. If we see no major problem in castigating a deity, person, or cultural value that is deeply held by anybody, then there should be no problem with it. Having been served notice about this already in 2005, and the fact that they continued, the question still is: if other people on the other side did things deliberately over a period of time, and they showed no remorse about it, it would mean that it's an intentional insult.

GM: There is definitely a form of lingering cultural imperialism, even on the left. In all the former empires, this notion that we can do anything we want because we're British, or we're French, or Americans. My partner and co-editor in chief, Dady Chery, has written a couple of articles on what she called colonialism of the mind. When I write a story, I always try to write it from many perspectives and see what that could entail for people, wherever they are, in Qatar, in Israel. You really need to do that as a journalist. Those people at *Charlie Hebdo,* they dealt with humor. They are cartoonists.

UL: It's humor to them! It's not funny, obviously, to quite a significant sector of people. Let's move on. This event occurs at a particular time in geopolitics. Where does France fit in geopolitically with the group supposedly identified as al-Nusra or the jidahists of ISIS?

GM: Some people might remember that Hollande was really pushing, about a year and half ago, to attack Assad, when the Obama administration was contemplating an attack, after the sarin gas episode, which was either true or not true. Hollande's administration is active in Mali, Republique de Centre Afrique, and West Africa. They are also helping out in the new war against ISIS, which by the way they helped create. One of the reasons why this brand of Islam is growing very fast is because the money of Saudis and Qataris is building huge mosques, from Italy all the way to Sweden. What filtered from some sources that I found in Saudi Arabia is that they're trying to say that the attack on *Charlie Hebdo* was financed by Iran. This is complete PSYOP, because it doesn't make any sense at all. Those two guys were Sunni Arabs. They had nothing to do with Iran. There are all sorts of disinformation. You cannot look at the kingdoms of Saudi Arabia or Qatar as innocent bystanders, because they are not. They manipulate and brainwash their own population. One of the reasons why Muslims have radicalized is because for them it's a form of resistance against the West. That's the only form of resistance that they know, because there's no more secular type of resistance. They don't have their own Ho Chi Min; they don't have their own Fidel Castro. What they have is Imans. They are tired of what's happening in their countries. They have no real possibility, and they want to fight. It is understandable, in a sense, but they are getting completely manipulated.

UL: This is how history works. You look at how things come together to form a perfect storm: things that would seem ordinarily disconnected from each other. What does a magazine, taking what many people in the Muslim world consider to be blasphemous attacks against Islam and the holiest of prophets, have to do with France's colonial tentacles still reaching out into Africa and the Middle East, and France working together with the West, notably Britain and the United States in this kind of formation against the Middle East and other places of the world, and NATO, and the European Union against China. All of this is coming together. Here we have this event. Within France, we have the building of anti-immigrant sentiment, and we have blatant racism that's been building and is out of control. Even a government minister, an African woman, has been attacked as being a monkey.

GM: Yes, the minister of justice.

UL: You have all these things happening and causing people to decide: I have to take a stand somewhere, and if I can't take a stand on the basis of the European Union, maybe I could take a stand against anti-immigrant sentiment. But definitely, if I feel strongly as a Muslim, and I see this in a magazine as being a direct hit against one of the holiest precepts of my religion, maybe that's where I want to start.

GM: As a French person, I don't exactly share your view. First of all, I'm not a cartoonist, and words are a different thing. Always, images are very strong. The motto of all the crew at *Charlie Hebdo* since 1971 was to be provocative. It was irreverence against every form of what they viewed as authority: anti-religious, anti-government, anti-police, anti everything. This is a direct line from the mini revolution of May 1968. It has to be put in that context. Now, is this a good idea right now? Apparently not. It's very tricky to define limits on freedom of expression and freedom of speech. What is the limit?

UL: In my experience, the US media understand implicitly what the limits are. They observe those limits when they are dealing with communities that will stand up against being belittled, defamed or harmed by the work these publications do. But they observe no limits when they believe that the constituencies affected are completely vulnerable and they expect no reactions from them.

GM: To go back to *Charlie Hebdo:* it all started when Stephane Charbonnier, a cartoonist and one of the persons who got killed yesterday, decided to republish in 2006 the work of a cartoonist from Denmark after he received threats and had a fatwa issued against him. Charb then had a fatwa issued against him as well. This tit for tat is what they were doing. It might be a little bit childish. As a publisher, there's stuff that I won't publish, because I don't think it's worth creating a bunch of problems. What you need to think as a publisher is: what is the point? Should that be said?

UL: I can't say this too often. A lot of this is still latent racism even in the left. It's usually done against communities that are powerless to do anything about the harm done to them. I've been in this business for about 40 years. I respect the right of independent journalists. I understand how important it is to have the freedom to write and present the truth. In the end, these things are not about truth; they are editorial expressions. The consideration ought to have been, in a mature way, to what degree am I harming any community or person by what I do?

GM: Also, everything circulates a lot faster nowadays. So you have to use reason. I would agree with you. There is a form of neocolonialism pretty much always coming from Western journalists. Number one, they have a much bigger bullhorn than anyone else, and number two, there's also this cultural assumption: "we know better than you."

Free-Speech Guidelines Curtail All Democratic Principles

In the above radio conversation and others about *Charlie Hebdo,* it transpired that even some journalists or radio hosts, who make their business entirely under the premise of their own free-speech rights, find that the cornerstone principle of any democracy is not an absolute, and that some topics, such as religious creed in the case of *Charlie Hebdo,* should be off limit. But who can define the criteria about where and when freedom of expression goes too far? To introduce some sort of free speech code of conduct would be to enact the very opposite of free speech, which is censorship. The brave satirists of *Charlie Hebdo* were the victims of religious fanatics who believed that some Iman had the right to issue a fatwa to kill them. If it were up to Islamist fundamentalists, they would burn every single book written except for the Koran, just like they have destroyed countless major artifacts such as the giant sculptures of Buddha in Afghanistan. ISIS has done this already in Iraq and Syria.

Islamist fundamentalists are not the only examples. Monotheist religions and secular authoritarian ideologies have a long tradition of shutting down freedom of expression. The Christian Inquisition banned books. When scientists put into question the notion peddled by the church that the earth was the center of the universe, they were put on trial. When Christian fundamentalists colonized the Americas, non-submissive women were put on trial, convicted of possession by Satan and burned alive. Adolf Hitler organized systematic destructions of books. That said: absolute power did not always historically entail restrictions on free speech. In France, during the 17th and 18th centuries, Louis XIV and Louis XV not only did not crack down on dissent and critics but also enjoyed the plays by Molière. Catherine the Great in Russia was an avid reader of philosophers such as Voltaire, Rousseau, Diderot and Montesquieu, which was quite incredible considering that the seeds of the French Revolution were in the books of the thinkers of the age of Enlightenment. The killing of the satirists of *Charlie Hebdo,* and the way it was hijacked by politicians and media alike, paradoxically, to increase the repression apparatus, was yet another troubling side of this Orwellian age of darkness, which considers restrictions on freedom of expression to be a perfectly acceptable way to protect certain groups or show cultural sensitivity. In the cases of Bradley Manning and *Charlie Hebdo,* free speech became a collateral damage of the global police state and its repression apparatus, in the names of national security, political correctness and respect for others.

18

The US War Culture Has Come Home to Roost

A NOTHER EPISODE of the schizophrenic sociological roller-coaster ride that has become a part of daily life in contemporary US took place in Aurora, Colorado, in July 2012.[58][59] A delusional young man, obviously in the middle of a psychotic episode, probably thought of himself as the Dark Knight on a mission to save his victims from an even worse fate than reality.[59] He killed 12 people and injured 70 others. One week later, gun sales were skyrocketing in Colorado.

Guns are everywhere in the US. Guns bought in the US and taken across the border have armed the Mexican drug cartels to the teeth. If Mexico has become a narco-state where drug lords keep the police, army, and many politicians on their payroll, it is in large part because of the superior firepower that they have acquired due to the large influx of guns from the US. American violence is not only a good export in its real form, such as guns and the US military, but also a mighty force in the field of its entertainment exports. On screens, big and small, all over the world, violence is a hot commodity; it is constantly sexualized, but US censors challenge it less than depictions of human sexuality.

In between the unspeakable acts of savagery, mayhem and murder sprees, Americans need to be sedated. Many of them look into prescription pills of all sorts for this, but most find their opiates watching the countless reality shows on TV. The locations are really irrelevant, because all of them are about gossip, staged fights and a lifestyle that most viewers do not have, cannot have and never will have. The mechanics of all those shows are the same: they are about convincing people that the American dream is alive and well, that if you have talent, you can become a star and, finally, that everyone can and will find love.

Simultaneously, the aspiration for peace between nations, and for the triumph of the human spirit, which was formerly celebrated in events like the Olympic Games, has morphed into another mass celebration of consumerism at its worst. The athletes have become living billboards, and instead of an atmosphere of peace, fear, paranoia and an Orwellian ambiance of a police state rule the cities where they perform. Corporations like McDonald's and Coke are the games' main sponsors, despite their products being major causes of heart attacks, obesity and diabetes. It is no surprise that in such a schizophrenic world some people have cracked. Indeed, one wonders why it does not happen more often.

After every incident of random shooting, the National Rifle Association (NRA) becomes public enemy number one amongst left-leaning Americans. A transfer of blame to the NRA appears to be a convenient way for Americans to avoid some necessary soul searching: a refusal to address the deeply-rooted cultural problem of violence being the preferred method of conflict resolution as well as the most popular source of entertainment in areas that include sports, movies, TV, and video games. In essence, violence provides the backdrop to nearly all aspects of life in the US. The government has glamorized violence by conducting endless wars, maintaining a gargantuan prison system, and keeping the death penalty legal. The US economy has increasingly become a war economy since 2001, and the business of death is booming. Recruitment centers for the military are popping up in every high school and shopping mall. Television and cinema advertisements for the Marines have the slick and sexy look of Hollywood trailers. "Be all you can be!" says Uncle Sam, who carefully omits from his sales pitch that the main requirements for the job are the willingness to kill and get killed.

Can one blame the NRA when a US president runs a kill list from the White House? Obama's approval rating jumped up more than five percent a couple of days after the assassination of Osama bin-Laden. Mr. Obama was proud and excited to take responsibility for the extrajudicial killing: "shortly after taking office, I directed Leon Panetta, the director of the CIA, to make the killing or capture of bin-Laden the top priority of our war against al-Qaeda."[60] Everywhere, newspaper headlines shouted "We took him out!" and the US public glowed from the pleasure of doing away with their favorite bogeyman. Killing people for the US federal government has become a quite simple affair that can even be done remotely, as in a video game, with drones that reach anywhere in the world from Yemen to

Pakistan. The countless innocent victims of these drone attacks are called collateral damage. Most people in the US could care less about them, the understanding being that it is all right to kill people who had the bad luck to go to a market, mosque, or wedding at the wrong time.

So a man loses his job and kills his boss and numerous colleagues at his place of work. This has become so common that it is called going postal, or more politely, workplace violence. Every year, more than 10 Americans on average are gunned down in such workplace killing sprees. The enemy is quite close, especially for women. For example, of 429,729 homicide FBI files examined by evolutionary psychologist David Buss, 13,670 (or 3 percent) were cases in which a husband killed his wife.[61] Thus, in their more intimate roles as jilted lovers or unloved sons, a small fraction of men murder not only their mates or parents but also everyone else who happens to be nearby at the wrong time. Why should collateral damage be solely the privilege of the president? After all, he is considered to be the country's ultimate role model. And why should Americans be surprised by an endemic violence problem when their role model, their foremost example of what one does with power, runs an assassination program directly from the White House?[62]

One week after the December 2012 fatal shootings of 20 children and six adults at Sandy Hook Elementary School by a 20-year old man who subsequently committed suicide, Mr. Wayne LaPierre broke the NRA's silence with a press conference.[63][64] LaPierre argued that only more guns in the hands of good guys could stop America's killing spree. "I call on Congress today to appropriate whatever is necessary to put armed police officers in every single school in this nation. Innocent lives might have been spared if armed security was present at Sandy Hook. The only thing that stops a bad guy with a gun is a good guy with a gun," said LaPierre.[64] Besides this good guy with gun versus bad guy with gun argument, reminiscent of a John Wayne Western movie cliché, LaPierre blamed the mass shootings on popular culture like "vicious, violent video games" such as Bulletstorm, Grand Theft Auto, Mortal Kombat and Splatterhouse, and on movies such as American Psycho and Natural Born Killer for "portraying life as a joke and murder as a way of life. In a race to the bottom, media conglomerates compete with one another to shock, violate, and offend every standard of civilized society by bringing on ever-more-toxic mix of reckless behavior and criminal cruelty into our homes," added LaPierre. The supposed adverse effect of popular culture on vulnerable minds is a perennial argument that gets brought up after each shooting, although the details vary. But this argument is about as sound as blaming a flood on the movie Waterworld. Violence is ubiquitous in American life, and it is quite natural that it should pervade American fantasies and popular culture.

Who are LaPierre's good guys? Might they be the policemen who routinely criminalize and kill innocent black youths in urban centers? Might they be part of the growing security sector? Or could they be the teenage students who meet a life-size cardboard cutout of a machine-gun toting soldier at the entrance to their high schools every day? One moment of impatience about growing into full adulthood is all it takes for them to sign away their lives. So the dear children survive elementary school, junior high school, and finally high school, only to be sent off to kill people in places like Haiti, Iraq and Afghanistan. There they learn not to distinguish those who are defending their countries from invasion from those who either cannot fight, like children and the elderly, or choose not to fight. The cost is their very soul. Many return hollowed out and suicidal.

Police violence in the US has reached epidemic proportions. Ferguson, Missouri, has witnessed the use against US citizens of Iraq-tested war technologies. On August 17, 2014, a police force, using armored vehicles and military tactics, fired rubber bullets and tear gas canisters at peaceful protesters who had been demanding justice against Darren Wilson, a policeman who had killed Michael Brown, an unarmed black teenager. Wilson discharged 12 shots. According to an autopsy, Michael Brown was shot six times: four times in the right arm and twice in the head. One of the head shots blasted his right eye, rattled through his head, then came out through his jaw to penetrate his collar bone; another penetrated his head from above, which suggested an execution style for the killing attributed to Wilson. A return to violent tactics, rather than the community policing promised by the authorities to the people of Ferguson, and a decision by Governor Jay Nixon to call up the National Guard were very much part of an escalation.[65]

For decades and all over the world, the US has worked to spread, via warfare, what it calls freedom and democracy. As long as this was being done in the towns of Vietnam, Afghanistan or Iraq, ordinary Americans often applauded the endeavor, lured by the disinformation. Mostly, they ignored the crimes being committed in their names because these were not in their own backyard. As the streets of Ferguson looked more and more like those of Fallujah, it was impossible to dismiss that the US' best exports, warfare and civilian repression, had come home to roost. When the war machine runs out of places to occupy abroad, it mutates into an occupying force at home, starting in Black or Latino neighborhoods, and it manifests itself as police violence, curfews and a state of emergency. This is what happens when the military-industrial complex becomes the cornerstone of an economy.

The US economy is a war economy. Together with fostering warfare abroad, a climate of insecurity at home has become a necessary business model for the growth of the war and security business. Between 2001 and

2014, US military spending more than doubled to exceed the staggering level of $700 billion dollars a year. This represents about 20 percent of the overall federal budget despite not including retirement and medical care for veterans, which represent an additional 3.5 percent of the budget. Furthermore, this 23.5 percent of the budget per year does not include emergency and supplemental bills for the specific wars in Afghanistan and Iraq, nor does it include moneys for the vast domestic security apparatus that comprises the DHS, FBI counter-terrorism or NSA intelligence gathering. To give a sense of the gargantuan size represented by a more than $700 billion expenditure on defense per year, consider the fact that the US spends more on its military per year than on benefits for federal retirees, transportation infrastructure, education, and scientific research combined. Or if you prefer, consider the fact that the US spends more on its military budget per year than the military expenditures of China, Russia, the UK, France, Japan, India, Saudi Arabia, Germany, Italy, South Korea, Australia and Canada combined.

Police and military have become almost impossible to tell apart due to two little-known Federal programs: the Department of Defense Excess Property Program (DOD 1033) and the 1122 Federal Program. The DOD 1033 Program lets the DOD provide surplus equipment to state and local police under the pretext of "counter-narcotic, counter-terrorism operations and to enhance public safety."[66] The 1122 expansion was voted in 2009 under the Duncan Hunter National Authorization Act. According to the US General Service Administration, the 1122 Program offers Americans peace of mind. The 1122 Program enabled state and local police to become militarized by getting gear from the Pentagon, which is allowed to give local US forces billions of dollars worth of sophisticated weapons of war, including high-caliber automatic weapons, armored vehicles, armed drones, and stun grenades. The 1122 Catalog for all your local war needs is extensive.[67] The state of Missouri benefits from both the DOD 1033 and the 1122 Federal Programs.

Police officers are supposed to enforce the public safety against crimes. Community policing should never include high levels of militarization, systematic intimidation and denial of constitutional rights. Police officers were never supposed to be used to crack down on dissent and protest. Some people still call them peace officers, although this is a role they no longer fulfill. It is not surprising that protests and riots have erupted in Ferguson. What is surprising is that they have not occurred simultaneously in more towns on a much larger scale.

Many times in the past few years, unacceptable police brutality went largely unchallenged. In Florida, policemen riddled an unarmed 22-year-old Haitian called Raymond Herisse with 116 bullets, in spring 2011.[68] This followed the killings of six other youths in Florida by police in 10 months, without so much as an investigation.[68] In New York, the death of a Jamaican 18-year-old, Ramarley Graham, at the hands of a policeman in summer 2012 was one of three police killings of black youths in one week.[69] The reaction in Ferguson was the first time since the Rodney King riots in Los Angeles in 1992 when people, driven by a need for justice, took their anger to the streets.[70] Popular anger is justified when the clear and present danger to freedom is the introduction of militarized forces into vanishing democracies.

By far the most violent practice of the US is capital punishment, in which a person is made completely defenseless and then killed in cold blood by the state with the collusion of its citizens. The shooters, who are well aware of this, typically conclude their sprees in a quick suicide, thus depriving the state of the sadistic process involving a protracted stay on death row and numerous appeals. The practice of the death penalty is all the more gruesome for its discrimination based on race and the innocence of many of those killed. An Innocence Project study has discovered that, of 333 individuals exonerated in the US by DNA testing, 16 had been charged with capital crimes but not sentenced to die, and 20 had been sentenced to die and served time on death row.[71]

For US presidential candidates, the support of capital punishment has become what appears to be a rite of passage: the ultimate proof of their willingness to kill the innocent so as to support an expansion of US wars and weapons sales. Former US President Clinton suspended his presidential campaign so he could return to Arkansas to make sure Ricky Ray Rector was executed. Rector was so mentally impaired and clueless about his fate that, before his execution, he asked the guards to save his pecan pie for later.[72] On the evening of George W. Bush's inauguration as governor, the state of Texas executed Mario Marquez, who was brain damaged and had the skills of a seven-year old; later, when Mr. Bush was a presidential candidate, he mocked Karla Faye Tucker in an interview a year after her execution.[73] [74] On November 6, 2012, while Mr. Obama celebrated his reelection with an elated public by hugging his wife, mentally ill Oklahoma inmate Garry Thomas Allen, who had been watching the election with great enthusiasm, was executed.[75] The violence of the state, domestically and abroad, is pervasive. It is celebrated: even sexy. Violence breeds more violence and, in a sense, we have all become collateral damage.

VII. Call for a Paradigm Shift

19

Our Broken World

OVER THREE BILLION PEOPLE in the world have to survive on less than $2.50 per day, and more than 80 percent of people live on less than $10 a day.[1] Many of the crises that are unfolding globally have much more to do with the problems of poverty and social injustice than ideology. In Thailand, for example, the Red Shirts were the poor from the rural areas, who were fighting for a small share of the pie controlled by the urban elites and the military. In India, the Maoist movement is popular because the economic boom has left most Indians behind. If, as a global community, we do not reconsider our model of development and urgently address the issues of poverty, social injustice, climate change and overpopulation, social unrest will become yet more widespread. If anything can be learned from world history, it is that once a society reaches a breaking point, where a miniscule percentage of the population controls the wealth and most of the resources, the poor eventually organize to revolt against the existing order. This was the case in France in 1789 when the revolution toppled the monarchy; in Haiti in 1804 when the slaves overthrew their colonial masters; in Russia in 1917 when the Communist Revolution took down the Czar; in China when Mao Zedong's long march established a Chinese brand of Marxism in the country; in Vietnam when Ho Chi Min defeated, first the French Empire in

1951, then the US in 1975; and in Cuba when Castro's revolution brought down a US client and America's crime families.

The statistics on worldwide poverty are overwhelming and getting worse all the time. More than 80 percent of the world's population lives in countries where income differentials are widening. Globalization is having a negative impact on the poor in the industrialized as well as the developing worlds. Not only the gap between rich industrialized nations and poor developing countries is growing, but also the income differentials within the boundaries of rich nations and poor nations alike. For example, the poorest 40 percent of the world's population accounts for only 5 percent of the global income, while the richest 20 percent accounts for 75 percent of world income.

The total wealth of the top 8.3 million people around the world is rising dramatically, effectively giving them control of nearly a quarter of the world's financial assets. Specifically, in 2004 about 0.13 percent of the world's population controlled 25 percent of the wealth. If we consider the global spending priorities of 1998, the trends were already alarming: in the US, $8 billion were spent on cosmetics; in Europe, $11 billion were spent on ice cream, $50 billion on cigarettes, and $105 billion on alcoholic drinks; in Europe and the US combined, $12 billion were spent on perfumes and $17 billion on pet foods; and worldwide, $400 billion were spent on narcotics and $780 billion on the military.[2]

By contrast, according to Anup Shah from Global Issues, the costs of universal access to basic social services in all developing countries would be: $6 billion to provide basic education for all, $9 billion to bring everyone water and sanitation, $12 billion to provide reproductive health care for all women, and $13 billion for basic health care and nutrition.[2] Instead, among the 2.2 billion children worldwide, an estimated 1 billion live in poverty, and about 24,000 die each day due to poverty, according to UNICEF. Currently, 121 million children lack access to education worldwide, and for the 1.9 billion children from the developing world, 270 million are without health care, 640 million lack adequate shelter, and 400 million have no access to safe drinking water.

Globalization has not leveled the social playing field at all, but has instead increased the unsustainable gap between rich and poor. After the financial crash of 2008, the poor's experience of the collapse of the labor, housing, and stock markets was very different from the rich. By 2013, the stock markets and housing markets were undergoing a boom; but this deceptively bubble-like recovery mostly benefited the super-rich, as corporations sat on trillions of dollars and hired as few people as possible. The global financial collapse was a unique opportunity to adjust the mode of economic development and make it more sustainable. Unfortunately, because of a general lack of political vision and will from government, the process of re-thinking capitalism to address the issues of poverty and social justice in the context of globalization never took place.

The deadly disease of the global capitalist system is rather easy to understand from a philosophical standpoint. The crisis is ontological, a profound existential turmoil. Human beings are currently defined and valued by what they have, not by what they are. The quantitative aspect of our lives is in the forefront of all human interactions, either between groups or individuals within a group, while the qualitative aspect has been pushed aside, not even on the back burner of our collective consciousness, but into the trash of our social interactions. People are gauged by their assets, incomes, and the cars they drive: not by the contributions they make to the common good. We live in a world where a person is defined by quantity not quality, and this is probably our biggest systemic problem. This is reflected by countless examples in the popular culture of expressions like show me the money, money talks, or the famous line in Brian De Palma's movie Scarface: "You gotta make the money first. Then when you get the money, you get the power." Poor kids, who dream of a better future, are bombarded by the spectacle of the "bling, the cool cribs, the fancy rides and the sexy babes," which are the trademarks of most Hip Hop music videos. Money is always center stage in this out-of-reach universe of players who, without any tangible cultural significance, serve as heroes and role models for the disenfranchised. It is the deadly equation of money = success + happiness + self-respect = power. The same toxic components motivate some of the brightest and best-educated young people in the world to opt for a career in finance instead of becoming doctors, engineers or scientists.

In our global society, money gives a few people access to power, which in turn allows the very same people the possibility to accumulate yet more wealth. A typical example of this vicious cycle is the constantly revolving door between investment banks, such as Goldman Sachs, and the highest jobs at the US Treasury Department. Top finance executives with a taste for power, such as Hank Paulson or Larry Summers, under the premise of an interest in public service, work for governmental branches for a few years and then go back to their lucrative jobs in finance, etc.[3] Some people still live under the pretense that things in our broken global system will eventually fix themselves spontaneously by some kind of miracle. Of course it will not happen, and this model is, by essence, the definition of magical thinking. A Haitian woman, interviewed on the second anniversary of the earthquake, said that she was "putting her trust in god, not in people," to rebuild Haiti from the horrific disaster. With a rising uncertainty and global anxiety building up like a pressure cooker, most people are scared. They either try to escape reality by putting their heads in the sand or convince themselves that the global system can be salvaged by changes from within.

What they refuse to see is that this model of a business-as-usual mentality impairs their judgment and locks them into the box of paradigm paralysis.

Even though most people feel that we have already entered an extraordinary period of global paradigm shift, the fear of the unknown makes them want to hang on to a system in an advanced state of decay. More people worldwide are becoming aware of the fact that it is not a question of if the system will collapse but, rather, when. A potentially successful global movement will have at least two functions: first, to be the main catalyst for systemic change, second, to be an architect to set up the foundations for a new global system where quality, not quantity, shall finally prevail in human relationships. To turn what seems to be a Utopian ideal into a reality and dismantle the current Orwellian construct is the challenge. It will be a question of reaching a certain critical mass and developing the psychological ability to welcome the unknown, without fear, and enter uncharted territories.

Capitalism: Back to the Dark Ages of Feudalism

History never repeats itself, but from time to time, consciously or not, some influential men attempt to force us into the monstrosity of their imaginary time machines to try to reverse decades, and in the case of feudalism, almost a millennium of social progress. The mid-20th century brought the years of collective psychosis of Adolf Hitler's thousand-year Reich, and more recently what can be viewed as the US' imperialist manifesto, or so-called Project for the New American Century, concocted in 1997 but still in effect today, with the self-proclaimed objective to "promote American global leadership" resolutely and by military force, if necessary.[4]

Montesquieu and his colleagues of the mid-18th century, such as Voltaire, Diderot and Rousseau of the Age of Enlightenment, denounced feudalism as being a system exclusively dominated by aristocrats who possessed all the financial, political and social power. During that time, which incubated the French Revolution and built its ideological foundations, feudalism became synonymous with the French monarchy. To the Enlightenment writers, feudalism symbolized everything that was wrong with a system based on birth privilege, inequality and brutal exploitation. In August 1789, shortly after the takeover of La Bastille on July 14, one of the first actions of the Assemblée Constituante was to proclaim the official abolition of the feudal regime.

Ironically, feudalism is making a comeback in the latest evolution of, and under the impulse of, predatory global capitalism. After all, Karl Marx, in the mid-19th century, considered feudalism to be a precursor of capitalism. Typically a feudal system can be defined as a society with inherited social rank. In the Middle Ages, wealth came exclusively from agriculture: the aristocracy strictly assumed ownership of the land while the serfs provided the labor. The feudal system of the Dark Ages was the social and economic exploitation of peasants by lords. This led to an economy always marked by poverty, sometimes famine, extreme exploitation and wide gaps between rich and poor. The feudal era relation of a serf to his lord is essentially identical to the relation of a so-called Walmart associate to an heir of the Walton family. If one looks objectively at the power stratum in the US in 2015, and the one of, let us say, France circa 1750, it is hard to ignore the startling similarity. For example, attendance at Ivy-League schools in the US is principally an inherited privilege; the same can be said for elected positions in Congress. The concept of dynasties rules, not personal merit.

A powerful network of oligarchs worldwide seems to be pursuing the objective to set back the social clock to before the era of the Enlightenment, so as to return us to the Dark Ages of lords and serfs: a new era of global slavery to benefit Wall Street's masters of the universe. Compared to the Middle Ages, today's servitude is more insidious: the IMF, World Bank, and many private banks operate like mega drug dealers. The IMF and World Bank do so with countries, while the banks do so with individuals. Once Greece, Detroit or John Doe is addicted to its fix — loans in this case — the trick is done. After a while, money must be borrowed even to service the debt.

In a cynical opinion piece on July 21, 2013 titled "Detroit, the new Greece," *New York Times* columnist and Nobel-Prize winning economist Paul Krugman reasoned more like a callous Wall Street operator than someone with the self-proclaimed humanist conscience of a liberal, by casually calling Detroit a victim of market forces.[5] "Sometimes the losers from economic change are individuals whose skills have become redundant; sometimes they are companies serving a market niche that no longer exists; and sometimes they are whole cities that lose their place in the economic ecosystem," wrote Krugman, forgetting Greece in his laundry list of innocent victims of these mysterious market forces.[5] Krugman concluded his paragraph with: "Decline happens," as if this were a physical phenomenon, like gravity or magnetism. Like most of the leading international economists, Krugman had adamantly supported NAFTA and the WTO. Detroit and Greece are not some sort of collateral damage of market forces, as suggested by Krugman's decline happens scenario. Detroit was demolished wholesale by NAFTA, and Greece was enticed to borrow money to join the euro zone.

The IMF itself has conceded that the policies it had implemented for Greece had resulted in notable failures. It failed to push for an immediate restructuring of Greece's debt, but it did not prevent money owed by the country before 2010 to private-sector creditors from being fully repaid at the onset of the fiscal crisis. Greece's overall debt level remained the same, except it was now owed to the euro-zone taxpayers and the IMF, instead of banks and hedge funds. Both Greece and Detroit were targets of a predatory capitalism that had sought to downgrade and then shut down all the public sectors of an economy.

The market forces are not physical phenomena; they are the hyenas and vultures from Wall Street who rip apart and then feed on the carcasses of a city or country. Decline does not just happen; it is engineered by the corporate entities of global disaster capitalism to maximize profit without regard for human costs. It is ultimately up to us, for the common good of humankind, to put wrenches into the well-oiled wheels of this global corporate machine that is breaking our backs by grinding and crushing our accomplishments of more than 250 years, to return us to the servitude of feudalism.

20

The Inspiration of Tunisia

IN A DRAMATIC TURN of events, on January 14, 2011, Tunisian auto-cratic President Ben Ali panicked and fled to Saudi Arabia after being forced out of office by the will of the Tunisian people.[6] The popular uprising had started in mid-December 2010, originally triggered by rising food prices and food shortages. It quickly expanded to become more about social justice, freedom of expression and denouncements of the corruption of Ben Ali's regime. A catalyst in unleashing the expansion of the wave of protests, which became known as the Jasmine Revolution, was the case of 26-year-old Mohammed Bouazizi, who set himself on fire on January 4, 2011, after police humiliated him and prevented him from making his living as a street vendor of fruits and vegetables.[6] He later died from his burns.

Ben Ali's departure closely followed the dissolution of his own government, the declaration of a state of national emergency, and his call to hold elections in six months. Tunisia's opposition parties, legal and banned, had called on him to resign. "We demand that Ben Ali go and a provisional government be set up and put in charge of organizing free elections in six months," the parties said, in a joint declaration during a press conference held in France. Ben Ali had been in office for 23 years. After his resignation, Prime Minister Mohammed Ghannouchi announced that he would take over as the interim leader. Weeks of clashes between protestors and police had left at least 66 people dead although, during the final two days before his departure, Ben Ali said he had ordered police not to fire live rounds at demonstrators.

Unlike the police, the army had sided with the protestors against Ben Ali's own security apparatus. Ali Seriati, Ben Ali's security chief and a key figure behind the authoritarian regime, was arrested for plotting against the new leadership that emerged after Ben Ali's departure. Credible reports confirmed that Seriati's security forces had staged looting and violence in the aftermath of Ben Ali's resignation, to try to create conditions favorable for Ben Ali's return to power. On January 24, 2011, General Rachid Ammar, who had refused to back the crackdown on protesters, vowed to protect the revolution as the transition government went through a reshuffle to exclude elements of Ben Ali's regime. General Ammar, who was hugely popular for his role in ousting Ben Ali, said that the Tunisian army would act as guarantor of the revolution. "Our revolution, your revolution, the revolution of the young risks being lost. There are forces that are calling for a void, a power vacuum," General Ammar told a cheering crowd, speaking through a megaphone.[7] Two days before, thousands had marched to the capital, Tunis, in what they called a caravan of liberation. The protesters wanted anybody who had been affiliated with Ben Ali's regime out of the government. "You stole the wealth of the country, but you are not going to steal the revolution," they chanted.

The Jasmine Revolution had set an historical precedent that was making all the dictators in the region very uneasy. It was the first popular uprising to succeed in removing a president in the Arab world. It was also a secular movement, ironically inspired by the principles of Liberty, Equality and Fraternity of the revolution of the former colonial power, France. In Algeria, Egypt, Jordan, Morocco, Syria, Yemen, Libya and even the Emirates and Saudi Arabia, the Arab autocratic rulers had a new fear: a popular uprising from their own respective oppressed populations inspired by Tunisia's Jasmine Revolution. In Algeria, several cities, including the capital Algiers, experienced riots over unemployment and a sharp rise in food prices. In Yemen, on January 16, 2011, thousands of protesters marched in the capital Sanaa, in solidarity with Tunisians, calling on Arabs to "wage a revolution against their scared and deceitful leaders." In Egypt, people voiced similar grievances as Tunisians in terms of economic hardship, corruption, social injustice, and the lack of free speech. The iron-fist regime of Mubarak had kept a lid on social progress and freedom for decades with an emergency law that had stayed in place for 30 years while half of Egypt's 80 million people became reduced to living in extreme poverty. They organized their first protests on January 25 in Cairo and Alexandria.

Gaddafi, in Libya, was one of the only Arab leaders to voice his support officially for Ben Ali. "The bloodshed in Tunisia was for nothing, and Ben

Ali is still the legitimate president," said the autocrat Gaddafi in a speech on state-controlled TV the day after Ben Ali's departure.[8] In Syria, the daily *Al-Watan* said that the events in Tunisia were "a lesson that no Arab regime should ignore."[9] According to an editorial in the Syrian daily, "Arab leaders on sale to the West should learn from the Tunisian lesson. They should make decisions according to what is favorable to the interest of the Arab people."[9] In Israel, PM Netanyahu said: "The region in which we live is an unstable region. Everybody can see that today. There can be changes in government that we do not foresee today but will take place tomorrow."[9]

Nobody in Israel, the US and Europe had foreseen these revolts in the Middle East, which had been in the making for decades. Following a Cold-War logic, the US had supported autocratic governments in the region, providing they were anti-communist and would not challenge US power or threaten Israel. This problematic and shortsighted policy had made the US support Islamist fundamentalists in Egypt with the Muslim Brotherhood, as well as in Afghanistan with the mujahideen. They were considered to be natural allies against the so-called spread of communism, and the CIA had financed both in the context of a proxy war against the Soviet Union. After 2001 however, the new scarecrow used to justify US imperialist policies became the supposed spread of radical Islam. The events in the Middle East in early 2011 proved once again that Washington policymakers were a couple of trains behind historical trends. What appeared to be a domino effect in the Middle East had nothing to do with radical Islam but everything to do with oppressed people taking their destinies into their own hands. The growing unity of the Arab street, across national boundaries, was not in the name of religious fundamentalism but for the sake of real democracy. The Western geopolitical calculation in favor of a so-called stability, at the expense of any real democratic change, had backfired.

In the two years before 2011, there had been a few instances during which the hope for change and reforms was squashed before it could blossom, including the Green movement in Iran, the Red Shirts in Thailand, and the social unrest in Greece in the aftermath of the global financial crisis. Political activists had tried to keep these movements alive with social media but, on the whole, had failed to make them gel. Other key ingredients for the success of Tunisia, in addition to Bouazizi's sacrifice, were probably the sacrifices that Bradley Manning and Julian Assange had made to expose the conduct of the US and its client states. Despite Manning and Assange's persecution, *WikiLeaks* had made available to the public an astronomical amount of information that governments had until then kept secret. It was from the leaked US State Department cables, for example, that Tunisians discovered that Ben Ali had been hosting lavish dinners at one of his palaces, where fancy French ice cream was served after being shipped, by air from Saint Tropez, on one of Ben Ali's private jets.[10]

Following Mohammed Bouazizi's example in Tunisia, within a week of his death, several men in the Middle East embraced self-immolation as the ultimate form of political protest. In Algeria, during the second week of 2011, there were at least four attempted public suicides using the same method as the one that had been used by Bouazizi, all of them in protest over unemployment, food prices and scarcity of housing. On January 17, a man set himself on fire outside Egypt's parliament, and another one torched himself in front of Mauritania's presidential palace in an apparent replay of the self-immolation. All these men had witnessed the success of the Tunisian revolution; they were obviously willing to become martyrs on behalf of their own people, and to illustrate graphically their people's suffering and desperation.[11]

It was somewhat reductive to view these men merely as Bouazizi copycats. These actions were disturbing but bigger and deeper than that. They were a political act. By torching themselves, these men had tried to make Tunisia's Jasmine Revolution spread like wildfire through the region, and to act as symbols of their people's common misery. In other words, their martyrdom was not an act of personal desperation like most suicides but had a collective value in the desire to become a catalyst for change. While suicide is one of the most despicable forms of political action, whatever the reasons may be when suicide bombers commit it, the motivation and moral predicament of public suicide by self-immolation belong to a different realm. Even though it is a violent act, it is not violence directed at others, and it can have peaceful implications for the common good.

Two historic examples during the Vietnam War should be discussed here, to help understand the paradox of self-immolation in the context of a reflection on the possible justification and effectiveness of such extreme acts. One of these episodes happened in Vietnam and the other in the US. On June 11, 1963 in Saigon, a Buddhist monk, Thich Quang Duc immolated himself in the middle of a busy intersection. A crowd of Buddhist monks watched as the 73-year-old lit a match, and in a few moments, burned to death while he remained seated perfectly still in the lotus position.[12] "Flames were coming from a human being; his body was slowly withering and shriveling up, his head blackening and charring. In the air was the smell of burning flesh; human beings burn surprisingly quickly. As he burned, he never moved a muscle, never uttered a sound," wrote an emotional David Halberstam who was filing daily reports for the *New York Times* from Vietnam.[12] The event and Malcom Brown's photographs of it for *AP* had a deep impact on the global consciousness and were a catalyst in changing the course of the war.[12] This action in Vietnam was followed a couple of years later by the November 2, 1965 suicide of Norman Morrison, a Quaker and anti-war activist.[13] Morrison doused himself with kerosene and set himself on fire in front of the Pentagon, just below Secretary of Defense McNamara's office. The public suicide was done as a tribute to the innocent men, women and children of Vietnam, and to protest the war. Norman Morrison's self-immolation shocked McNamara and the US, and it had a significant role in turning public opinion against the war.[13]

Tunisia's Jasmine revolution was a geopolitical seismic wave that challenged the global status quo and still reverberates throughout North Africa and the Middle East. Despite differences between the countries where the larger uprising called the Arab Spring had spread, the common and universal threads were remarkable. In all cases, it was about social justice, freedom of speech, and the establishment of democracies where people would have a voice. The problems and the aspirations of the Arabs in 2011 were similar to what people were tackling everywhere else. In fall 2011, it was the turn of Europeans to protest the financial crisis that gripped such countries as Greece, Spain, Ireland and Portugal. In the UK, a growing number of people viewed the austerity measures as a disaster in the making. The global system of governance, manipulated by a transnational global elite, was unjust, amoral, idiotic, and unsustainable. There would be setbacks, but the debates about its replacement had begun.

Can We Invent a World Based on Morals, Ethics and Empathy?

In the coming decades, the global food crisis will continue to worsen. Worldwide, there are some major systemic problems on both sides of the food scarcity equation: supply and demand. On the demand side, the main factors responsible for driving up food prices are a population explosion, the use of crops for fuel, and runaway speculation on commodities and land by global financial markets. On the supply side, the loss of cropland to non-farming activities, diversion of water to cities, and climate change, with its heat waves and floods, are taking a dramatic toll on much of world's capacity to produce more food. What global capitalism, both at the level of governments and of mega-corporations, would have to do for its own survival, would be to redefine security, and shift spending from military and policing purposes to investments in solutions to tackle the emergency of overpopulation, climate change, and water scarcity. The world is on an unsustainable path that will surely lead to a major confrontation between the people and the national and transnational ruling elites.

There was nothing revolutionary about the industrial revolution. The industrial Leviathan has enslaved workers and attacked the planet's ecosystems. If communism died in the late 1980s with the collapse of the Soviet Union, capitalism is not faring much better and is on life support. The current world order of corporate imperialism is an extreme version of capitalism. It has no national boundaries, and it can engage in predatory practices worldwide with complete disregard for local populations and no legal consequences. Globalization has become a fact of our daily life. Decisions made in the US, China or Europe by governments or corporations, affect what we eat, the energy we use, what we buy, and have an impact on how we are kept informed of world events. This is, of course, considering that a large fraction of news outlets are controlled by diversified mega-corporations with either an economic or a political agenda at stake. Globalization has made capitalism into a destructive machine of wealth concentration without concern for the worker bees that produce the wealth, and for the damage this creates by polluting our environment and draining our resources. To a US businessman, it does not matter if his hometown experiences double-digit unemployment, if he can find a cheaper way to fabricate a product in China or India. Workers in China and India are paid meager wages, which barely allow them to survive but allow Chinese, Indian and US businessmen to become very wealthy. Some multinational corporations operate like states. They even hire their own private armies. Oil companies such as Shell do it in Nigeria. It is alleged that the US fruit giant Dole hired ex-right-wing militia to threaten or kill union organizers in Central America.

In the US-led corporate world order, the US military-industrial complex provides the technology and muscle to control key resources, while corporations share of the spoils of wars. Wars and prisons are for profit, and good education and decent health care are for the rich. This world order operates as a wealth and power concentrator for the few. It is the case for the so-called masters of the universe on Wall Street, and it was so for Mubarak in Egypt. Gaddafi and Berlusconi, for example, were similar in substance if not style: both men were in love with power and wanted to hold on to it at any cost. Globalization profits from disasters, creates disasters, and then profits again from the supposed reconstruction that never takes place. Furthermore, the current world order is a disaster in itself for not addressing the urgent global issues of climate change, overpopulation and hunger. It is a world where the rules are dictated by commerce and profit, not by ethics and moral principles.

Every year, the transnational elite meets in Davos, Switzerland to discuss the global economy. During the turmoil in 2011, the thematic for this meeting was: "Shared Norms for the New Reality."[14] The global elite presumably had to ponder on "the fact that we live in a world that is becoming increasingly complex and interconnected, but also experiencing an erosion of common values and principles." It was ironic and insulting for the organizers to mention an "erosion of common values and principles" when they clearly belonged to the very small group of people who were plundering the world. Only profit matters for global disaster capitalism, not conscience or even real analytical abilities. Billionaire Warren Buffett has said: "Yes, there is a class warfare, all right. But it is my class, the rich class, that is making war, and we are winning."[15] Mr. Buffett was right, the rich and super-rich like himself are making war on the middle class and the poor. The class warfare mentioned by Buffett is not limited to the US; it is a global phenomenon. Similar concentrations of wealth can be seen in Russia, China, India, Brazil, South America, and Europe.

The global community has reached an impasse. Our mode of development is vertical, and the levers of power are concentrated at a rarefied top where outsiders are not welcome. Corporations and the politicians in bed with them could care less about real problems such as climate change, food shortage, inequality and overpopulation. The entire system is rigged for maximum profit at the top of the food chain. For most countries, the political process is locked under the tight control of a small group of individuals. It is a vicious cycle where politicians have to be at the mercy of corporate interests in order to get elected, and once elected they have to pay back the favors by protecting the interests of their donors. In all these sordid backroom deals, what is forgotten is the interest of the people whom these politicians are supposed to represent. Some people may think that the global elite has some sort of grandiose master plan. In fact, the only plan is profit, and not even for the long term. It is time to look into horizontal social configurations, where power and money do not get concentrated into so few hands. It is time to rethink the basic principles of a just, global, and sustainable governance and ask if, for example, it is necessary to be ruled by a king substitute in the person of a president or prime minister.

Ancient Chinese culture, inspired by Confucius, placed at the core of its value system the notion of balance and harmony. A vicious cycle has engulfed our global reality: wars, food crisis, financial crisis, natural and man-made disasters. The inexorable cycle of death and destruction is a fast-spreading global disease, and no one is immune from it. The storms have become tornadoes or hurricanes that aim straight at us and, to make it into the headlines, the waves must be killer tsunamis. It cannot be contested by anyone that we live in a period of deep turmoil, but few propose solutions that are not purely cosmetic and merely peripheral to the core issues. Most people put the entire blame for the global crisis on corporations or governments, which, as noted above, could be called a global system of governance and production, or exploitation of people and resources. First of all, we could have resisted this global system a long time ago. Secondly and most importantly, most of us carry within ourselves the psychological attributes we so vehemently reject in the global social context: character traits such as greed, quest for power, narcissism and a lack of empathy.

Years ago, the US was called the heart of the beast, in Marxist circles, and identified as being the center of capitalism. This colorful Marxist imagery does not portray today's reality at all. Capitalism does not have a conscience, even less a heart. It has become a hydra, a giant octopus, with no heart, many twisted brains and countless tentacles reaching across the planet. It is not centered in the US alone, and it would be ludicrous to think that the capitalist beast can be killed by a shot in the heart. All the tentacles chocking us must be severed, and then the hydra must be dragged ashore to die in the bright sunlight and away from the sea of profit where it has dwelled for decades. And even if this giant capitalist squid dies, unless we change our own psychological makeup at an individual level, another hydra will be born soon thereafter from the seeds of our inhumanity, amorality, unethical behavior and deeply-rooted conscious or unconscious selfishness. The world is broken, and some of us talk about the need for a global revolution, but we will never make lasting progress in a global consciousness where brutality, selfishness, corruption and amorality are the driving forces of social success. We can only challenge the order of this ruthless, amoral, dog-eat-dog mentality that is our global reality by having a revolution within ourselves to change our own psychology. To mend the world, we must understand what should be changed within ourselves to make us better humans.

21

Toward a Global Revolution

PHILOSOPHER THOMAS KUHN gave the word paradigm its modern definition, in reference to the principles and practices that define a scientific discipline at a particular period. In his seminal book, *The Structure of Scientific Revolutions,* Kuhn introduced the notion that most significant scientific advances are made by quantum leaps, which he called paradigm shifts.[16] These are the vectors of scientific revolutions: the challenges to the former paradigms in the evolution of a scientific discipline.[16] A major example was Albert Einstein's groundbreaking notion of relativity, which radically challenged the simple rules that had been laid down by Newtonian physics. The same can be said about the communication revolution of the information super-highway, which happened about 25 years ago. A paradigm shift of this magnitude is a colossal thinking-outside-the-box process and a leap forward into a new reality.

The greatest barrier to a paradigm shift is the incredible inertia of paradigm paralysis, which may be defined as the inability or refusal to see beyond the current models of thinking. There are countless examples of paradigm paralysis in the history of mankind. In Europe, up until the 17th century, physicians used to draw substantial volumes of blood from their patients to purify their bodies from some imaginary miasma. This would weaken the patients and hasten their death. The first physicians to challenge this absurdity were banned from the profession. A better-known example of paradigm paralysis is the rejection of Galileo's theory of a heliocentric universe, in which the earth and other planets revolve around the sun. This revolutionized the field of astronomy.

If paradigm shifts are mega-phenomena of thinking outside the box, then paradigm paralyses are the enemies of progress and may be regarded as the sclerosis of thinking inside the box. In today's world of social turmoil, fast-pace change, globalization, communication revolution, overpopulation, shrinking resources and growing ecological threats, paradigms are double-edged swords. On one hand, they provide a structure and the illusion of permanence, which is a false sense of security. On the other hand, the current paradigms often fall into the category of paradigm paralysis, and they prevent us from tackling challenges and major problems to keep life sustainable on this planet for future generations. In other words we need to step, individually and collectively, out of the illusion box of established thought paradigms and jump courageously into the uncharted reality that unfolds with significant paradigm shifts.

Thomas Kuhn was on the fence about applying his concept of paradigm shifts to revolutions in fields such as sociology, history, and psychology. In retrospect, Kuhn's ambiguity might have been shortsighted. Just like science, history can move at an incredibly brisk pace during social paradigm shifts. It was the case in France during the 1789 revolution, and again in Russia in 1917. Today, there are countless indications that we are going through a major global paradigm shift. The list of symptoms is extensive. People worldwide are anxious even about their immediate tomorrow. The global system of governance is broken or in an advanced state of decay. Our global laissez faire and the lack of vision to address critical issues have already produced catastrophic consequences.

In 2013 alone, Pakistan had its worst floods on record, Russia had much of its forests and wheat crop destroyed by fire, and Somalia faced a killer drought. Within two generations, the rise of sea levels will make coastal areas uninhabitable for 600 million people; simultaneously, other areas including large sections of North America's southwest, such as Arizona and Nevada, could become uninhabitable from a lack of water. Nevertheless, climate change is still not treated as a global priority. If we had a halfway intelligent system of governance, the foremost questions would be: How can we slow down climate change? How are we going to feed all these people? Will there be major migrations because of climate change and overpopulation and how can we prepare for this?

Inspired by the Arab Spring, American radicals started a US Day of Rage movement in August 2011. This was quickly co-opted and transformed into the Occupy movement, which was inaugurated in New York on September 17, 2011. By its first-year anniversary, the celebration of Occupy had become a sentimental fare that illustrated not only the movement's originally good intentions but also its enormous limitations. In

New York, the police pushed the Occupiers around without much resistance; 200 of them got handcuffed in plastic ties and briefly arrested as they applied, above all, their golden rule of peaceful non-violent protest. While the strategy of turning and giving the other cheek is a cornerstone of the Christian faith, it is not exactly a useful tool for revolutions. Jesus' rejection of an eye for an eye to offer the other cheek indicated a submission to oppressors. Such calls to submit to total non-violence become in fact calls for complete non-resistance, and they facilitate aggressions from police states that are bent on using force. Jesus' non-violent message was made powerful by his self-sacrifice in the extremely violent act of the crucifixion, and this is reminiscent of the self-immolation of Bouazizi, the modest street vendor who lit up the torch for the Arab Spring with his very person. Martyrdom is what gave Christianity the political power with which it eventually sapped the Roman Empire.

The beauty of Occupy was its grassroots birth and horizontal structure. The problems began when intellectuals and pundits, from the comfort of their respective ivory towers, started telling the supposed base what to think. Even though the people in this so-called radical-left intelligentsia had not started the global movement, some quickly pretended they did, for the sake of their over-inflated egos and, more prosaically, to garner book sales and TV appearances. Considering everybody knows who they are, why not name the usual suspects? They are, in no particular order, Noam Chomsky, Naomi Klein and, last but not least, Chris Hedges. Hedges, in particular, quickly made it his business to tell the Occupiers what to do and think. Occupy was a patchwork of different ideologies, from peace activists to neo-Marxists and anarchists. In my view, Hedges' actions, including his label of the Black Bloc anarchists as the cancer of Occupy, did the bidding of the Obama administration: it drove a wedge in the movement and completely emasculated it in North America.[17]

Some have decided to re-brand the movement. It is Los Indignados in Spain, and Les Indignés in France, but the branding is still weak, a bit scared. To occupy public places or to be indignant is unlikely to move the dial. Those who want a much-needed global revolution must crank up the volume and call themselves by what they have to be: revolutionaries. In response to the violent demonstrations in the Middle East in fall 2012 against the US, Israel and the West, US Secretary of State Hillary Clinton said: "The Arab Revolutions did not trade the tyranny of dictators for the tyranny of the mob."[18] She neglected to mention that the dictators in question were US clients, and that some of the so-called revolutions were military interventions by the US and NATO. By then, many Arabs were mad as hell that the West, with the help of Saudi Arabia, had stolen their revolution. Afghans and Pakistanis were mad about being invaded, exploited and killed by American drones. A healthy dose of anger and rage was also propelling Greeks and Spaniards to take over their streets in protest against the slavery imposed on them by the IMF and the global banking system through austerity policies. General strikes turned violent in Greece on September 26, 2012 because, when the police attacked the demonstrators with tear gas, they fought back with stones and Molotov cocktails.

Like all Americans, Hillary Clinton was taught that the US grew out of a revolution. In what Americans call their revolution, slavery continued, and the land and slave owners stayed in power, leaving the socioeconomic power structure unchanged. Instead of a revolution, the former British colony that became the US had a successful colonial war, with critical help from France, against the British Empire. Absolutely no social change or wealth and power redistribution occurred in the process. None. Because of this lack of revolutionary experience, it is unlikely that a global revolution could ever start in the US. A key ingredient in this is a terror of the police state's repression apparatus. I would say that, as opposed to the Occupiers' lofty non-violent credos, this paralytic fear is what kept them from fighting back.

In October 2013, a collaboration of nine groups, called the International Network of Civil Liberties Organizations, published a report that presented a series of alarming case studies of the criminalization of political and social dissent around the world.[19] The report exposed disturbing governmental policies and law enforcement practices where the fundamental democratic right to protest publicly was viewed as a threat that required a brutal police response. Ironically, the name of the report, *Take Back the Streets,* had come from an order from Toronto's police commander to his force in June 2010, when more than 100,000 Canadians took to the street to protest the G20 summit. Despite the fact that this protest was peaceful, within 36 hours, more than 1,000 people, protesters and journalists alike, were arrested and detained.

The nine case studies covered nine countries: Argentina, Canada, Egypt, Israel and the Occupied Territories, Kenya, Hungary, South Africa, the UK, and the US.[19] All the cases reflected instances of repression of democratic rights through the legal system, criminalization of leaders, and excessive use of force by police that resulted in injuries and deaths. "These cases collectively illustrate the use of lethal and deadly force in response to largely peaceful gatherings seeking to express social and political viewpoints," said the report. The deaths and injuries were mostly caused by firearms with live ammunition: for example, against protesters in Egypt; but some were also caused by so-called non-lethal weapons such as tear gas or rubber bullets fired directly into crowds.

In a case involving police brutality in Puerto Rico, the ACLU mentioned violent beatings and low-flying helicopters that sprayed toxic chemicals over crowds of protesters.[19] In the US, only the NYPD is larger than the Puerto Rico Police Department (PRPD). The PRPD regularly applies excessive force with pepper spray, tear gas, rubber bullets, stinger rounds, sting-ball grenades, high-power Taser guns, and batons. According to the ACLU, police in Puerto Rico have routinely used 36-inch batons in riot control to jab, strike and beat protesters.

In the Israeli Occupied Territories of the West Bank, the Association for Civil Rights in Israel documented the persecution and arrest of leaders and organizers, such as Bassem Tamimi who was jailed by Israel for more than 13 months for organizing peaceful protests. "These cases demonstrate how the justice system not only frequently fails to provide accountability for the illegal acts committed by law enforcement, but can also, at times, act as a repressive force towards demonstrators and social organizations," said the report.[19] In Egypt, in November 2011, the police shot thousands of gas canisters directly into the crowds that caused many deaths by asphyxiation in addition to the deaths by live ammunition. In one instance, Egyptian police fired numerous gas canisters into a building where the protesters had found refuge, then proceeded to seal the building.[19]

The report pointed to 9/11 as being the turning point that allowed governments to crack down on social dissent using the subterfuge of broad anti-terrorist laws. There are alarming signs, perfectly illustrated by these nine case studies, that these legal structures concocted by most governments worldwide are, in effect, tools of repression. Law-enforcement actions such as arrests, random searches, detentions without probable cause or right to a trial, have been redirected to suppress peaceful political activities. Furthermore, police forces are getting consolidated into militarized extrajudicial bodies. In Europe, police organizations are being gathered into multinational military structures like the European Gendarmerie Force (EuroGenFor, or EGF).[20] Global military organizations like the so-called UN peacekeepers are tasked with repressive policing when they come back home from military occupations overseas, habituated to urban warfare. Brazil's favelas, for example, suffered a pacification process prior to the 2014 World Cup, administered in large part by former UN troops that had been recalled from Haiti.[21] These soldiers also wind up populating private mercenary forces.

The erosion of basic democratic rights, like dissent and protest, is obvious and global. Despair is not an option, global solidarity is. The only hope to stop the final rise of an Orwellian world, under the boots of a global police state, is for all people to unite in a fight to take back the streets and government from the police. Some will pay a heavy price, but the streets must be reclaimed at any cost and without fear. Historically troubled times, such as the rise of fascism in Europe during the 1930s, have proven that people must remain watchful about basic human rights being swept away by tyranny. Globalization of policing must be countered by global vigilance about state-sanctioned abuses and a massive and coordinated globalization of revolt.

If one considers any successful real revolution in history, some form of violence has always been present. The mechanics and social forces that drive countries to revolution have many things in common. If you take either the French, Haitian, Russian or Cuban revolutions, they only became successful when the misery of most people reached a point of no return. In Spain more than 25 percent of people are unemployed, and it is getting worse every day. What magical percentage of unemployment will drive Los Indignados to storm their parliament and get rid of the government? This factor of misery reaching critical mass applies also to Greece, Egypt, Pakistan, etc. To become united in a global revolution, the 99 percent worldwide must first overthrow fear. Revolutions have villains, heroes, martyrs, traitors and footnotes. They are very much like omelets: eggs must be broken to make them.

Despite humanity's considerable leaps in science and technology in the past 200 years, the collective consciousness of humankind appears to have stood still or even, in many instances, to have regressed to a stage of brutality and irrationality. This regression of the collective psyche has expressed itself by a revival of fundamentalist non-inclusive monotheist religions and a quest for providential men. This journey back to the darkness of magical thinking, ignorance and permanent conflict would have puzzled the Enlightenment philosophers.

Too many believe that some ideological constructs and special men can save them from their condition. Sometimes for the better, but usually for the worse, a few individuals have changed history, but providence did not bring them forth like a stroke from a magic wand. They grew in the right place and time to serve as the catalysts in complex chain reactions that were largely beyond their control. The vectors of significant historical change belong to two different, rarely intersecting categories: people of ideas and people of action. Those few who can combine ideas with actions become the historical catalysts. The Enlightenment thinkers, Voltaire, Rousseau, Diderot and Montesquieu provided the intellectual foundation for the 1789 French Revolution, but it was the men of ideas put into action such as Danton, Mirabeau, Saint-Just, and Robespierre who rose to the occasion and became the leaders in the turmoil of the revolutionary process. The revolution's main driving force was the opposition of rationality and social justice to the notion of a French king being picked by divine providence. The psychotic megalomania of Robespierre almost jeopardized the entire process. The Girondins versus Jacobins infighting nearly dealt a deadly blow to the revolution. Drunk from his own power, Robespierre saw himself as a providential man and acted accordingly during the fratricidal period called La Terreur.

If some ideas and people may be considered vectors of progress, other ideologies and leaders can also be catalysts for disaster. Charismatic leaders and their permanent quest for power, combined with the collective hypnosis they can induce, usually have dire consequences. Very few men who became historical catalysts have managed to stay grounded in reality and to keep in mind that sound leadership can only have a positive and lasting impact if it is for the greater good. The stratospheric rise of General Napoleon Bonaparte was due, not only to his military genius but also his ability to bring order from the chaos of the French Revolution. He quickly established himself as the sword to protect the new republic, a providential man with the extraordinary charisma to lead men and women on and off the battlefield. If Bonaparte started his ascent as a pragmatic leader, with his feet firmly on the ground, his trajectory took a dramatic wrong turn when he betrayed the revolutionary principles that had brought him to power and crowned himself emperor on December 2, 1804. On that fateful day, which was supposed to celebrate his apogee, Napoleon became a believer of his own mythology. Paradoxically, this marked the beginning of the end of the Napoleonic adventures. Sword and protector of the great revolution no more, Napoleon had become a despot like Rome's Julius Caesar.

Again and again, seemingly reasonable people become hypnotized by individuals like Napoleon and come to regard them as godlike father figures. The key to trigger this collective hypnosis is a crafting of myths that are often based on the pretense of having a privileged connection to the truth or having an intimate knowledge of the people's needs. Manipulation by myths allows leaders to become the pseudo-omniscient shepherds of powerless men. Adolf Hitler, Joseph Stalin and, more recently, Pol Pot, wound up believing their own myths and playing god in the delusional scenarios of their paranoia. Added to the manipulation of myths is mass seduction: a prerequisite for the providential men. "Power is the ultimate aphrodisiac," said Henry Kissinger. The fake providential men and worst mass murderers of the 20th century, including Hitler and Stalin, have successfully staged this collective seduction. By contrast, real leaders such as Haiti's Toussaint L'Ouverture, India's Mohandas Gandhi, Cuba's Fidel Castro, Vietnam's Ho Chi Minh, China's Mao Zedong and France's Charles De Gaulle have used the undeniable connection between power and personal charisma for the greater good. These leaders were not only unquestionable historical catalysts, but also firmly anchored in reality. Their motivations and vision were altruistic in essence, and they were ultimately willing to yield power.

In our days, the genuine leaders, i.e. the charismatic historical catalysts, are an endangered species. The interchangeable technocrats of capitalism have displaced them. Since the rise of corporatism, money has become a deity for a diffuse leadership in a godless and faceless system, and we have witnessed the revival of a brutal religious fundamentalism unseen in centuries. The murderous religious fervor tearing apart the Middle East today is a reaction to the lack of morality and brutality of the hyper-capitalist system. This brand of imperialism does not build anything; it destroys so as to loot. It does not require an emperor but, rather, some temporary and nominal chairman of the board. The foreign legions of ISIS and other Islamists were seeded in Syria, Libya, and Iraq by the global corporate empire in the hope to destroy these countries' statehood. The revival of the 600-year old secular conflict between Sunnis and Shiites might have been, at first, a plan conceived by the board members of Global Empire Inc. to divide and conquer Islam in a fratricidal all-out war. ISIS has, however, acquired considerable momentum and its own imperialist folly: the Caliphate of the Islamic State. Pseudo-providential men and want-to-be messiahs, on Sunni as well as Shiite sides, are persuading their adoring foot soldiers that they speak and act in the name of Allah and will carve, in blood, a name for themselves. It hardly matters whether the inception of ISIS was stupid or Machiavellian; it has run amok, and the mercenaries of the corporate empire will likely end up in the crosshairs of assorted jihadists. The anachronism of religious fundamentalism's revival confirms yet again that history can suffer collective regressions.

The ideologies of the 19th century, based almost solely on the economic realities of the industrial revolution, have become irrelevant. After the collapse of the Soviet Union, it is the turn of global capitalist neoliberalism to fall. There have been setbacks, but this is expected. Many times in history, social paradigm shifts have taken a wrong turn. This was the case during the French Revolution when the madness of Robespierre turned the streets of Paris into rivers of blood. The same applies to Joseph Stalin's murderous spree after he took over the apparatus of power in the aftermath of Russia's Communist Revolution. Nevertheless, France and Russia have grown into republics that kings or czars will never again rule. The setbacks to the French and Russian revolutions were due to a deep-rooted psychological problem: for humans, a latent desire for the unchallenged power of a benevolent father figure is too often transferred to authoritarian regimes. This was the psychological makeup of France and Russia during the centuries when absolute monarchs ruled. As long as our infantile collective psyche continues to seek refuge in magical thinking, which is a major component of religions, or to long for father figures, which is the fault of our lengthy childhood, we will not enjoy the peace that a new age of reason could bring. A new Enlightenment will only be possible if we toss magical thinking into the dustbin of history and swear off the habit of turning to religion or self-proclaimed providential men to save us from ourselves. If power truly belonged to the people, it would not have to be so regularly reclaimed. A lasting global paradigm shift must do nothing less than psychologically and socially reconstruct us.

Notes

Part I. Fair Is Foul

1. Rousseau, Jean-Jacques, *The Social Contract*. Trans. Maurice Cranston. Penguin Books, London (1968).
2. Ayres, Alex, ed. *The Wit and Wisdom of Mark Twain: A Book of Quotations*. Meridian, New York (1989).
3. Zinn, Howard, *Writings on Disobedience and Democracy*. Seven Stories Press, New York (1997).
4. "Foreign-connected PACS, election cycle 2010," *opensecrets.org*
5. Moyers, Bill. "Common Cause anniversary, October 6, 2010." Moyers & Company speeches, 6 October 2010.
6. Stein Ben. "In class warfare, guess which class is winning." *The New York Times*, 26 November 2006.
7. Stevens, J. "Opinion. Supreme Court of the United States, Citizens United, Appellant V. Federal Election Commission." Cornell University Law School, Legal Information Institute, 21 January 2010.
8. "Supreme Court decision creates political crisis." Common Cause press release, 21 January 2010.
9. "Letter to the Department of Justice re: conflicts of interest in the Citizens United case." Common Cause press release, 19 January 2011.
10. "What else haven't they told us?" Common Cause press release, 21 January 2011.
11. Obama, Barack. "Remarks by the President in state of union address." White House press release, 27 January 2010.
12. "Obama's 2010 'shellacking' is like Bush's 2006 'thumping.'" *CBS News*, 3 November 2010.
13. Jones, Jeffrey, M. "Obama approval rallies six points to 52% after bin Laden death." *Gallup*, 5 May 2011.
14. Newport, Frank. "Congress approval at 17% in June," *Gallup*, 11 June 2012.
15. Vidal, Gore. "State of the union, 2004" *The Collected Essays of Gore Vidal*. Ed. Jay Parini. Vintage, New York (2008).
16. Lewis, Sinclair. *It Can't Happen Here*. New American Library, New York (2005).
17. Becker, Jo and Shane, Scott. "Secret 'kill list' proves a test of Obama's principles and will." *The New York Times*, 29 May 2012.

18. King, Martin Luther Jr. "Letter from Birmingham jail." *Why We Can't Wait.* Beacon Press, Boston (1964).

19. King, Martin Luther Jr. "Beyond Vietnam — A time to break the silence." American Rhetoric Only Speech Tank, 4 April 1967.

20. Bricmont, Jean. *Humanitarian Imperialism: Using Human Rights to Sell War.* Monthly Review Press, New York (2007).

21. Bricmont, Jean. "The case for a non-interventionist foreign policy." *Counterpunch*, 20 February 2012.

22. King, Martin Luther Jr. "I have a dream." American Rhetoric Top 100 Speeches, 28 August 1963.

23. Obama, Barack. "Remarks by the President to the United Nations General Assembly." White House press release, 23 September 2010.

24. Greenwald, Glenn. "Obama argues his assassination program is a 'state secret.'" *Salon,* 25 September 2010.

25. "Opposition to plaintiff's motion for preliminary injunction and memorandum in support of defendants' motion to dismiss." US District Court for the District of Columbia, 25 September 2010.

26. Grimm, Andy and Dizikes, Cynthia. "FBI raids anti-war activists' homes." *Chicago Tribune,* 24 September 2010.

27. Roberts, Paul Craig. "It is now official: the U.S. is a police state." *Antiwar.com,* 25 September 2010.

28. "Executive Order 13567- Periodic review of individuals detained at Guantánamo Bay Naval Station pursuant to the authorization for use of military force." White House press release, 7 March 2011.

29. Finn, Peter and Kornblut, Anne E. "Obama creates indefinite detention system for prisoners at Guantanamo Bay," *The Washington Post,* 8 March 2011.

30. "Administration also announces it will use military commissions for new terrorism cases." ACLU press release, 7 March 2011.

31. Obama, Barack. "Military Commission legislation statement." US Senate, 28 September 2006.

32. Savage, David G. "Constitution applies to detainees, justices say. It's third Supreme Court rebuke of Bush's policy." *Los Angeles Times,* 13 June 2008.

33. Rosenberg, Carol. "Clinton would seek to try 9/11 plotters in established courts." *McClatchy DC,* 17 February 2008.

Part II. Lowest Common Denominator Empire

1. Reagan, Ronald. John Winthrop's 1630 sermon, "a model of Christian charity." 1974.

2. Zinn, Howard. *A People's History of the United States 1492 - Present.* Harper Perennial Modern Classics, New York (2005).

3. "ESEA reauthorization: a blueprint for reform." US Department of Education, 13 March 2010.

4. Pyarelal. *Mahatma Gandhi: The Last Phase. Vol. 2.* Navajivan Publishing House, Ahmedabad (1956).

5. *The Teaching of Buddha: The Buddhist Bible, a Compendium of Many Scriptures Translated from the Japanese.* Federation of all young Buddhist associations of Japan (1934).

6. "U.S. economic confidence improves during Christmas week." *Gallup,* 28 December 2010.

7. Timberlake, Cotton. "U.S. retailers' holiday sales jump 5.5% on apparel." *Bloomberg,* 28 December 2010.

8. "GE investing $500 million in Brazil operations." *AP,* 10 November 2010.

9. AmericanCrossroads.org, accessed on 22 October 2010.

10. Thomma, Steven. "Kennedy to Democrats: keep the faith." *Philly.com,* 12 January 1995.

11. Strentz, Thomas. *Psychological Aspects of Crisis Negotiation.* CRC Press, Boca Raton (2011).

12. Shear, Michael D. "Petraeus quits; evidence of affair was found by F.B.I." *The New York Times,* 9 November 2012.

13. Williams, Matt. "Dominique Strauss-Kahn settles sexual assault case with hotel maid." *The Guardian,* 10 December 2012.

14. Parodi, Emilio. "Berlusconi 'directed' bunga bunga sex parties: court." *Reuters,* 21 November 2013.

15. "Haiti's unconventional new president shows off his moves." *The Telegraph,* 6 April 2011.

16. York, Anthony. "Arnold Schwarzenegger discusses affair in interview." *Los Angeles Times,* 1 October 2012.

17. "Former senator and presidential candidate John Edwards charged for alleged role in scheme to violate federal campaign finance laws." US Department of Justice, 3 June 2011.

18. Lipset, Seymour Martin. *American Exceptionalism: A Double-Edged Sword.* W. W. Norton & Company, New York (1996).

19. Obama, Barack. "Remarks by the President at the United States Military Academy commencement ceremony." White House press release, 28 May 2014.

20. De Tocqueville, Alexis. *Democracy in America. Vol. 1.* Trans. Henry Reeve. Project Gutenberg EBook (2006).

21. "Hurricane Katrina." NOAA National Climatic Data Center, 29 December 2005.

22. "Episode 17." Counterpunch radio, 1 September 2015.

23. "Death toll from Chile earthquake soars." *AFP* via *The Age,* 1 March 2010.

24. "California budget deficit tops $25 billion." *AP* via *CBS Los Angeles,* 10 November 2010.

25. "The 2010 annual homeless assessment report to Congress." US Department of Housing and Urban Development (HUD), Office of Community Planning and Development.

26. "Profile of sheltered homeless veterans for fiscal years 2009 and 2010." National Center for Veterans Analysis and Statistics.

27. "America's youngest outcasts 2010." The National Center on Family Homelessness, December 2011.

28. "World Wealth Report 2010." Capemini, 18 June 2010.
29. "Forbes announces its 32nd annual Forbes 400 ranking of the richest Americans." *Forbes*, 16 September 2013.
30. Chery, Dady. "Humanitarian imperialism: charity for power." *News Junkie Post*, 10 March 2013.
31. Colorni, Ruben Rosenberg. "Bill Gates, big pharma, bogus philanthropy." *News Junkie Post*, 7 June 2013.
32. Shaefer, H. Luke and Edin Kathryn. "Rising extreme poverty in the United States and the response of federal means-tested transfer programs." *National Poverty Center Working Paper Series #13-06*, May 2013.
33. "H.R.2642 - Agricultural Act of 2014 (Enrolled Bill [Final as Passed Both House and Senate] - ENR)" The Library of Congress, 3 January 2014.
34. Obama, Barack. "Remarks by the President at Cairo University, 6-04-09." White House press release, 4 June 2009.
35. Obama, Barack. "Press conference by the President." White House press release, 15 February 2011.
36. "Rebuilding America's defenses: strategy, forces and resources for a new century." Project for the New American Century, September 2000.
37. Truman, Harry. "Unsent draft letter from President Harry S. Truman to Arthur Krock, October 7, 1951. President's secretary's files, Truman papers." Harry S. Truman Library & Museum.
38. "TARP programs." US Department of the Treasury, 14 October 2015.
39. "Ben Bernanke wants to resign." *RT*, 23 October 2012.
40. "Ben Bernanke isn't the problem, the system is the problem." *The Atlantic*, 16 April 2015.
41. "Major foreign holders of treasury securities (in billions of dollars)." US Department of the Treasury, 16 October 2015.
42. Hart, Alexander C. "The case for more federal aid." *New Republic*, 16 February 2011.
43. Lav, Iris J. and McNichol, Elizabeth. "Misunderstandings regarding state debt, pensions, and retiree health costs create unnecessary alarm." Center on Budget and Policy Priorities, 20 January 2011.
44. Obama, Barack. "Remarks by the President in state of the union address." White House press release, 25 January 2011.
45. "Budget for a millennial America." Roosevelt Institute Campus Network, May 2011.
46. Hobson, Jeremy and Bufacchi, Isabella "Italy: 'too big to fail.'" *Marketplace*, 12 July 2011.
47. McMorris-Santoro, Evan. "'We get the sacrifice, they get the wealth': a fired-up Pelosi tears into GOP deficit plan." *Talking Points Memo*, 26 July 2011.

Part III. War Is Peace

1. Grimmett, Richard E. and Kerr, Paul K. "Conventional arms transfers to developing nations, 2004-2011." Congressional Research Service, 24 August 2012.
2. Stone, Chad and Sherman, Arloc. "Income gaps between very rich and everyone else more than tripled in last three decades, new data show." Center on Budget and Policy Priorities, 25 June 2010.
3. "Growth of DoD's budget from 2000 to 2014." Congressional Budget Office, 20 November 2014.
4. Garamone, Jim. "Budget request continues defense reform agenda." US Department of Defense, 1 February 2010.
5. Obama, Barack. "Letter from the President — authorization for the use of United States Armed Forces in connection with the Islamic State of Iraq and the Levant." White House press release, 11 February 2015.
6. "United States Department of Defense fiscal year 2016 budget request." Office of the Under Secretary of Defense (Comptroller) Chief Financial Officer, 20 January 2015.
7. Obama, Barack. "Remarks by the President in address to the nation on the end of combat operations in Iraq." White House press release, 31 August 2010.
8. Druzin, Heath. "As U.S. combat troops exit Iraq, unresolved issues are left behind in a country facing an uncertain future." *Stars and Stripes*, 15 August 2010.
9. McEvers, Kelley. "Iraqi leader reconsiders U.S. troop withdrawal." *NPR*, 28 May 2011.
10. Gatehouse, Gabriel. "Iraq's Moqtada al-Sadr warns Mehdi Army ready to fight." *BBC News*, 6 June 2011.
11. Kelemen, Michele. "Huge embassy keeps U.S. presence in Iraq." *NPR*, 17 December 2011.
12. "Treaty of Maastricht on European Union." EUR-Lex, accessed 1 February 2014.
13. Stuenkel, Oliver. "Looking back: the 2nd BRIC summit in Brasília in 2010." Post-Western World, 15 June 2014.
14. "Full text of Sanya Declaration of the BRICS Leaders Meeting." *GOV.cn*, 14 April 2011.
15. Putin, Vladimir interview with *ITAR-TASS* "BRICS key element of emerging multipolar world — Putin." *RT*, 22 March 2013.
16. "Ukraine crisis: Transcript of leaked Nuland-Pyatt call." *BBC News*, 7 February 2014.
17. Orwell, George. *1984*. New American Library, New York (1961).
18. "Hillary Clinton says Vladimir Putin's Crimea occupation echoes Hitler." *AP* via *The Guardian*, 6 March 2014.
19. Svan, Jennifer H. and Mathis, Adam L. "Lakenheath fighters headed to Baltics to beef up air space patrolling as Ukraine crisis continues." *Stars and Stripes*, 6 March 2014.

20. Chivers, C. J. and Herszenhorn David M. "*NYT*: in Crimea, Russia showcases a rebooted army." *Council on Foreign Relations*, 2 April 2014.

21. O'Dwyer Gerard. "Russia surges in global arms sales." *Defense News*, 31 January 2014.

22. "Russia vetoes UN resolution declaring Crimean referendum illegal." *AP* via *National Post*, 15 March 2014.

23. "5 Year crude oil prices and price charts." InvestmentMine, accessed on 29 January 2015.

24. "Petroleum reserves." Energy.gov, accessed on 29 January 2015.

25. "The Universal Declaration of Human Rights." United Nations, accessed 29 January 2015.

26. Obama, Barack. "Remarks by the President at the acceptance of the Nobel Peace Prize." White House press release, 10 December 2009.

27. Bacevich, Andrew J. *Washington Rules: America's Path to Permanent War*. Metropolitan Books, New York (2011).

Part IV. Engineering Failed States

1. "Toyota suspenderá producción en Venezuela desde el 13 de febrero." *EFE* via *RPP Noticias*, 11 February 2014.

2. Regan, James. "France to send 400 more troops to Central African Republic." *Reuters*, 14 February 2014.

3. Lejeune, Lea. "En Egypte, Hollande assure le service après-vente du Rafale auprès de Sissi." *Le Monde*, 6 August 2015.

4. "L'offensive de charme de François Hollande dans la Silicon Valley." *Le Monde*, 13 February 2014.

5. Kassam, Raheem. "WikiLeaks issues whopping €100,000 bounty for leaked TTIP, TPP documents." *Breitbart*, 11 August 2015.

6. "NATO and Afghanistan launch transition and embark on a long-term partnership." NATO press release, 20 November 2010.

7. Rozoff, Rick. "Global warfare: after NATO summit, U.S. to intensify military drive into Asia." *Global Research Canada*, 18 November 2010.

8. Obama, Barack. "Letter from the President — authorization for the use of United States Armed Forces in connection with the Islamic State of Iraq and the Levant." White House press release, 11 February 2015.

9. "National security strategy." The White House, February 2015.

10. Oliphant, James. "Charlie Wilson dies at 76; hard-partying Texas congressman backed Afghan resistance fighters." *Los Angeles Times*, 10 February 2010.

11. Zaeef, Abdul Salam. *My Life with the Taliban*. Hurst & Company, London (2011).

12. Waldman, Matt. "The sun in the sky: the relationship between Pakistan's ISI and Afghan insurgents." *Crisis States Discussion Papers*, June 2010.

13. Ray, Ashis. "7 of Taliban's top 15 are ISI agents." *The Times of India*, 14 June 2010.

14. Amoore, Miles. "Pakistan puppet masters guide the Taliban killers." *The Sunday Times*, 13 June 2010.

15. Walsh, Declan. "Air strike kills Taliban leader Baitullah Mehsud." *The Guardian,* 7 August 2009.
16. "Obituary: Baitullah Mehsud." *BBC News,* 25 August 2009.
17. Hoh, Matthew interview with Block, Melissa. "A sudden exit driven by an 'irrational' war." *NPR,* 29 October 2009.
18. "Kabul shuts down as Taliban target city centre." *AFP* via *The Telegraph,* 18 January 2010.
19. "Afghan capital Kabul hit by Taliban attack." *BBC News,* 18 January 2010.
20. "Operation Moshtarak in Marjah, Afghanistan." *The Guardian,* 15 February 2010.
21. Georgy, Michael. "NATO Afghanistan airstrike kills 27 civilians." *Reuters,* 22 February 2010.
22. "McChrystal apologizes as airstrike kills dozens in Afghanistan." *CNN,* 23 February 2010.
23. "Taliban warlord Haji Zaman killed in suicide blast that claimed 15 victims" *Daily News,* 22 February 2010.
24. "Indians, Europeans dead in Taliban attack in Kabul." *RFI,* 26 February 2010.
25. "Taliban fighters attack Kabul." *Al Jazeera,* 27 February 2010.
26. "Operation Moshtarak: lessons learned." International Council on Security and Development (ICOS), May 2010.
27. "Terrorist bombing in lower Dir." Embassy of the US in Islamabad, Pakistan, statement, 3 February 2010.
28. "Taliban claim responsibility for suicide bombing: Dir attack kills US troops, schoolgirls." *Dawn,* 4 February 2010.
29. Khan, Ismail. "U.S. Consulate in Pakistan attacked by militants." *The New York Times,* 5 April 2010.
30. "Pakistani public opinion ever more critical of U.S." Pew Research Center, 27 June 2012.
31. Woodward, Bob. *Obama's Wars.* Simon & Schuster, New York (2010).
32. Bowman, Tom. "Woodward book details secret Afghan force." *NPR,* 22 September 2010.
33. Northam, Jackie. "Dissent grows over U.S. presence in Afghanistan." *NPR,* 23 September 2010.
34. Jones, Jeffrey, M. "Obama approval rallies six points to 52% after bin Laden death." *Gallup,* 5 May 2011.
35. Sands, Chris. "In Afghanistan, bin Laden's dream lives on." *Le Monde Diplomatique,* June 2011.
36. Nelson, Dean. "Leon Panetta says US Marines urinating video 'utterly deplorable.'" *The Telegraph,* 12 January 2012.
37. "Dutch cabinet collapses over Afghanistan deployment." *Radio Free Europe,* 20 February 2010.
38. "Afghan reinforcements: Germany pledges 500 extra troops plus big aid increase." *Spiegel,* 26 January 2010.
39. Samuel, Henry. "France will not send any more troops to Afghanistan, says Nicolas Sarkozy." *The Telegraph,* 15 October 2009.

40. Haass, Richard N. "Time to draw down in Afghanistan." *Newsweek,* 18 July 2010.

41. "Afghanistan leak exposes NATO's incoherent civilian casualty policy." Amnesty International, 26 July 2010.

42. Bumiller, Elisabeth. "Pentagon says Afghan forces still need assistance." *The New York Times,* 10 December 2012.

43. Obama, Barack. "Statement by the President on Afghanistan." White House press release, 15 October 2015.

44. Baker, Peter and Gordon, Michael, R. "U.S. Warns Syria on Chemical Weapons." *The New York Times,* 3 December 2012.

45. Tavernise, Sabrina. "Cleric said to lose reins of parts of Iraqi militia." *The New York Times,* 28 September 2006.

46. Rapoport Yossef and Ahmed, Shahab, eds. *Ibn Taymiyya and His Times.* Oxford University Press, Oxford (2010).

47. Pipes, Daniel. "Stay out of the Syrian morass." *The Washington Times,* 12 June 2012.

48. Annan, Kofi. "Opening remarks by Joint Special Envoy Kofi Annan at the Meeting of Action Group on Syria – Geneva." UN press release, 30 June 2012.

49. Ajami, Fouad. "The ways of Syria." *Foreign Affairs,* May/June 2009.

50. "No concrete Syria plan after U.S., Russia meet." *CBS News,* 6 December 2012.

51. "Assad threatens retaliation for alleged Israeli strike." *AP* and *The Times of Israel,* 3 February 2013.

52. Lev, David. "Hizbullah: Israeli attack aimed at Syria." *Israel National News,* 31 January 2013.

53. "Russia 'deeply concerned' over Israeli attack on Syria." *The Telegraph,* 31 January 2013.

54. "Israel tight-lipped over air raid on Syrian site." *France 24,* 31 January 2013.

55. "Iraq PM warns of Syria crisis spillover." *AP* via *Al Jazeera,* 28 February 2013.

56. Solomon, Erika and Bassam, Laila. "Nasrallah says Hezbollah will bring victory to Syrian ally Assad." *Reuters,* 25 May 2013.

57. Kerry, John. "Remarks on Syria." US Department of State, 26 August 2013.

58. Harris, Shane and Aid, Matthew, M. "Exclusive: CIA files prove America helped Saddam as he gassed Iran." *Foreign Policy,* 26 August 2013.

59. Cohen, Tom. "Syria quagmire? Warnings raised as U.S. contemplates military response." *CNN,* 29 August 2013.

60. Maguire, Mairead. "Mairead Maguire calls for end to military action in Syria." Peace Jam press release, 28 August 2013.

V. The New World Order Is Chaos

1. Nietzsche, Friedrich. *The Gay Science.* Dover Publications, Mineola (2006).

2. Nietzsche, Friedrich. *Thus Spoke Zarathustra.* Wilder Publications, Blacksburg (2009).

3. Kays, John. "A critical essay on Christine O'Donnell's speech for the Values Voters Summit." *News Blaze,* 19 September 2010.

4. Kirkpatrick, David D. "Anger over a film fuels anti-American attacks in Libya and Egypt." *The New York Times,* 11 September 2012.

5. Oz, Amos and Oz-Salzberger, Fania. *Jews and Words.* Yale University Press, New Haven (2012).

6. Pattisson, Pete. "Revealed: Qatar's World Cup 'slaves.'" *The Guardian,* 25 September 2013.

7. "Amnesty International Report 2014/15 – The state of the world's human rights." Amnesty International. Accessed on 1 October 2015.

8. Sanderson, A. B. "Saudi court sentences gang rape victim to 200 lashes and custodial sentence." *Breitbart,* 5 March 2015.

9. "Saudi Arabia beheads woman for 'sorcery.'" *Al Jazeera,* 13 December 2011.

10. Markey, Patrick. "More than 1,000 killed in Iraq violence in May." *Reuters,* 1 June 2013.

11. Maguire, Mairead. "Mairead Maguire calls for end to military action in Syria." Peace Jam press release, 28 August 2013.

12. McCoy, Terrence. "ISIS just stole $425 million, Iraqi governor says, and became the 'world's richest terrorist group.'" *The Washington Post,* 12 June 2014.

13. DeYoung, Karen and Gearan, Anne. "Obama sending up to 300 soldiers to Iraq as advisers, says move is limited." *The Washington Post,* 19 June 2014.

14. Mercier, Gilbert interview with Dzhashi, Marina. "Saudi Arabia: does a new king mean a new future?" *Sputnik,* 6 February 2015.

15. Mercier, Gilbert interview with Korybko, Andrew. "Refugee crisis: Putin blames the West." *Sputnik,* 12 September 2015.

16. Mercier, Gilbert interview with Leid, Utrice. "Europe's refugee crisis rooted in imperialism, says French journalist." *PRN,* 9 September 2015.

17. "Le maire de Roanne ne veut accueillir que des réfugiés chrétiens." *Le Monde,* 7 September 2015.

18. Beaumont, Peter. "Netanyahu meets Putin to discuss concerns over Russian activity in Syria." *The Guardian,* 21 September 2015.

19. Usher, Barbara Plett. "Joe Biden apologised over IS remarks, but was he right?" *BBC News,* 7 October 2014.

20. "Trafficking in Persons Report 2011." US Department of State. Accessed on 15 January 2012.

21. Merrill, Rebecca interview with Mercier, Gilbert. "Putting Human Trafficking in the Spotlight." *News Junkie Post,* 2 February 2012.

22. "World population projected to reach 9.6 billion by 2050." UN Department of Economic and Social Affairs, 13 June 2013.

23. "How to Feed the World in 2050." UN Food and Agriculture Organization, 12 October 2009.

24. Wilson, Jeff and McFerron, Whitney. "Farmers fail to meet demand as corn stockpiles drop to 1974 low." *Bloomberg,* 21 February 2011.

25. Weiner, Eric J. *The Shadow Market: How a Group of Wealthy Nations and Powerful Investors Secretly Dominate the World.* Scribner, New York (2010).

26. Weiner, Eric J. interview with Moon, Bob. "Using shadow markets to increase global power." *Marketplace,* 23 September 2010.

27. This section was written for *New Junkie Post* in collaboration with Dady Chery and is reprinted here with her permission.

28. Alister, Doyle. "G20 pledges lift Green Climate Fund towards $10 billion U.N. goal." *Reuters,* 16 November 2014.

29. Olivier, Jos G. J., Janssens-Maenhout, Greet, Muntean, Marilena, and Peters, Jeroen A. H. W. "Trends in global CO_2 emissions – 2013 report." PBL Netherlands Environmental Assessment Agency Institute for Environment and Sustainability (IES) of the European Commission's Joint Research Centre (JRC).

30. Ehrlich, Paul R. and Ehrlich, Anne H. "Too many people, too much consumption." *Yale Environment 360,* 4 August 2008.

31. Manning, Richard. "The oil we eat: following the food chain back to Iraq." *Harper's,* February 2004.

32. "Special report: world energy investment outlook." International Energy Agency, 2014.

33. Kaiman, Jonathan. "China's one-child policy to be relaxed as part of reforms package." *The Guardian,* 15 November 2013.

VI. Fear and Paranoia

1. Orwell, George. *1984.* New American Library, New York (1961).

2. Orwell, George. *A Life in Letters.* Ed. Peter Davison. Liveright Publishing Corporation, New York (2014).

3. Meyers, Jeffrey. *Orwell: Life and Art.* University of Illinois Press, Chicago (2010).

4. Cohen, Jon and Dropp, Kyle. "Most Americans object to planned Islamic center near Ground Zero, poll finds." *The Washington Post,* 9 September 2010.

5. "Obama says the West is not at war with Islam." *Al Jazeera,* 20 February 2015.

6. Tharoor, Ishaan. "Mosque protests add note of discord to 9/11 remembrances." *Time,* 11 September 2010.

7. "Counter the 9/11 rally against Park51 - Say no to bigotry and hate!" NYC Coalition to Stop Islamophobia, 11 September 2010.

8. "Secretary Napolitano Announces Expansion of "If You See Something, Say Something" Campaign to Walmart Stores Across the Nation." Department of Homeland Security press release, 6 December 2010.

9. "Walmart shoppers: Homeland Security wants you." *NPR,* 11 December 2010.

10. Schmidt, Michael S. and Moynihan, Colin. "F.B.I. counterterrorism agents monitored Occupy movement, records show." *The New York Times*, 24 December 2012.
11. Orwell, George. "Why I write." *A Collection of Essays*. Hartcourt Books, Orlando (1981).
12. "The USA Patriot Act." ALA Government Relations. Accessed on 29 October 2015.
13. Savage, Charlie. "U.S. tries to make it easier to wiretap the Internet." *The New York Times*, 27 September 2010.
14. "Executive branch spying powers already too broad, says ACLU." ACLU press release, 27 September 2010.
15. Kain, Erik. "President Obama signed the National Defense Authorization Act - Now What?" *Forbes*, 2 January 2012.
16. VN Sreeja. "Why NDAA 2012 is against the spirit of U.S human rights?" *International Business Times*, 19 December 2011.
17. "US: refusal to veto detainee bill a historic tragedy for rights." Human Rights Watch, 14 December 2011.
18. "'Appalled, but not surprised' by congressional NDAA vote and administration's veto threat withdrawal, says Amnesty International." Amnesty International press release, 15 December 2011.
19. This section was written for *New Junkie Post* in collaboration with Dady Chery and is reprinted here with her permission.
20. Obama, Barack. "Remarks by the President in the state of the union address." White House press release, 12 February 2013.
21. Moqbel, Samir Naji al Hasan. "Gitmo is killing me." *The New York Times*, 14 April 2013.
22. "Police chiefs head to US to meet with FBI in aftermath of Boston bombings." *The Times of Israel*, 17 April 2013.
23. Kafka, Franz. *The Trial*. Trans. David Wyllie. Tribeca Books, Lindenhurst (2011).
24. Kafka, Franz. *The Castle*. Trans. Mark Harman. Schocken Books, Inc., New York (1998).
25. Rosenzweig, Paul. "Reforming the NSA surveillance programs – The testimony I would have given." *Lawfare*, 24 October 2013.
26. Newell, Jim. "Thousands gather in Washington for anti-NSA 'Stop Watching Us' rally." *The Guardian*, 26 October 2013.
27. Traynor, Ian. "Swiss vote to ban construction of minarets on mosques." *The Guardian*, 29 November 2009.
28. "Switzerland approves minaret ban." *Al Arabiya News*, 29 November 2009.
29. "European far right pushes for more minaret referendums." *RFI*, 30 November 2009.
30. "Bernard Kouchner : 'Le vote suisse interdisant les minarets est une expression d'intolérance.'" *RTL*, 30 November 2009.
31. Williams, Alexandra. "Switzerland faces backlash over minaret ban." *The Telegraph*, 30 November 2009.
32. "Algeria protests French far right minarets poster." *RFI*, 20 March 2010.

33. "Le Pen daughter compares public Muslim prayers to German occupation." *RFI*, 12 December 2010.

34. "Italy: speed investigations of Rosarno attacks." Human Rights Watch, 4 February 2010.

35. Hooper, John. "We don't want multi-ethnic Italy, says Silvio Berlusconi." *The Guardian*, 10 May 2009.

36. Pilgrim, Sophie. "EU blame-game over Tunisian migrants turns sour." *France 24*, 13 April 2011.

37. "Marine Le Pen visits Lampedusa." *France 24*, 15 March 2011.

38. "Marine Le Pen: les sondages se suivent et ne se ressemblent pas." *Liberation*, 10 March 2011.

39. "Sondage: Marine Le Pen en tête au 1e tour de la présidentielle." *Le Parisien*, 5 March 2011.

40. Sahne, Scott and Lehren, Andrew W. "Leaked cables offer raw look at U.S. diplomacy." *The New York Times*, 28 November 2010.

41. "WikiLeaks unleashes flood of confidential US cables." *AFP* via *The Jordan Times*, 29 November 2010.

42. Black, Ian. "Saudi Arabia tells citizens to ignore latest WikiLeaks release." *The Guardian*, 21 June 2015.

43. "Top Chinese officials ordered attack on Google, WikiLeaks cables claim." *The Telegraph*, 4 December 2010.

44. Brady, Brian and Chorley Matt. "WikiLeaks set to reveal what US really thinks of David Cameron." *The Independent*, 22 October 2011.

45. "France joins WikiLeaks condemnation despite Sarkozy jibes." *RFI*, 29 November 2010.

46. Greenberg, Andy. "An interview with WikiLeaks' Julian Assange." *Forbes*, 29 November 2010.

47. Zetter, Kim and Poulsen, K. "Pentagon says Bradley Manning a possible suspect in Afghan leak." *Wired*, 26 July 2010.

48. "Soldier faces criminal charges." US Division – Center press release, 6 July 2010.

49. Traub, Courtney. "Free WikiLeaks suspect Manning, say activists." *RFI*, 20 August 2010.

50. "Barack Obama: connecting and empowering all Americans through technology and innovation." Obama'08. Accessed on 31 October 2008.

51. "The Obama-Biden plan." Change.gov. Accessed on 31 October 2008.

52. "Prosecuting WikiLeaks for publishing documents would raise serious constitutional concerns, says ACLU." ACLU press release, 1 December 2010.

53. "US accused of inhumane treatment over WikiLeaks soldier case." Amnesty International press release, 24 January 2011.

54. Brown, Matthew Hay. "Accused WikiLeaker Manning says he was punished before trial." *The Baltimore Sun*, 25 November 2012.

55. "Solitary confinement should be banned in most cases, UN expert says." UN press release, 18 October 2011.

56. Savage, Charlie and Huetteman, Emmarie. "Manning sentenced to 35 years for a pivotal leak of U.S. files." *The New York Times*, 21 August 2013.

57. Mercier, Gilbert interview with Leid, Utrice. "French journalist: before terror attack in Paris, rampant racism, anti-Arab sentiment, and the rise of the rabid right." *PRN*, 8 January 2015.

58. This chapter was written for *New Junkie Post* in collaboration with Dady Chery and is reprinted here with her permission.

59. Pilkington, Ed and Williams, Matt. "Colorado theater shooting: 12 shot dead during The Dark Knight Rises screening." *The Guardian*, 20 July 2012.

60. Obama, Barack. "Remarks by the President on Osama Bin Laden." White House press release, 2 May 2011.

61. Buss, David M. *"The murderer next door: why the mind is designed to kill."* Penguin Press, New York (2005).

62. Becker, Jo and Shane, Scott. "Secret 'kill list' proves a test of Obama's principles and will." *The New York Times*, 29 May 2012.

63. Candiotti, Susan and Aarthun, Sarah. "Police: 20 children among 26 victims of Connecticut school shooting." *CNN*, 15 December 2012.

64. Lichtblau, Eric and Rich, Motoko. "N.R.A. envisions 'a good guy with a gun' in every school." *The New York Times*, 21 December 2012.

65. Taylor, Alan. "National Guard sent to Ferguson, Missouri, after week of chaos and protest." *The Atlantic*, 18 August 2014.

66. Patrick, Robert. "Ferguson police began seeking military assault rifles days before Michael Brown shooting." *St. Louis Post-Dispatch*, 9 September 2014.

67. "1122 Program equipment and supplies catalog." US General Services Administration, February 2014.

68. Allard, Jean-Guy. "In Miami, 12 officers shoot Haitian over 100 times: where is international press?" Trans. Natasha Mann. *Watching America*, 9 June 2011.

69. Daniels, Peter. "Third police killing in one week in New York City." *WSWS*, 6 February 2012.

70. Polner, Rob. "Riots erupt in L.A. after cops acquitted in Rodney King case in 1992." *Daily News*, 30 April 1992.

71. "DNA exonerations nationwide." Innocence Project, 26 October 2015.

72. "Death for the mentally disabled." *The Economist*, 8 March 2014.

73. Bonner, Raymond. "Argument escalates on executing retarded." *The New York Times*, 23 July 2001.

74. Will, George F. "Bush's revealing interview." *The Baltimore Sun*, 12 August 1999.

75. "Oklahoma executes Garry Thomas Allen despite claims of insanity." *AP* via *The Guardian*, 7 November 2012.

VII. Call for a Paradigm Shift

1. Chandy, Laurence and Dews, Fred. "Ending extreme global poverty." Brookings, 8 November 2013.

2. Shah, Anup. "Poverty facts and stats." Global Issues. Accessed on 7 January 2013.

3.   Wachtel, Katya. "The revolving door: 29 people who went from Wall Street to Washington to Wall Street." *Business Insider,* 31 July 2011.

4.   "Rebuilding America's defenses: strategy, forces and resources for a new century." Project for the New American Century, September 2000.

5.   Krugman, Paul. "Detroit, the new Greece." *The New York Times,* 21 July 2013.

6.   Fisher, Marc. "In Tunisia, act of one fruit vendor sparks wave of revolution through Arab world." *The Washington Post,* 26 March 2011.

7.   "Tunisian army chief warns against power vacuum." *AFP* via *Dawn,* 24 January 2011.

8.   "Bloodshed in Tunisia was for nothing: Libya's Gaddafi." *Al Arabiya News,* 15 January 2011.

9.   "Mideast rulers watch Tunisia in fear of repeat." *AFP* via *Dawn,* 16 January 2011.

10. Freeman, Colin. "Tunisian President Zine el-Abidine Ben Ali and his family's 'Mafia rule.'" *The Telegraph,* 16 January 2011.

11. Fadel, Leila. "Self-immolation cases in Egypt and Mauritania follow Tunisian incident." *The Washington Post,* 17 January 2011.

12. "The burning monk, 1963." Rare Historical Photos, 23 June 2015.

13. Steinbach, Alice. "The sacrifice of Norman Morrison." *The Baltimore Sun,* 30 June 2015.

14. "World Economic Forum Annual Meeting to focus on shared norms for the new reality." World Economic Forum press release, 19 January 2011.

15. Stein, Ben. "In class warfare, guess which class is winning." *The New York Times,* 26 November 2006.

16. Kuhn, Thomas S. *The Structure of Scientific Revolutions.* The University of Chicago Press, Ltd., London (1996).

17. Hedges, Chris. "The cancer in Occupy." *Truthout,* 6 February 2012.

18. Alhomayed, Tariq. "Hillary Clinton, dictators and the mob!" *Asharq Al-Awsat,* 17 September 2012.

19. "Take back the streets: repression and criminalization of protest around the world." International Network of Civil Liberties Organizations (INCLO), October 2013.

20. Colorni, Ruben Rosenberg. "EGF: Europe's multinational militarized police." *News Junkie Post,* 20 July 2013.

21. Chery, Dady. *We Have Dared to Be Free: Haiti's Struggle Against Occupation.* News Junkie Post Press, Dallas (2015).